Praise for

A Team for America

★   ★   ★

"*A Team for America* carries a special meaning for me because the Class of 1944, of which I was a member, reported to West Point at the same time that Earl Blaik was taking over as the academy's head football coach. We therefore shared the frustrating period, which included three losses to Navy, in which Colonel Blaik built the team that dominated the national football scene between 1944 and 1946. Thoroughly researched, and containing many acute character analyses, Randy Roberts has taken me back in time as if the events had occurred only yesterday." —**John S.D. Eisenhower**

"There are days I'll never forget. One was Sunday, December 7, 1941, when a victory celebration in the previous week's Army-Navy game at the Admiral's Quarters was interrupted by news of Pearl Harbor. Another was December 2, 1944, the day Army and Navy went at it on a Baltimore gridiron. Seven all-Americans were part of the greatest 'all out' game I have ever seen. Randy Roberts captures the saga of Army-Navy wartime football, and so much more. The rest of us are in his debt."

—**Robert Woods, West Point First Cadet, class of 1945**

"An engrossing tale full of 20th-century military icons."
— *Publishers Weekly*

"Supplementing the extensive newspaper accounts of the game with a decade's worth of personal interviews, veteran biographer Roberts brings to life not only the game itself but also its context, supplying capsule histories of the service academies and their performances on the gridiron. Most important, he places the game firmly in its moment of wartime history, for without the war, this watershed event would have had little meaning beyond the field on which it was played."
— *Booklist*

"A gripping portrait of a game that was emblematic of a nation at war. Highly recommended for World War II-era buffs, military enthusiasts, and sports fans."
— *Library Journal*

A Team for America

A Team for America

✦ ✦ ✦

The
ARMY-NAVY
GAME
THAT RALLIED
A NATION AT WAR

Randy Roberts

Mariner Books · Houghton Mifflin Harcourt · BOSTON · NEW YORK

First Mariner Books edition 2012
Copyright © 2011 by Randy Roberts

For information about permission to reproduce selections from this book,
write to Permissions, Houghton Mifflin Harcourt Publishing Company,
215 Park Avenue South, New York, New York 10003.

www.hmhbooks.com

Library of Congress Cataloging-in-Publication Data
Roberts, Randy, date.
A team for America : the Army-Navy game that rallied a nation at war / Randy Roberts.
p. cm.
ISBN 978-0-547-51106-1 (hardback)   ISBN 978-0-547-84460-2 (pbk.)
1. United States Military Academy—Football—History. 2. United States
Naval Academy—Football—History. 3. Football—United States—
History. 4. Sports rivalries—United States. 5. World War, 1939–1945—
Influence. I. Title.
GV958.U5R64 2011
796.332'630974731—dc22
2011016065

Book design by Brian Moore

Printed in the United States of America
DOC 10 9 8 7 6 5 4 3 2 1

For Doug Kenna,
West Point Class of 1945, and for his teammates and friends at the Academy who have served their country in war and peace

Contents

Prologue

Far off I hear the rolling, roaring cheers.
They come to me from many yesterdays,
From record deeds that cross the fading years,
And light the landscape with their brilliant plays,
Great stars that knew their days in fame's bright sun.
I hear them tramping to oblivion.

— GRANTLAND RICE

BUT OUR SON played at Harvard," the couple explained
when they were refused tickets at the gate of Michie
Stadium for the 1943 Army-Navy game. It seemed like
a perfectly valid reason, irrefutable to them. Still, unless they
had spent the previous few weeks in quarantine, they must have
known what everyone else who read a newspaper, listened to a
radio, or heard any of the football gossip knew—anyone who
lived beyond a ten-mile radius of West Point and who failed to
send in a verified application for a ticket would be banned from
the contest. Gasoline and tire rubber were too valuable. Army
officials would not sell any tickets at the gate. That was football
near the end of the second year of the war. Even in an age when
college football was king, its most important annual game could
not escape the impact of the war.[1]

"Use it up, wear it out, make it do or do without," was the

mantra of 1943. What with rationing, shortages, and continual privations, nothing seemed to look or taste like it had before Pearl Harbor. What American ever heard of making rubber from desert shrub guayule, rabbit bush, goldenrod, or milkweed? What self-respecting coffee drinker could abide the brew made of soybeans, chicory, or used grounds? And meatless Tuesdays and Fridays were one thing, but quite another was being served lungs, tripe, or heart on the other days. It was enough to make people long wistfully for the Great Depression.

An Army-Navy game played before a half-filled Michie Stadium at West Point instead of a packed house of more than 100,000 in Philadelphia's Municipal Stadium was a sorry sight. Even worse was the spectacle of the Army band busting onto the field playing "Anchors Aweigh" before swinging into "On, Brave Old Army Team," and the entire First Regiment of cadets sitting in the Annapolis cheering section wearing Navy's distinctive white peak hats. They actually shouted "We want Bill" and followed the command of the Navy cheerleaders. Demanding to see the Navy goat and rooting for the blue-and-gold appeared to many gray-clad men a clear signal that wartime unity had been stretched too tightly. But President Franklin Roosevelt had ordered the low-key affair. Midshipmen were not allowed to travel, so Army cadets had to root for the enemy in their stead. It was all part of college football in 1943 in a time of rubber shortages, gas rationing, and travel restrictions.

Pacing the sideline, Earl "Red" Blaik hardly noticed the tomfoolery. The hard, uncompromising aspect of his face looked as if it had been chiseled in the rock of Mount Rushmore. His nickname was the product of his bronze hair, cut short in a no-nonsense fashion. His nose was full, his mouth slightly turned up on the left side, and his lips thin as razor blades when he was concentrating, but his jaw and eyes attracted most people's attention. His jaw looked as if it had been squared with a bevel and fixed into place with screws—strong, tight, unmoving. His pale blue eyes, normally shaded under a baseball cap during practice or a neat, gray fedora during a game, were not so much cold as distant, as if he were always thinking about the next move on a chessboard. Joe Williams of the *New York World-Telegram* thought that if you didn't know Blaik and had to guess his profession, "you'd probably catalogue him as a professor of mathematics."[2]

Doug Kenna played for and coached under Blaik, becoming one of his closest friends over the years. "The thing that you've got to understand," he began, "is that Red Blaik didn't have a shred of an iota of a sense of humor. He was serious when he woke in the morning and he just stayed that way until he went to sleep at night." The day was never long enough for all the important work he needed to accomplish, so he drove himself relentlessly, measuring days into fifteen-minute units, eating meals at his desk, laboring to bring order to a game whose outcome often resulted from some whim of the gods.[3]

No game would be lost because the other coach outworked Red Blaik. His commitment to his profession was so single-mindedly complete, so numbingly uncompromising, that during his son's high school football career he saw him play only one half of one period, about six minutes of action. He watched from behind a shrubbery that guarded the Highland Falls High School football field. Later he remarked, "I had to leave for Army practice before the first period was over, but I stayed long enough to see that Bob's team was going to get a good licking."[4]

Blaik's schedule left no time for frivolous activities or what he considered questionable behavior by his strict Scot Presbyterian standards. He didn't drink alcohol, smoke, or swear—except for an occasional "Jeepers Katy!" and a very rare "Jesus Katy!" Well into his forties, he was the same size and weight as when he played end at West Point. At 6-2, 180 pounds, he was rock solid and could still fit into the same uniform he had worn as a first lieutenant in the early 1920s out on the dusty plains of Texas.

Over the years other coaches put on weight and aged; Blaik just didn't seem to do either. It was not part of his plan.

And his life was all about precise plans. Robert Woods played for him at West Point and remembered that he was "like a ballet teacher. He drilled everyone on their exact moves. His plays were not designed to pick up 5 or 6 yards. He was sure that if every player performed his job they would end in touchdowns." Glenn Davis, who earned All-American honors and won a Heisman Trophy playing for Blaik, recalled that his coach never praised him or anyone else. Praise was not required for simply performing his role perfectly. That was expected. Nor did Blaik berate anyone for failure. "I never heard him degrade anyone in the presence of anyone else," Davis said. "Never heard him raise his voice, hardly, in the presence of or to any player." "Red Blaik didn't yell," Kenna noted, "but he remembered. Fail once too often and you would never get another chance on his team."[5]

More than any other emotions, Blaik inspired respect and loyalty from his players, coaches, and associates. Robert Chabot, who played for him in the mid-1940s, said he was a "tough, hardworking type of guy" but also, in a chilly way, "compassionate." He demanded everything from a player, but he also cared for each one. John Sauer, who played and coached for Blaik, agreed. Whenever he went into the coach's office and saw him sitting at his desk, a framed picture of General Douglas MacArthur behind him on the wall, his knees started shaking. "I had more respect for that man," he said. "I was a smoker in those days, not a big one. . . . No way Earl Blaik ever saw me with a cigarette. I mean, that's just the respect you had for the man."[6]

Now his team was in trouble. His jaw visibly tightened as it always did when he faced adversity. With a nervous tic, he turned his class ring—West Point, 1920—on his finger. There had to be some adjustment, some bit of fine-tuning, that he could make to change the momentum of the game. Behind its mammoth, bruising linemen, Navy was taking over the contest. Ben Chase, Jack Martin, and Don Whitmire—especially the quick, violent Whitmire—were punishing Army's linemen, beating them up and wearing them out. The game was won between the tackles, Blaik knew, and that was exactly where Army was now losing it.

His team had started strong, biting off chunks of yards on end runs and battling the bigger Navy line on defense. In the first series, the sensational plebe Glenn Davis broke off tackle and streaked down the sidelines for a first down. He had another beautiful run in Army's second offensive series. But then he began to play erratically. After breaking off a nice end run on Army's third possession, he fumbled a handoff and on the next play bobbled an easy pitch.[7]

Suddenly the brilliance was gone, and he played like his mind was not in the game. On the fourth Army series he failed to catch another easy underhand pitch, resulting in a large loss and another punt. Later, in the second quarter, he threw an interception. By then Army's offense appeared AWOL, and time after time Navy's defense smothered Army's runners near the line of scrimmage. At the half the score was 0–0, but Army's players seemed to drag toward their locker room.

Navy had a powerful squad in 1943, ranked sixth in the nation going into the Army game. Their only loss was to undefeated, number-one-ranked Notre Dame. The Midshipmen's strength was their line play and their powerful, fleet backs. Whitmire had been an All-American tackle at the University of Alabama before transferring to Navy, and in 1942 he was a consensus All-American. His teammates called him Rock; sportswriters referred to him as a Neanderthal. Both described his physical, take-no-prisoners play. His role on offense was to open holes for Bobby Tom Jenkins, another Alabama transfer described as "190 lbs. of fluid force." In both the starting lineup and the reserves, Navy's power threatened to overwhelm Army.[8]

Blaik had foreseen the challenge before the season even began.

To give Army a chance in the game, he had installed a T offense that took advantage of Army's speed and discipline. Army was deep in exceptionally fast backs—Doug Kenna from Mississippi, Max Minor from Texas, and especially Glenn Davis from California. But the season had taken its toll. Kenna badly injured his right knee, Minor suffered a series of nagging smaller injuries, and Davis became mired in academic troubles. Before the big game they spent more time healing and studying than preparing to face Navy.

Now that lack of preparation was painfully apparent. In the middle of the third quarter Navy's offense stirred awake. Their march began when the smallest player on the field, a transfer from the University of Arkansas named Hal Hamberg, punted the ball 50 yards to the Army 8. After Davis was tackled for a 6-yard loss, Army punted the ball back to Navy. Hamberg fielded the kick, carrying it 10 yards to the Army 42.

The speed of the game seemed to change. As he had the year before, "little" Hal Hamberg simply took over. He carried the ball twice for 11 yards to the Army 31. On the next play he took off to the right, cut off tackle, veered toward the sideline, and, just as two Army tacklers slammed into him, pitched the ball to fullback Hillis Hume, who raced down to the Army 6. The play covered 25 yards. On Navy's sideline, the cadets in white peak hats followed orders and cheered loudly, if not quite enthusiastically.

Their backs to the goal line, Army's line stiffened. In three plays Navy advanced only to the 2. Fourth and goal. Navy's captain, John Whelchel, coaching his last game before receiving a combat assignment, sent in his power back, Bobby Tom Jenkins, to replace Hamberg. Like all single-wing offenses, Navy's running game was built for power, designed for its toughest back to carry the ball close to the goal line. Blaik knew—hell, his players and everyone with any knowledge of the game knew—that as sure as football was played without face masks, Jenkins would carry the ball off right tackle behind Whitmire's and Ben Chase's double-team block.

And he did. Jenkins lined up 4 yards behind the center, in back of a Navy line unbalanced to the right. He took a direct snap and, without a fake or attempt at deception, ran toward Whitmire's ample rear. As he did, Joe Stanowicz, Army's best tackle and an NCAA heavyweight wrestling champion, knifed through the line and hit Jenkins on the 4, wrapping his right arm around his waist and his left arm around his neck. He looked like a rodeo cowboy grabbing a calf to throw it to the dirt. It was a perfect high hit, fully executed to stop Jenkins's forward momentum and throw him backward.

The tackle straightened Jenkins, who stood erect, almost like a boxer who had just been hit with a devastating uppercut, but he just kept moving forward. With Stanowicz draped across him, attempting to rip his head back, Jenkins struggled like a soldier who had been shot, in a slow-motion death run, one, two, three, four steps then collapsed across the goal line. Touchdown. Extra point. It was 7–0 Navy.

Army battled back. Blaik replaced Davis with Kenna, who hobbled onto the field favoring his injured knee, fortified with frequent injections of Novocain. "I knew the knee was gimpy, no question about it, but I wasn't in pain, and Colonel Blaik put me in the game to pass, not run," Kenna recalled. Later in life he claimed that he was verifiably the worst passer in the history of Army football. "I really was," he said, "and I've got the statistics to prove it." In truth, Kenna was not a classic quarterback with a short, quick delivery but a gifted tailback with a long delivery and a fluid, graceful motion. And he immediately began to complete passes.[9]

The problem was not Kenna's throws but Army's fighting spirit. From the first kickoff the play had been intense, bordering on combative. As the last minutes of the third quarter ticked away, the action crossed the border into dirty. At times it seemed like a fight night at Madison Square Garden as players hit after the whistle and slugged each other at the slightest provocation. Both Army and Navy players were guilty. In the 1930s and 1940s rough play was common, and officials turned a blind eye to occasional punches and late hits. But this Army-Navy game careened out of control. One reporter counted seven fights involving at least fourteen different players. The bloody noses and cut lips finally overcame the officials' laissez-faire, boys-will-be-boys attitude. Red penalty flags began to litter the playing field. Time and again Kenna's passes were nullified by drive-killing penalties.[10]

Near the end of the third quarter, one penalty-plagued series forced Army to punt from deep in its own end of the field. Once again, Navy simply overwhelmed Army as they powered their way to a second touchdown. Allison Danzig of the *New York Times* commented, "Army, fighting its heart out in desperation to end Navy's long supremacy, simply could not stand up to that power. . . ."[11]

In the fourth quarter, penalties, mistakes, and interceptions halted each Army drive. Final score: 13–0 Navy. It was Army's fifth straight loss to its rival and the fourth shutout of the five. For Red Blaik, Glenn Davis, Doug Kenna, the Army team, the Corps of Cadets, and every member of the Long Gray Line, from the new second lieutenant fresh out of the Academy to General Douglas MacArthur in the Pacific Theater and General Dwight Eisenhower in the European Theater, it was a bitter loss.

The newspapers of the day had yet more trouble for Army, questioning its leadership at the highest levels. A few months earlier, in Sicily in August, General George Patton verbally attacked and slapped several soldiers hospitalized for shell shock. In one case he exploded at a traumatized GI, "You dirty no-good son-of-a-bitch! You cowardly bastard! You're a disgrace to the army and you're going right back to the front to fight, although that's too good for you. You ought to be lined up against a wall and shot, although that's too good for you. In fact, I ought to shoot you myself, right now, God damn you!" Then he shouted at the attending physician, "There's no such thing as shell shock. It's an invention of the Jews."[12]

On his November 21 radio broadcast, Washington columnist Drew Pearson went public with the story, reporting, according to Eisenhower's chief aide, "a very vicious and exaggerated version of the Sicilian hospital incident." The timing could hardly have been worse. The bloody Marine landing on the Tarawa Atoll in the Gilbert Islands was just days away.

Now the newspapers were full of charges and countercharges, General Eisenhower's official explanations and congressional hand-wringing, and columns editorializing on the insensitivity of Army officers and the bungling of military strategists. West Point's performance at Michie Stadium only provided more fodder.

Red Blaik had returned to West Point to accomplish a task. And he had failed. Every plebe learned on arriving at the Academy that there were only four responses: "Yes, sir." "No, sir." "Sir, I do not understand." "No excuse, sir."

Red Blaik had no excuse.

A Team for America

1

★ ★ ★

A Week in November

The sand of the desert is sodden red,—
Red with the wreck of a square that broke;—
The Gatling's jammed and the colonel dead,
And the regiment blind with dust and smoke.
The river of death has brimmed his banks
And England's far and Honour a name,
But the voice of schoolboy rallies the ranks,
"Play up! play up! and play the game!"

— SIR HENRY NEWBOLT

RED BLAIK HAD dug himself out of holes before the one at Army. His career, an unending uphill battle, was epitomized by two games in November 1940. It had been a raw month. Across the nation, extreme weather conditions buffeted people and buildings. In the Pacific Northwest, near gale force winds peeled shingles off houses, blew over flimsy structures, knocked down thousands of hardy citizens, and forced the less sturdy indoors. On November 7, 40- to 50-mile-an-hour winds in Tacoma, Washington, caused the First Narrows Bridge—aptly dubbed "Galloping Gertie"—across Puget Sound to undulate and sway like a belly dancer. Shortly after frightened officials closed the structure, its rhythmic dance turned into a spastic two-way twist, increasing from 5 to 28 feet while the roadbed twisted from a 45-degree angle in one direction to 45 degrees in the other. It performed its danse macabre for half an hour before breaking apart, piece by piece, into the water hundreds of feet below.

The Armistice Day blizzard that swept across the Rockies into the Midwest was less spectacular but more deadly. It came virtually without warning, catching duck hunters out on the rivers, lakes, and wetlands. One moment, a Minnesota hunter recalled, it was so warm that he had to remove his heavy jacket. Then the winds stirred, the skies darkened with ominous, smoky clouds and ducks looking for shelter—and it rained, sleeted, and snowed to depths of more than 2 feet. Forty-nine people died in Minnesota, and over a hundred more in the rest of the Midwest.

In the Northeast, the conditions were merely uncomfortable. Gray sheets of cold rain drenched New England and the Middle Atlantic States. Shoppers in Boston, New York, and Philadelphia sought something wool and warm, and when they left, their shoulders were hunched against the cold, wet winds that broke umbrellas like twigs.[1]

It was not exactly football weather, but it was November, and the race for the national championship was heading into the home stretch. Football players then as now were the postmen of sports, performing their appointed tasks in rain, sleet, or snow. For teams like Cornell and Minnesota, locked in a close race for the national championship, bad weather was simply a factor in a game plan, not a reason to postpone a contest. The same was true for such other midwestern and eastern powerhouses as Michigan, Notre Dame, Boston College, and Pennsylvania. On November 16, 1940, they would all play in conditions that recalled Noah and his ark.

The premier game in the East was Cornell-Dartmouth. With an eighteen-game winning streak, Carl Snavely's Big Red team had not been beaten since 1938. They started the 1940 season ranked first in the nation, and although they slipped to second in the November 11 poll, they had given up only 13 points in their first six games. Their closest contest was a 21–7 victory over Ohio State; their other victories were lopsided walkovers. Meanwhile, Red Blaik's Dartmouth squad suffered a series of disappointments, including last-minute losses to Franklin & Marshall, Yale, and Princeton. They lost four of their first seven games. Yet the Indians were stronger than their record indicated, and certainly better than a 4-1 underdog.

Blaik devised a brilliant game plan. Cornell's single-wing attack used a dazzling variety of traps, reverses, spins, and sleight-of-hand plays. Blaik's new defense featured most of his players set off the line of scrimmage. They would play a cat-and-mouse game, refusing to commit and patiently waiting for Cornell to come to them. Only when Cornell committed would the Dartmouth players angle toward the ball, effectively neutralizing the Big Red's trickery. In addition, the wet field would make it more difficult for Cornell to execute its sophisticated offense.[2]

Following their normal routine, Blaik's team spent the night before the game at the Bonnie Oaks Inn on Lake Fairlee, just over the state line in Vermont. After breakfasting on a cup of tea, Blaik called for his captain, Lou Young, instructing him that he should play "some of that hot jazz" for the team. "We want to go up to the stadium relaxed," Blaik explained.[3]

Slightly more than 10,000 spectators, most dressed in green, trudged into Hanover's rain-soaked Memorial Stadium to cheer on their team. They sat on towels and blankets, their muddy shoes resting in puddles, and gazed down at a field that had tried to absorb several weeks of near-steady rainfall. It was a defensive field, the sort that promised a low-scoring contest with a circus of fumbles, dropped passes, miscues, slips, and other unplanned acrobatics.

From the opening whistle, the smaller, lighter, hot-jazz-relaxed Dartmouth team played inspired football. During the first half, their defense confused Cornell and kept them pinned on their own side of the 50. Dartmouth also mounted several drives. One ended when Bob Krieger missed a 26-yard field goal; another stalled on the 6-yard line. In the third quarter Ray Wolfe, Dartmouth's stellar back, stopped a Cornell drive with a brilliant interception in the end zone. A short time later, the Indians held Cornell once again, forcing them to punt from their own end zone. One-hundred-and-fifty-pound Joe Arico returned the ball to the Big Red 26, and three plays later Krieger booted a 27-yard field goal.

Krieger's kick came early in the fourth quarter as a light snow fell, making the ball even slicker. In response, Cornell took to the air. Twice in the last quarter the Big Red mounted drives. Twice interceptions by Dartmouth defensive backs stopped them. With only 2½ minutes remaining in the game, Cornell fashioned a final drive from their own 42-yard line. A series of passes took them to the Dartmouth 46 and then the 31. Then Mort Landsberg got open for what would have been a sure touchdown pass, but before he could get to the ball an Indian defender tackled him. The resulting pass interference call advanced the ball to the 18, and another first-down pass moved Cornell to the 6. They now had four plays and 45 seconds to win the game.

On the first play Landsberg carried the ball on a reverse, avoided a tackler in the backfield, and gained 3 yards. Then Walt Scholl picked up another yard on a slant off right tackle. Finally, Landsberg rushed into the Big Green line and pushed the ball to the 1.

Memories of what happened next differ. Only seconds remained when either Cornell attempted to rush in a substitute, triggering a 5-yard penalty for an extra time-out, or called a time-out it did not have. Whatever the case, a referee moved the ball back to the 6. On fourth and goal Scholl attempted a pass into the end zone. Defensive back Ray Hall easily batted the ball to the turf, ending the drive and the game.[4]

Or so it seemed to everyone except the chief official, William

H. "Red" Friesell. First, he marched the ball to the 20, where it should have been Dartmouth's ball with 3 seconds on the clock. There he was intercepted by Cornell's captain, Walter Matuszczak, who evidently convinced him that a double offside penalty had been called on the play, though all three of the other officials denied that they had made such a call. Nevertheless, Friesell executed an about-face and placed the ball back on the 6, giving Cornell a final play. Reporters looked at one another and checked their play-by-play cards, and spectators glared and shouted. Captain Lou Young protested "vociferously and vehemently," but Friesell refused to argue the matter. Rule 13, Section 1, Article 13 of the Football Code manual stated that field captains could appeal only to a referee about the interpretation of the rules. "They are not allowed to question the jurisdiction of any official or to argue questions of fact"—as Cornell's Matuszczak had just done. Coach Snavely assumed that both teams had been called offside on the previous play and Friesell was replaying the down. Actually, Friesell was hopelessly, sadly confused. And in his numbed state he rewarded Cornell with another shot—a fifth down, a final chance to keep their unbeaten streak alive.[5]

Walt Scholl took the snap, rolled to his right, and threw a pass to the corner of the end zone, where a streaking Bill Murphy leaped and caught it for the touchdown. The point after gave Cornell a 7–3 victory. Young again complained to Friesell, and most of the reporters agreed that he had bungled the affair, but Cornell ran off the field as victors in what a *New York Times* writer called "one of the most thrilling gridiron encounters that had ever been waged."[6]

Red Blaik took the loss hard. There was no such thing as a gallant defeat, no substitute for winning. But he refused to whine to reporters. "I have every confidence in Referee Friesell," he said, before retreating into the locker room.

The world in November 1940 was at war—Germany was

bombing English civilians, Italy had invaded Greece, Japan had stormed French Indochina, and the United States had begun a peacetime military draft. The result of a football game might not have seemed to amount to a hill of beans in a crazy world charging toward total, catastrophic war—but it did. Outside the locker room, about 1,500 students took to the streets and campus green in protest, hailing their "victorious heroes" and chanting "no fifth downs."

Outside his home, Blaik tried to calm the student mob. Friesell is "a great referee," he offered, and Dartmouth was a law-abiding school. He steadfastly refused to throw gasoline on the fires of discontent. "As far as I can see, . . . the score is on the board."[7]

Cornell officials immediately took the high road. President Edmund Ezra Day and Athletic Director Jim Lynah issued a joint statement: "If the officials in charge of today's Dartmouth-Cornell game ruled after investigation that there were five downs in the final series of plays; and that the winning touchdown was made on an illegal fifth down, the score of the game between Dartmouth and Cornell will be recorded as Dartmouth 3, Cornell 0."[8]

Daily newspapers followed the story as if it were an important diplomatic negotiation. Asa Bushnell, the first commissioner of the Eastern Intercollegiate Football Conference, headed the organization that should have exerted a decisive role in what was becoming "l'affaire du futbol Américain." As the editor of a Princeton University humor magazine, he had once rejected a submission by F. Scott Fitzgerald, a recent alumnus. But this time Bushnell froze and tried to wash his hands of the matter. Neither he nor the officials had the power to change the 7–3 score after the fact. He hoped the record would demonstrate that Friesell "was right." But, he concluded, "if they show he was wrong, we still can't do anything." Only the schools themselves had any power to change the final score.[9]

The films of the game were developed on Monday. By then, Friesell was clearly having second thoughts about his call. Not long after the game, Blaik and Dartmouth's President Ernest Martin Hopkins had driven him across the Connecticut River to White River Junction Station. During the somber ride the referee confessed that he might have lost track of a down. After reviewing the press charts and two different sets of game films, Friesell admitted, "I am now convinced beyond a shadow of a doubt that I was in error in allowing Cornell possession of the ball for the play on which they scored." He insisted that the mistake was his and his alone, and that the other officials were blameless. He was now powerless to correct his error, but he wanted to acknowledge it to the commissioner and "the football public."[10]

Cornell's athletic director, Lynah, and Coach Snavely immediately wired Blaik and Dartmouth's graduate manager William H. McCarter that in view of Friesell's announcement, Cornell relinquished any claim to victory. "I accept the final conclusions of the officials," Snavely told Blaik, "and without reservation concede the victory to Dartmouth with hearty congratulations to you and a gallant Dartmouth team."

President Day fully agreed: "If we hadn't made that decision we'd have been explaining that game as long as football has a place in intercollegiate athletics — and I want no long count in Cornell's athletic history." The reference to the 1927 Gene Tunney–Jack Dempsey "long count" fight reinforced Day's belief that college football and professional boxing were two different animals. Bungled calls, misinterpreted rules, and bad decisions were part of the seedy world of prizefighting. But college football, a game that taught the great lessons of life, adhered to a higher code.

Cornell's handling of the affair, commented a *New York Times* editorial, demonstrated something about the school and the sport. More than all its victories, it showed the character, honesty, and sportsmanship of its administrators and coaches. And it proved that football, "which is too often described as a 'struggle,' a 'battle,' even a 'Blitzkrieg,' is just a game." For Americans who had recently witnessed the Nazi bombings of British civilians and Japanese brutalities in the Far East, the verdict about a football game confirmed something deep and implacable about the American character. It provided a comforting yardstick to measure the moral distance between "us" and "them."[11]

By the time news of the victory reached Dartmouth, Red Blaik already had one foot out of Hanover. One game remained in the 1940 season, and his five-year contract with the college had reached its countdown stage. Not that he was looking to flee Dartmouth. He genuinely loved the school. He admired President Hopkins, respected the college's traditions and academic standards, enjoyed the friendships he had formed there, and slept contentedly in the new home that had been built for his family. Dartmouth, he liked to repeat, was "the closest place to heaven." Still, he was on his way out.

Another November 16 game, played at virtually the same time as the Dartmouth-Cornell contest, changed Blaik's life. Under gray skies in a less than half full Franklin Field in Philadelphia, the University of Pennsylvania battled the United States Military Academy. Penn entered the game 4-1-1, a team that had displayed early-season promise but had slipped in its last three games. Army had shown not a glimmer of promise since they opened the 1940 campaign by squeaking out a 20–19 victory over a weak Williams College squad. The nadir of the season was a 45–0 drubbing by Cornell, at the time the worst defeat in Army's proud football history.

The Army-Penn encounter was even worse. Penn scored on its first drive, stopped Army's only first-quarter threat, then turned the game into a track meet, scoring 42 points in the last three quarters. Final score: Penn 48, Army 0.

Sitting on the Army side of the field, cold, cheerless, consumed by anger and embarrassment, Brigadier General Robert L. Eichelberger looked on glumly. At 6-3 he was tall, but he stooped slightly and had recently begun to put on weight. As he watched the game, the forehead above his thick, coarse eyebrows furrowed. He took on the aspect—as he often did when he was angry—of a predatory bird with unblinking, narrowed eyes and a prominent, beaklike nose.

It was Eichelberger's eyes that people remembered most. They dominated his face and often revealed his feelings. Watery blue, they could shift from warm and inviting to cold and forbidding in a heartbeat. When he talked to a man, he looked straight into his eyes, intently, constantly, taking full measure. When he watched action on the field—as he did Army's play against Penn—he seemed to miss nothing and understand everything.[12]

When Robin Olds was a young football player at West Point he met Eichelberger. "He wasn't the sort of person who invited idle conversation," Olds recalled. "If you had something to say, you said it, waited for a response, saluted, and got the hell out of there." There were no MacArthur flourishes or Patton eccentricities to Eichelberger's dress. He wore the uniform of the U.S. Army strictly according to regulations, and he expected every officer and soldier under his command to do the same. On occasion, he stopped jeeps carrying soldiers and dressed them down for some uniform infraction. A sloppy soldier sent the wrong message about the country's strength and pride.[13]

A month before the Army-Penn game, Eichelberger had been on the first list of colonels to be promoted to brigadier general. A few days later, he received a message from a West Point 1909 classmate who had also received his first star. "At last they have had the sense enough to promote the two best damn officers in the U.S. Army," the new general modestly announced. It was signed "George S. Patton."[14]

Eichelberger's life took on a dizzying pace. The United States, as virtually every army officer knew, was careering toward war.

As a new general, Eichelberger was ordered to report to General Joe Stilwell in Monterey to become assistant division commander of the new 7th Division. Before he could pack for the move, however, he was directed to go to Columbus, Ohio, and take command of the VII Corps area. Not long after purchasing a railroad ticket he received yet another order: He was named superintendent of the United States Military Academy. He would be training cadets to assume junior officer commands in the upcoming war.

He would also be defending the institution against blunt frontal assaults and vicious flanking attacks in Washington, D.C. There were senators, congressmen, and even officials in the War Department who believed that West Point was intellectually and tactically out of date, an inefficient trainer of soldiers, and a drain on taxpayers' dollars. Many West Pointers believed that if Chief of Staff George C. Marshall had his way, the Academy was doomed. A Virginia Military Institute graduate, Marshall advocated original thinking and discouraged numb reliance on the "school solution." In private he occasionally expressed the idea that there was no need for a four-year college program to train officers. ROTC programs and staff schools could do the job just as well and train many thousands of officers, not just hundreds.

In truth, the Academy did march to a different drummer, one whose beat had not changed dramatically during much of the twentieth century. In an age of automobiles, cadets still learned to ride like lancers, as if the cavalry was about to mount a heroic comeback. When cadets appeared in the pages of the *New York Times* or *Life* magazine—which they did with some frequency—more often than not they were pictured on a jumping horse or white-gloved, escorting an attractive young woman at a cotillion.

Eichelberger knew that few places in the United States were more tradition-bound than West Point and that any change was customarily regarded as vaguely sinister. He also realized that the Academy's survival depended on just such change, that the insights of Darwin and his followers were as applicable to West Point as they were to dinosaurs and dodo birds. He thought more about airplanes than horses, officers in combat fatigues than cadets in dress grays at dinner parties. He envisioned a modern institution, not a quaint relic. With war looming, he knew he had to take immediate action.

Attending the Army-Penn game was Eichelberger's first act as superintendent. "How Army's prestige has fallen!" he thought. The next day he continued to West Point and moved into the Superintendent's Quarters, a white Federal home. Dwarfed by the granite Washington Hall and the brick Arvin Gymnasium, the house is a study in simplicity, a reminder of the modest origins of the republic. From the sweeping front porch, Eichelberger could look out across the Plain toward Trophy Point and the bluffs of the Hudson River. It was an inspiring view. Every superintendent since Sylvanus Thayer had gazed across the Plain; almost every American president since the third decade of the nineteenth century had been greeted at the door. Robert E. Lee and Douglas MacArthur had lived there; the Marquis de Lafayette and Abraham Lincoln had spent a night there. It was the heart of the Academy, the beginning of the Long Gray Line. Eichelberger was not about to see the Academy diminished.[15]

On November 18, his first Monday on post, he addressed the football team's sorry state. Meeting with the Athletic Board, he gave his impressions of the Army-Penn game. He applauded the enthusiasm of the cadets who cheered on their Brave Old Army Team to the humiliating end, standing throughout the game, never flagging or grumbling. It appeared that the Academy was developing "the finest bunch of losers in the world." "By the Gods," he added, "I believe the cadets deserve a football team which will teach them how to be good winners."[16]

Eichelberger rejected the general "concept of graceful losing," especially as it applied to the military. "[I]n combat warfare there may be no game next week." He demanded cadets who expected to win and a football team that did win. In 1939 Army had finished the season with 3 wins, 4 losses, and 2 ties; in 1940, with 1 win, 7 losses, and 1 tie. They were losers, especially in the major games. In two years they had generally been outclassed by the Ivy teams and had failed to score a point against either Notre Dame or Navy.[17]

The superintendent focused first on the size of the young men who were admitted to the Academy. In 1931 the surgeon general had mandated strict height and weight standards for all cadets. An ideal seventeen-year-old cadet standing 6 feet tall was supposed to weigh 160 pounds and could not weigh more than 176. A 6-4 candidate (the height limit for the Academy) could not weigh more than 198 pounds. The surgeon general refused to grant waivers, believing that slender men lived longer than overweight ones. "This may be true from an actuarial viewpoint," Eichelberger observed, "but it is a hell of a way to run a football team. And the fact that an athlete by his mere size and appearance may make a compelling combat leader apparently had been lost sight of by the yardstick experts; life expectancy in battle for big or little men is just about the same." The superintendent gave notice to the Athletic Board that he intended to fight for a change.[18]

But he had a more important fight to pick with the Academy's own policy that the head football coach be an officer on active duty. This had led to a series of coaches who lacked professional expertise. Since the formation of the first football team at West Point in 1890, only one man had served as long as five years as head coach. Most of the recent coaches had done a three- or four-year tour of duty and then moved on to their next post. For Eichelberger, the approach made about as much sense as selecting combat generals from the ranks of football coaches.

Eichelberger didn't just want any professional coach. He wanted one particular coach—Red Blaik. After meeting with the

Athletic Board, he slipped a sheet of USMA stationery into his typewriter and pecked out "confidential" on the top of the page. "First, let me congratulate you on your wonderful victory over Cornell," he began. Then he shifted gears. "That, however, has nothing at all to do with this note that I am sending to you. . . ." Even as he was preparing to travel to Washington, D.C., to attend his first budget hearing, Eichelberger wrote, "[M]y thoughts turn to you and Fats [Harry Ellinger] with the feeling that you might want to come back to your old Alma Mater as head coach and line coach."[19]

The note was not an offer. Eichelberger had no authority to make one. It was a feeler. "[I]f you are at all interested, please have a letter waiting for me when I come back from Washington towards the end of this week," he wrote.[20]

Blaik's response was as quick as a salute. He had graduated from West Point with the Class of 1920, and his assistant coach, "Fats" Ellinger, had graduated in 1925. West Point represented duty, honor, and country to both. The Army-Navy game was less than a week away, prompting Blaik to suggest that they meet in Philadelphia. On the chilly, blustery night before the game, Blaik and Ellinger conferred with Eichelberger at the stately Benjamin Franklin Hotel on Chestnut Street. They talked about the days when Blaik was an assistant coach on the Ralph Sasse teams that beat Navy three straight years and compiled a 25-5-2 record. It was less than a decade before but seemed like a century ago.[21]

Over several hours, Eichelberger kept returning to the same message: "[I]t was urgent that Academy football be restored." There was a war on the horizon, and the Army had to project strength on the gridiron and battlefield. Blaik understood, but he would need time to talk to his wife, assistant coaches, and President Hopkins. He loved Dartmouth, and it would be a hard place to leave.

Eichelberger understood, but only as a career officer could grasp such matters. He knew about friends and pleasing towns, but they were secondary to his commitment to the Army. He went where he was ordered without a comment or a second thought. "Take all the time you want, Earl," he said. "But just remember one thing: West Point needs you."

The next day Navy defeated Army, 14–0, in a game that was not as close as the score indicated.

Two weeks later Red and his wife, Merle, visited West Point. Blaik knew he had friends at the Academy, but he was also aware that there was a coterie who had opposed his appointment as head coach in 1932 and were still against him. They resisted any talk of changing the active-duty coach tradition. During a meeting with Eichelberger, Blaik voiced his concerns. What was his standing at the Academy? Even if the superintendent forced through his appointment, would the opposition ensure his failure?[22]

Eichelberger suggested a test. He told Blaik to wander over to the Officers' Club and get Tom Impel to cut his hair. Impel could give a standard high-and-tight to a noncom or cadet in no time at all. For a second lieutenant he took 5 minutes. The higher the rank, the more time—and conversation—he expended. Eichelberger, at the top of the pecking order, would lounge for 45 minutes in Impel's chair.

Blaik returned to Eichelberger's office about an hour later, reporting that it had taken Impel 35 minutes to complete his job. "You're in," Eichelberger replied. "If Tom took that long, you'll be about the second-ranking person on the post."

Eichelberger pushed hard. He promised the Blaiks a new home above the Lusk Reservoir, control over the choice of staff, and an attractive salary. But he kept returning to his main point: West Point needed Blaik. "[I]t wasn't safe for the nation to have the West Point cadets walking around with an inferiority complex in anything," he recalled saying. His message fell a bit short of a direct order, but it had the same sense of urgency. The fate of

Army's football team, he implied, would soon be linked to that of a country at war. It was a burden, a patriotic responsibility, that Blaik carried back to Hanover.[23]

Back at Dartmouth, Blaik and Ellinger considered every aspect of the decision. Fats had been an outstanding guard at Army in the mid-1920s, "a chunky human dynamo tearing around the gridiron," commented John Kieran in the *New York Times*. He loved football, the Academy, and fun, and when he graduated he had looked forward to a career in the Army. But he was "busted" by the Medical Board. Because of a heart condition, he could not receive a commission and, further, was told to avoid all violent exercise. In response, Fats dashed out of the room, ran to the Hudson River, dove in wearing his uniform and shoes, swam to an island and back, ran up the steep hill, burst into the examining room, and demanded another physical. The Medical Board complied and "busted" him a second time.[24]

Ellinger took the news badly, dropping out of sight for a few years and living hard. But when he surfaced, he returned to the Academy as a civilian assistant football coach. If he could not be an officer, he could help train officers, he reasoned. He ignored his medical condition and trained with his players, pushing them and himself to the limits. He had no fear of death. "I never knew a more unafraid guy," one of his players commented. "He wasn't scared of anything, and he had a laugh for every situation and every job he got into. He had the most infectious chuckle I ever heard."[25]

Fats had gone to Dartmouth with Blaik and he too enjoyed it there. But a call from West Point trumped any other job. It was Blaik's call, but Fats still considered himself all Army, commission or no commission, and he told Red as much. No one was closer to the tight-lipped head coach. They were each other's opposite—a Mutt and Jeff, Laurel and Hardy odd couple. Blaik, the quiet, reserved Scot, stingy with words and feelings;

Ellinger, the boisterous, gregarious prankster. Blaik needed Ellinger, needed his humor and carefree attitude to help the team
relax and himself unwind.

Ten days before Christmas, Blaik sat at his desk and in neat,
crisp handwriting on Dartmouth College Athletic Council stationery began a letter to Eichelberger. Over the next two days
he wrote several drafts. "The fact that all of our discussions have
been above the board has prompted me to write this letter with
the same spirit of candidness," he began. Before he accepted the
position he required several concessions:

- First, the physical requirements for entering cadets had to
  be formally changed.
- Second, he demanded a five-year contract with an annual salary of $12,000 and "quarters as you have outlined
  them." He expected the Army Athletic Association to pay
  for his moving expenses and quartering costs until his family moved to the Academy.
- Third, his staff, including Harry Ellinger, A. F. Gustafson,
  Roland Bevan, Frank Moore, and Averell Daniel, had to be
  hired. For each he requested a specific salary, but he was
  more cavalier about their quarters: "A football coach knows
  no hours during the season & has no reason for anything
  but a comfortable bed."

He closed his letter with a word on his philosophy of football:
"At all times, but particularly under present conditions, West
Point in all endeavor[s] should command the respect of the nation. Football can be no exception. . . . The Army can have but
one philosophy & that is the one of a winner."[26]

The first point was above Eichelberger's pay grade. It was a
policy issue, a matter for the surgeon general, chief of staff, and
politicians in the Capitol. Eichelberger explained to Blaik that

on November 6, 1940, West Point had requested that the surgeon general rewrite the physical standards for incoming cadets, but "the question of securing big men for football purposes was never in the picture. We built all our argument around the relative value of a big man as opposed to a runt for use as an Army officer."[27]

It was a ticklish point, he added. In the early 1930s, when he was in the office of the chief of staff with General Douglas MacArthur and General George Simonds, there had never been a problem with obtaining a waiver for an overweight recruit. "Both were keen football enthusiasts," he wrote. But General Stanley Embick, who replaced MacArthur as chief of staff, "took the opposite point of view and felt no particular consideration should be given to a man because he might prove to be a football player." It all depended on how committed the chief of staff was to the success of the Army team.[28]

With "a million other things" pressing for his attention at the Academy, Eichelberger went to Washington to meet with the chief of staff. The Capitol swarmed with activity and crises. British and Italians were fighting in Egypt; Germans were still bombing English cities; Joseph Kennedy had resigned as ambassador to the Court of St. James's to "help the president keep the U.S. out of the war"; and the president was preparing to deliver his "arsenal of democracy" speech to launch a massive industrial buildup of planes, tanks, and other weapons of war. Germany was completing its plans to attack Gibraltar, Greece, and Russia, and U.S. military planners were examining large maps on walls and asking "Where?" and "When?" And Eichelberger wanted to talk to George Catlett Marshall, perhaps the coldest fish in town, about getting some big lugs into West Point.

Fortunately Eichelberger had an ace in the hole: Roosevelt's appointments secretary, General Edwin "Pa" Watson. The Alabama-born officer had graduated from West Point in 1908 near the bottom of his class and was friends with such contemporaries as George S. Patton and Jonathan Wainwright. Although he had served in the Philippines, Mexico, and the Western Front in World War I, his métier was politics. When FDR took office in March 1933, he appointed Watson as his senior military aide and, in 1938, his appointments secretary, the equivalent of today's White House chief of staff. Watson became a key FDR confidant.

Roosevelt made no secret that he was a Navy man. He depended on Pa Watson to guide him through the maze of the Army and the War Department. And it was no secret that Watson hated losing Army-Navy game bets to other members of the Roosevelt administration.

No sooner had Eichelberger left his office than Watson began greasing the wheels of change in the War Department and the office of the surgeon general. His connections in the War Department went deep, and he was largely responsible for the appointment of Rear Admiral Thomas J. Parran, Jr., as surgeon general. Within a few days Eichelberger received unofficial notification to expect "early approval of our study which will modify the regulations."[29]

On December 22 Eichelberger and Blaik had a "six-hour powwow" at the Ritz-Carlton in New York. The superintendent explained that the major stumbling block was about to fall. To be sure, it did not have final approval, but the decision had been made. By the end of their marathon session, Blaik had agreed to move to West Point with his entire staff.[30]

"Red has asked that he be permitted to break the news at the latter part of the week at Hanover or in other words that he give Dartmouth College a chance to make the first press release," Eichelberger wrote to Watson. But the superintendent wanted his political patron "to know ahead of the crowd." And of course he added, "Whenever the question of the waiver comes up I shall communicate with you and I know your help will be more than appreciated."[31]

The deal was done. Eichelberger got the coach he wanted, and Blaik got a program that he could build and shape without having to worry about the size of his players. On Christmas Day an announcement from Dartmouth made it official. Blaik said that he would always feel a special bond with Dartmouth, adding, "It is difficult to leave, but in these times to return to West Point is not only a challenge but a duty and a privilege."[32]

It was his duty to return to West Point. Now he was expected to win.

2

★ ★ ★

Where the Most Football Games Are Lost

The Army team's the pride and dream
Of every heart in grey.
— "On, Brave Old Army Team"

EMERY "SWEDE" LARSON, Navy's head football coach, was a hardscrabble Marine, equally known for his toughness and his sportsmanship. As an All-American lineman at Navy he played hard and smart, winning the Thompson Trophy Cup as Navy's outstanding athlete his senior year. As a coach he told his players that he favored men like himself, the ones with a mean streak. But after a game Swede was the quintessence of sportsmanship. In 1941, after Harvard tied his undefeated team, the disappointed Larson nonetheless walked over to the opponents' locker room to shake the hand of every coach and player on the team, as he always did.

But in late October 1941, even Larson's grace off the field was being tested. Relations between Japan and the United States were worsening by the hour, and too many Americans were ignoring the war in Europe. In New York for a luncheon with sportswriters, Larson talked about Navy's chances during the rest of the season, tempering his remarks with comments about the fragile state of world affairs. "[T]here's a war coming. And our boys are going to fight," he commented. What about rumors that Swede would be the next commissioner of the National Football League, a reporter asked. The coach grimaced. "I don't have time to think about a job in the NFL," he replied. "I've got a football team and a war to worry about."[1]

Even during those last few months of 1941, many Americans seemed blissfully free of war worry. The month before Christmas, the streets of New York were crowded with shoppers. The sounds of Christmas music filled Macy's and the other department stores. Across the country, retail sales for 1941 were up $10 million — almost 20 percent — over 1940's and $6 million above the 1929 all-time high. Not only could people still purchase nylons, Scotch, and rye, they could get them cheap. In a good sale nylons went for $1.75 a pair, a fifth of Scotch for $3, and a fifth of rye for $2.

True, the news outside was terrible. The Russians were fighting to keep the Nazis out of Moscow, the British were holding fast to Tobruk in North Africa, talks between Japan and the United States were going nowhere, and (unbeknownst to the media) somewhere in the Pacific Ocean a Japanese Task Force was heading east. According to the recent Gallup polls, a significant percentage of Americans believed that the country was headed toward war, and a majority now finally agreed with Roosevelt's policies that were inching the country nearer a conflict.

Yet movie theaters were packed for *That Hamilton Woman* with Laurence Olivier and Vivien Leigh, *The Maltese Falcon* with Humphrey Bogart, *Suspicion* with Cary Grant and Joan Fontaine, *How Green Was My Valley* with the young Roddy McDowall, and *King's Row* with Ronald Reagan. Films that addressed the conflicts in Europe and Asia were hard to find. A few comedies, such as Abbott and Costello's *Buck Privates* and *Keep 'Em Flying*, along with Bob Hope's *Caught in the Draft*, found humor in America's preparedness efforts. Although studio chiefs in Hollywood actively supported intervention in the European war, the movies they made only mildly and obliquely featured those views.

For those who wanted to escape the events of the day, there was always a good, stiff drink. The restaurants, bars, and clubs in New York, like others across the country, were packed. If you wanted to get into El Morocco, the Stork Club, Toots Shor's, Lindy's, "21," or the Copacabana, you either had to know the doorman, tip big, or be Joe DiMaggio. Columnist Walter Lippmann might have accurately predicted that war was coming, but columnist Walter Winchell attracted more readers with his news about the comings and goings of celebrities. At the beginning of December 1941 America was star obsessed, more concerned with the next Fred Astaire and Ginger Rogers movie or the previous week's Army-Navy game than the reports from the battlefront. And those reports were murky. The phrase "as clear as the news from the Russian front" had become a new simile for "hopelessly confused."[2]

By Saturday, December 6, the football season was almost over. In the previous week's big games, Texas outclassed Texas A&M, Georgia trounced Georgia Tech, Mississippi State edged out Mississippi, and California beat Stanford. Navy, for the third year in a row, shut out Army, a reminder to its new coach that he had failed in his most important assignment. Most of the major teams had ended their regular season. But there were still a few games on December 6. In Los Angeles, Southern Cal and UCLA played to a harmonious 6–6 tie on a perfect California day. That morning the *Los Angeles Times* reported on the negotiations between the United States and Japan in an optimistic headline: FINAL PEACE MOVE SEEN.[3]

It was a homecoming of sorts. When Blaik arrived for that fall 1941 season, it was not his first experience of West Point during a national emergency. In June 1918, during the waning months of World War I, as America and France fought to stop the German offensive at Château-Thierry, Blaik arrived at West Point after graduating from the University of Miami in Oxford, Ohio. He was twenty-one years old, his tonsils just removed, and duty called.[4]

The United States was in the thick of the fighting in Europe and desperately short of junior officers. The training program for cadets had been abbreviated, and West Point graduated three-year emergency classes in August 1917 and June 1918. The next month the superintendent obtained the consent of the War Department for a fixed three-year course for all cadets. But the deal did not last long. The fall Meuse-Argonne offensive had produced alarming casualties, especially among lieutenants and captains leading platoons and companies. The War Department needed more trained officers. In October the Academy was ordered to graduate two classes on the first of November, effectively robbing the school of its cadet leadership. The second graduating class had spent less than a year and a half at West Point, and when they departed only the class that had entered in June 1918—Blaik's class—remained.[5]

On November 1 the graduating classes marched across the Plain to the bouncing tune of "The Dashing White Sergeant." On November 2 a new emergency class entered the Academy, making Blaik's the new upper class. The two classes expected to graduate after merely a year and a half at West Point and be shipped to the Western Front to carry the fight into Germany. But nine days later Germany surrendered, ending not only the war but also the crushing demand for junior officers. Now suddenly awash in junior officers, the War Department decided to send the younger class back to the Academy for more training, designating them student officers rather than cadets.

The Academy sought normalcy and a return to its prewar traditions, including a type of hazing that often crossed the line into pathological behavior. Hazing at its best was fairly mild and encouraged esprit de corps. Serving as an upperclassman's alarm clock or polishing his boots resulted in no real harm. But at its worst hazing was brutal, dangerous, and sadistic. Forcing a plebe to swim across the Hudson in the winter or depriving him of food went beyond an innocent prank.

Hazing tragically crossed the line in the case of Stephen Bird, one of the new cadets. When it was discovered that Bird wrote poetry, a few cadets circled him like sharks. Exactly what they did is unclear, but the hazing was continual and unmerciful. Finally, in the early hours of New Year's Day, 1919, Bird tied a string to the trigger of a 30.06-caliber Springfield rifle, set the gun on a table, aimed it at his heart, and pulled the string. The bullet missed his heart but pierced his lung. He died later that day.

Bird's suicide provided ammunition to the Academy's opponents in Washington. Army Chief of Staff Peyton March concluded that West Point needed a complete academic and cultural overhaul. Looking for someone who could drag the Academy into the new century, he passed over dozens of more senior officers and chose Brigadier General Douglas MacArthur as the new superintendent.[6]

MacArthur had a host of good reasons for accepting the appointment, not the least of which was the certainty of maintaining his general's rank when other officers with wartime brevet generalships had been returned to their prewar ranks. Furthermore, the young general would become one of the youngest superintendents since Sylvanus Thayer in the early nineteenth century. And March wanted him to follow Thayer's example and remake the place. "West Point is forty years behind the times," he said, and in the months since the end of the Great War it had fallen into "a state of disorder and confusion." He issued a direct mandate to MacArthur: "Revitalize and revamp the Academy."[7]

In June 1919 MacArthur returned to West Point, once again,

as in his cadet years, with his mother, but this time he moved into the Superintendent's Quarters. He was not the choice of the Academic Board and was not a popular selection with the Academy's most powerful graduates. "There was no ceremony, not even a review of the Corps, when MacArthur took command," Blaik remembered. But the general had not come to the Academy for a final, glorious post before retirement. He had come to breathe new life into West Point, to create an atmosphere that would guarantee the continuation of the Long Gray Line.[8]

Perhaps it was inevitable that the general would court Cadet Blaik. Blaik was the outstanding athlete at the Academy, a three-letter starter in football, basketball, and baseball, and respected by his peers and professors. MacArthur loved sports and was always attracted to athletes, but Blaik was also one of the leaders of the First Class, a potential political ally in the general's assault on the Academy's entrenched traditions.

Not long after he arrived, MacArthur summoned Blaik and a small group of first classmen to his office. The cadets reported as they had been trained, wearing their dress grays and white gloves and prepared to salute and say, "Sir, Cadet So-and-So reports to the superintendent as ordered." But the general brushed aside the formalities and greeted each cadet with a handshake, "a cordial MacArthur pat on the arm," and the suggestion that they take a seat. Then, contrary to regulations, he offered each man a cigarette. Years later, Blaik recalled that the brand was Fatima or Melachrino, one of the exotically named cigarettes of the era. MacArthur then turned to the reason for the meeting, leading the cadets in a discussion of the corps' problems.

West Point in 1919 was still a small, insular place, and post news spread at the speed of light. MacArthur knew it. He fully understood that by retreat that day every cadet would have learned that "our new Supe was great. He didn't even know the blue-book regs prohibiting the smoking of cigarettes by cadets."

Of course, he knew every regulation. As Blaik later grasped, "The meeting had set the stage for a calculated break with parochialism."[9]

At the top of the new Supe's agenda was reforming the hazing system. Cadets should be taught to lead men, not torture them. Officers needed compassion for their soldiers, not the impulse to inflict pain and torment them on a whim. Rather than rule by fiat, MacArthur appointed a group known as the First Class Committee to solve the hazing problem. Blaik was part of the committee, and over the summer of 1919 the group met and discussed the problem, finally producing a pamphlet representing their opinions. The Class of 1920 then met in the gymnasium and debated the pamphlet, finally approving it. Almost a generation later, a respected general told Blaik that the action of the First Class Committee "was the most important single accomplishment of the Corps."[10]

During Blaik's last year at the Academy he formed a deep bond with MacArthur, mostly founded on their mutual love of sports. At one level the general harbored an almost mystical belief in the importance of sports for soldiers. On the Western Front during the Great War, he had been equally alarmed at the poor conditions of many officers and soldiers and heartened by the performance of troops with athletic backgrounds. Of course, athletes were on the whole better conditioned than their less active peers, but MacArthur maintained that they were more aggressive, quicker thinking, and more decisive as well. Now, as superintendent, he mandated that all cadets had to participate in intramural sports. The idea, he said, was "not only to fit future officers physically for the rigors of military service, but also to qualify them as physical directors and instructors for future commands." He thought that "the training of the athletic field, which produces in a superlative degree the attributes of fortitude, self-control, resolution, courage, mental agility, and, of course, physical development, is one completely fundamental to an efficient soldiery." His motto for the Academy was: "Every man an athlete."[11]

Soon the cheers of cadets were heard across the Academy on every baseball diamond, football field, basketball court, and boxing ring. The rule was to play hard and win. The intense competition led to intramural sports being dubbed "intramurder" sports. In case any cadet did not grasp the big picture, MacArthur wrote an inscription and had it chiseled over the entrance of the gymnasium:

> *Upon the fields of friendly strife,*
> *Are sown the seeds that,*
> *Upon other fields, on other days,*
> *Will bear the fruits of victory.*

Everyone, he decreed, should play, but his heart belonged to the best, and in his first year as superintendent the best was Red Blaik. MacArthur's interest in varsity sports, especially football and baseball, was extreme, bodering on obsessive. In 1902, as a cadet, he had been the manager of the varsity football team, and he never lost his love of the sport. An authority on Army football noted that throughout his career, in the Philippines, Japan, and Korea, and after he retired, the general closely followed the team and could "rattle off the names, heights, and weights of substitutes, their strong points and their weaknesses." The starters he seemed to know as if they were his own children. Blaik learned in September 1919 when football practice began that "the greatest enthusiast for the game was General MacArthur." He later wrote, "Never a practice period passed that did not see the Supe, carrying a riding crop, jauntily stride onto the practice field." The Supe was a bachelor, and "all varsity teams became his family." He advised, he comforted, he encouraged; he was equal parts coach, trainer, and cheerleader.[12]

Blaik remembered one day when he approached the general

during baseball practice. He knew that MacArthur had played varsity baseball at the Academy, and he was desperate to master the technique for hitting a curve ball. The Supe complied, loosening his collar, removing his Sam Browne belt, and taking his place in the batter's box. It was a magnanimous gesture but futile. Blaik emerged from the lesson unable to hit a curve or any other kind of pitch.

MacArthur's first year as superintendent—and Blaik's last as a player—was far from distinguished on the football field. The team lacked experience—understandably, since the classes of 1917, 1918, 1919, and 1920 had been pushed out of the Academy between April 1917 and November 1918. After playing only one game in the 1918 season, Army finished 1919 with 6 wins and 3 losses, but the wins were against weaker schools and two of the losses were against the teams that mattered most, Notre Dame and Navy.

Both losses nagged at Blaik for years. He missed the Notre Dame game because of a bout of the Spanish Flu, which killed millions of people in 1918 and 1919. Bedridden, he got an orderly to bring him reports of the progress of the game. Although Army took an early 9–0 lead, the running and passing of the legendary George Gipp carried Notre Dame to a 12–9 victory.

Blaik was back in action a few weeks later, however, for the Navy game. It was played at the Polo Grounds in New York under dark clouds and a drizzling rain. Unlike Army, Navy had not been crippled by emergency graduations, and they were strong and talented. The game resembled the fighting on the Western Front—brutal frontal assaults by both sides. The conditions permitted few passes, though Blaik claimed that "neither team would have darkened the skies with passes, had it been dry and clear."[13]

The two teams fought in the trenches between the ends. The linemen had wrapped their hands in yards of bicycle tape, and they pounded each other without fear of penalty. "Spare the blood and spoil the lineman," Blaik's line coach often said, and there were no pampered linemen in that contest. A maxim of Army's head coach, Captain Charles Daly, was, "Break any rule to win the game." And rules were shattered. Several players left the game missing a few teeth. A Navy lineman stuck a well-aimed finger into Blaik's eye, which resulted in an ulcerated cornea. Neither team could force the ball into the opponent's end zone, but Navy kicked two field goals to win, 6–0.[14]

That game ended Blaik's playing career at West Point. He had clearly been the team's best player, and Walter Camp named him third-team end on his All-American team. In addition, Blaik won the Athletic Association Saber, awarded to the best athlete in the class. In June 1920, only two years after he had arrived at the Academy, Blaik graduated, finishing 107th in a class of 287 and leaving as a commissioned officer.

His military career was brief, uneventful, and undistinguished. He entered an Army that had been hastily demobilized and deemphasized after the Great War. The Army sent Red to cavalry school at Fort Riley, Kansas, to learn how to break, bridle, saddle, and shoe horses. If the Army seemed obsolete in 1920, the cavalry was doubly so. In an age of airplanes and trucks, the usefulness of horses for reconnaissance and logistics was over. But Blaik mastered the skills of the old horse army, graduated, and was posted to the Eighth Cavalry Regiment of the First Cavalry Division at Fort Bliss, Texas.[15]

In the dust and the heat of the extreme Southwest, just across the Rio Grande from Ciudad Juárez, Blaik spent his days doing what he did best, competing in sports. The post commander, Major General Robert Lee Howze (West Point, 1888), assigned him as the player-coach for the football and baseball teams. A few months later, Blaik was also put in charge of a cavalry troop. He enjoyed the command, but he was in the wrong branch, at the wrong time, and in the wrong place. In early 1922, the government offered enlisted men and noncoms a year's pay to resign. The day the order arrived, Blaik's Troop E had 120 men, including 15 noncoms; the next day it had 15 men, mostly noncoms.

Later that year the War Department extended the offer to commissioned officers, hoping to reduce the officer corps from 14,000 to 9,000 by 1923. Blaik could see what lay ahead. He had sung the first stanza to "Benny Havens, Oh!" as a cadet:

> *Come fill your glasses, fellows, and stand up in a row,*
> *To singing sentimentally, we're going for to go,*
> *In the Army there's sobriety, promotion's very slow,*
> *So we'll sing our reminiscences of Benny Havens, oh!*

He was married, competitive, and ambitious, and in 1922 the U.S. Army did not seem the right place for him, so in February he tendered his resignation.

It was accepted on March 15, and two days later he was back in his hometown of Dayton, Ohio. On the eighteenth he received a letter from General MacArthur that had been forwarded from Fort Bliss. The general wrote that he was ending his tour as superintendent of the Academy and had been assigned to a post in the Philippines. He wanted Blaik to go with him as his aide. Without question, had Blaik received the offer a week earlier, he would have withdrawn his letter of resignation and in all likelihood would have ended his life as a general. Instead, he became a football coach.[16]

But he would still report to MacArthur.

In January 1941, only a few weeks after his return to West Point, Blaik was at the blackboard, a piece of chalk in his hand, teaching football to the remnant of a team that had gone 1-7-1 the year before. The players had come in their long gray winter coats, expecting a perfunctory introduction to the new coach. But the coach was not about to waste time on such matters. Young Robin

Olds, a big, handsome, square-jawed tackle on the plebe team, which had gone 3-4-1 in 1940, listened intently. The players had a lot to learn, and Red Blaik was starting at the beginning. "No football team can get anywhere without good tackles," he explained. "Tackle is the position where most football games are lost." Olds nodded his head in agreement.

But not all the players were listening as closely. Noticing a player looking vacantly into empty space, Blaik stopped talking in midsentence. "You, there!" he barked.

The player bolted to attention and replied, "Yes, sir!"

"Where are the most football games lost?"

The player paused, unsure of the answer, then replied, "Right here at West Point, sir!"[17]

Blaik enjoyed telling the story. It almost seems too perfect to be true, but he was not the sort of man who exaggerated. At least not much. And humor was not part of his verbal baggage. The story had a point. At the end of 1940 Army was a team of losers. In the previous two years they had won only four games. Both years they had lost to Navy, and it had been a decade since they had beaten Notre Dame. For the most part, Army had become a team of small, slow officers-in-training who looked great in dress uniforms but out of place in football uniforms.

Blaik was grimly determined to turn that around. The change in the height-weight requirements would eventually affect the size of his teams, but that would take several years. In the meantime he had to win with the cadets he had, and that required shaping them into a cohesive unit that believed they could win.

It was a daunting task. The first order of the day was that everyone—players, assistant coaches, and especially Blaik—had to outwork and outplan the opposing teams. When he had finished his initial meeting, he ordered the players to the field house to begin workouts. During the winter, spring, and fall he maintained a rigid schedule. By eight o'clock in the morning, Blaik arrived at his office on the top floor of the South Gym, where he spent his first hour taking care of correspondence. At nine the daily staff meeting began, and it lasted until midafternoon. The limitations on the cadets' time allowed for only short practices between 3:45 and 5:15, so Blaik and his staff had to make every minute count. He worked with his coaches, analyzing in minute detail everything they wanted to teach the players, every drill they planned to run. At practice, one drill followed another with the precision of a metronome—15 minutes line blocking, 15 minutes back blocking, 15 minutes specialized positional work for new plays, and so on, until the final whistle. He demanded that every player concentrate, work hard, and get the most out of every drill. "I wouldn't say that he was obsessed with detail," one of his coaches later said, "but I sure wouldn't say that he wasn't either."[18]

After practice the coaches returned to the South Gym and continued to work, often late into the night. "Our families saw little of us—a part of the price of the mission, and the steepest part of all," Blaik later admitted. He seldom thought of anything but football and improving the team. He jotted notes when an idea occurred, and if an especially promising one came to him late in the evening, he was apt to call an assistant and say, "We've got some work to do. I'll pick you up in fifteen minutes."

There was nothing glamorous about most of the work. Reviewing scouting reports, working out plays on a blackboard, charting opponents' tendencies, evaluating personnel—all of it involved mind-numbing attention to detail. Blaik was ahead of his time in the use of film. In every scrimmage and every game, each player on the field was filmed and graded. Whether a play was successful or not was irrelevant—each player had an assignment which he either accomplished or he didn't. Blaik was like the Scottish Presbyterian God on judgment day, weighing the successes and failures of each soul. The films were the final arbiter of performance, and so he watched, hour after hour, day after day. He and his staff studied practice film and game film "until our brain lobes felt as worn as the film sprocket holes looked."

Murray Warmath, an assistant to Blaik between 1949 and 1951, recalled one hot afternoon when the staff was reviewing Michigan game film. Blaik must have sensed that his assistants were flagging because he turned to Warmath and Vince Lombardi and said, "You guys want to have some fun?" A round of golf on the bucolic West Point course would have been made to order for Warmath. But the thought vanished quickly when Blaik called out to the projectionist, "Heck, open up the locker and get those Navy films out. Let's look at them for a while!" There were no cool dips in the reservoir, no shady rounds on the hillside course for Blaik. There was only football, football, and more football.[19]

For six months Blaik prepared for his first year as Army's head coach. At the end of August, in temperatures that climbed as high as 90 degrees, West Point commenced practice for the 1941 season. Despite the heat, Blaik appeared cool. Earlier in the year, before he had seen his team practice, he had sat around a table, sipping milk and fielding questions from reporters. "We may not be very good next fall, since opinion on our material is divided only as to 'bad' and 'not so bad,'" he said. "But we're going to be good before we're through."[20]

Now, his Army baseball cap pulled low on his forehead, he observed his team. Occasionally he barked an instruction in a stern but not overly dramatic voice, but mostly he just watched, allowing his assistants to do most of the coaching. Even when he was upset he seldom raised his voice, and he never swore, or condoned an assistant who did. Mostly he just watched quietly, one coach recalled, "but with a frightful intensity." He seemed to say more by saying nothing than any man alive.

The team was better than most sportswriters had predicted. The captain of the squad, lineman Ray Murphy from Anaconda, Montana, had worked as a logger during high school. He was powerfully built, explosive off the ball, and he played mean. He had fallen under the trance of the Academy listening to Army games on Saturdays with his father, and he thought that playing football at West Point was the summit of human ambition. Center Bob Evans and running back Hank Mazur were similarly talented. And from the previous season's plebe team, linemen Robin Olds and Henry Romanek impressed Blaik. Olds and Romanek had prepared for their West Point entrance exams together at Millard Military Prep in Washington, D.C., and had become close friends. The team's primary problem was depth. Although second-year men like Olds and Romanek would not start at the beginning of the season, both were only an injury or two from moving into the lineup. "I had no doubt that I would get my chance to play," Olds recalled. "And not at the end of the game. I'd play when the game was on the line."[21]

Blaik told his players that he would be tough but fair. He promised to work them till they dropped with exhaustion, then force them to get up and work some more. "No team in the United States will be as fit as us," he told Murphy. "That's why we'll win games. . . . In fact, we'll win a lot of games." Furthermore, he promised that he would run the team as a strict meritocracy. He did not care who had started the year before or who had watched from the bench. He would play the men who worked hard and proved their worth. "You'll have to earn the right to start," he said before the first practice. "All that matters is what you do right now until the first kickoff of the season."[22]

On the practice field Blaik was generally silent and dour. He watched everything closely, and if a player did something wrong, he would call him over to the side and calmly explain the mistake and how to fix it. He did not yell at or scold a player in front of his teammates. As he later told one of his fiery assistants who could not contain his emotions, "We just don't do it that way at West Point. You can't talk that way to cadets. You can't drive them that way because they're being driven all day." Blaik's players were men, not boys, and like men, they were expected to accept responsibility.[23]

His prediction to Murphy came true. Against weaker competition, Army charged out of the gate like Man o' War. In October, West Point defeated The Citadel 19–6, Virginia Military Institute 27–20, Yale 20–7, and Columbia 13–0. Sportswriters extolled the "spirit of the Army team." With war threatening, Robert F. Kelly of the *New York Times* commented, the cadets "have the feeling that it is important for Army to win for purposes of general morale. . . . [T]here is obvious, quiet determination that extends right through the squad from the top players to the lowliest assistant manager. And on the sidelines at practice sessions there are always in evidence the silver eagles of a colonel or two and, not infrequently, the gold stars of a general."[24]

In November, however, Army faced stiffer competition. All week before their Yankee Stadium contest with Notre Dame, players on the first and second teams sloshed through practices on the mud-soaked Plain. Blaik sent the remainder of the squad to the field house to practice, convinced that the top players needed the maximum amount of repetitions handling a muddy ball in the rain. The undefeated Fighting Irish were "terrific," he told reporters, bigger and faster than the Army opponents. In addition, injuries had begun to decimate the team. "We haven't anything like their speed and when it comes to replacements there just isn't any comparison." But Blaik promised that Army would play intelligent, inspired football.[25]

The mood at the Academy was more buoyant. The night before the game the cadets held a rally in the mess. The full corps, 1,800 strong, listened to speeches and sang fight songs. "On, Brave Old Army Team" echoed through the cavernous Washington Hall:

> *On, brave old Army team;*
> *On to the fray:*

Fight on to victory,
For that's the fearless Army way.

Singing and whistling the chorus, the cadets marched out of the hall to the practice field, following a torchlight parade past painted sheet banners unfurled from barracks windows. There they lit a bonfire and continued the celebrations. Their team had not defeated Notre Dame since 1931, but there was no mood of defeat on the cold, damp post. They vividly recalled the previous year's game, when a 10-1 Army underdog outplayed and outfought Notre Dame, only to lose on an improbable interception returned 80 yards for a touchdown.[26]

More than 76,000 spectators filled Yankee Stadium to watch the heavily favored Irish battle Army. Notre Dame's enormous number of subway alumni in New York braved the chilly winds and driving rain to cheer for their team. Army rooters were just as fanatical. The *New York Times'* Allison Danzig noted that the weather at the game never rose above "abominable." The rains that soaked the spectators turned the field into a slippery mess, confounding Notre Dame's runners and frustrating the passing game of star quarterback Angelo Bertelli. Coach Frank Leahy's team had been averaging more than 30 points a game, but the Irish could not move the ball against the "savage" Army defenders.

Army's offense faced the same problems as Notre Dame's. There were few first downs, even fewer successful passes, and almost no serious drives. Most of the game was a kicking duel between Army's Hank Mazur and Notre Dame's Dippy Evans. Once, in the first quarter, Army back Ralph Hill gained 37 yards on a reverse, reaching the Notre Dame 27 before being tackled. The full Corps of Cadets cheered wildly. But on the next play an errant snap from the center flew past the fullback and resulted in a 17-yard loss. In the second quarter, after a short punt, Army mounted another drive, reaching the Notre Dame 10-yard line before a penalty stopped their progress.

Mostly it was a game of fumbles, miscues, and penalties, with some good tackling but even more slipping and sliding. It ended as it began, 0–0. "A tie score was the logical reckoning and it reflected credit on both contestants, struggling as they were in such abysmal goo with a ball that was as slippery as a greased pig," wrote Danzig. When the final whistle sounded, the Notre Dame players looked crestfallen, their chance for an undefeated and untied season ended. Army's players did not dance through the puddles on their way to the locker room, but they were more satisfied. They had played and tied one of the finest teams in the country. Red Blaik, sportswriters were quick to note, had revived Army football.[27]

Halfway through the season Army was undefeated. At the Academy there was talk of winning all the remaining games and "beating the hell out of Navy." The players' spirits were high. It almost seemed as if there had never been a 1940 season, as if Army was the Brave Old Army Team of the 1920s, when Biff Jones had been coach and Red Cagle was the star running back. Superintendent Eichelberger wrote to General MacArthur in the Philippines that Blaik had taken essentially the same group as the previous year's and through expert coaching "built up an interesting team." In truth, however, Blaik was getting by with superior coaching, a limited number of good players, and outstanding team spirit. The reserves were hardly worth playing. Against Notre Dame, Bob Evans, Hank Mazur, Robin Olds, and fullback Jack Hatch played the full 60 minutes. Ralph Hill was on the field for 58. Just as Army was entering the meat of its schedule, the starters were beginning to tire. Many nursed injuries; others had lost weight and energy.[28]

"This won't be any undefeated team," Blaik told reporters the week after the Notre Dame game. "You don't have to worry about that, not with Harvard, Pennsylvania, West Virginia and Navy ahead." On November 8 Harvard soundly defeated Army, 20–6, and the following week Pennsylvania did the same by a

14–7 score. Although Army rebounded with a 7–6 victory over West Virginia, the team was clearly ailing. Robin Olds had been playing the entire season with a painful and debilitating shoulder injury, the result, he later noted, of "a dumb-ass diving incident." Added to the injured list were halfback Ralph Hill and end George Seip. Although Blaik limited contact during practice in the hope that the players would recover some of their lost strength, he must have realized that Army would face Navy undersized and undermanned. "Blaik acted like there was no such thing as an injury," Olds commented, "but by the end of November we were like a company of walking wounded. We needed reinforcements, but there was squat coming."[29]

What was coming on the last Saturday of November was a supremely talented Navy team, ranked eleventh in the nation and led by star tailback "Barnacle" Bill Busik. The atmosphere for the annual contest was fraught by the realization that war was undeniably near. The undeclared naval war with Germany on the Atlantic and the breakdown of negotiations with Japan left little hope of the United States avoiding the conflict. At the end of October, the USS *Reuben James* was sunk while carrying Lend-Lease supplies to Britain, and America's ambassador to Japan, Joseph Grew, warned of a potential surprise attack on American territory. The 1941 Army-Navy game, then, transcended its status as football's greatest rivalry, becoming something precious and fragile. To some reporters, the game seemed like the last peaceful event for a nation careering toward the abyss. As a reporter for the *Philadelphia Sun* wrote, "There probably never was a time when interest in the game was greater . . . , the international situation being as it is, the eyes of this nation being on its young men in the military and naval academies."[30]

For a week the contest consumed the academies. Across both institutions, BEAT NAVY and BEAT ARMY signs, most scrawled on sheets and accompanied by primitive drawings, hung out of windows and rippled in the late November wind. Cheers erupted spontaneously during mess, and torchlight and bonfires illuminated the dark. The night before the contest Swede Larson told his players, "You'll remember this game for the rest of your lives." No one doubted him. Olds recalled, "Blaik didn't have to say anything to get our juices flowing, which wasn't his style anyway. We all knew that we would never play in a more important game. It would be the game of our lives."[31]

Municipal Stadium in Philadelphia, with a standing-room capacity of about 102,000, had been sold out for months, and it began to fill early on November 29. The temperature, in the low 60s, was perfect for football, and the skies were clear and sunny. The kickoff was scheduled for one-thirty. At twelve-forty the Corps of Cadets, 1,850 future officers in their service grays, marched into the stadium, their band playing "Anchors Aweigh." Marching past the Navy stands, the band abruptly switched to "Fight On, Old Army Team," and wild cheers rose from the Army sections.[32]

In the locker room Blaik had his players lie on the floor and visualize their assignments, imagining perfect execution before achieving perfect execution. Larson took a more Rockne-esque approach, announcing to his players that this would be his last game as coach of Navy: "There's a war coming boys, and like all of you, I'm going to go and fight in it. All of us in this room have a more important duty than playing football." The words sent a shock of electricity through his players. They loved their coach, and they knew that as both a player and a coach Larson had never lost to Army. And they were not about to allow it to happen on their watch.[33]

Blaik believed that Army's only chance of winning was to control field position. He doubted that his offense could mount long drives, but he hoped that his defense could prevent Navy from executing them. His game plan called for patience, kicking often and deep, and playing for a game-deciding turnover or long gain. When Army won the coin toss Blaik chose to kick off. On the first series, Army's line held and forced Navy to punt. Army got the ball on their 35-yard line, ran once for a short gain, and then immediately quick-kicked. Army downed the ball on Navy's 16-yard line. Navy in turn ran one play, lost a yard, and then Busik attempted his own quick-kick. The punt was perfect, sailing over the Army defensive backs to land on the Army 20-yard line and roll to the 1-foot line, where it finally stopped. It was an 85-yard punt, the longest in Navy history. But Army's defense continued to hold Navy, forcing a fumble on one possession and intercepting a pass on another.[34]

The first quarter ended in a 0–0 tie. At the start of the second quarter Larson took a calculated gamble, substituting his entire second team into the game. He knew his team was deeper than Army's, and his plan was to wear down his opponent while resting his starters. Larson had used this strategy—dubbed "the Two-Ocean Navy"—throughout the year. Against fresh opponents, Army nevertheless pulled off its first big play. Hank Mazur fielded a punt, ran toward the Navy sideline, and as he was being tackled flipped the ball to Ralph Hill, who reversed field, sprinted toward the Army sideline, and carried the ball 56 yards to the Navy 22 before being forced out of bounds.

Blaik then uncorked his own surprise. Instead of lining up in its traditional single-wing offense, Army switched to the T formation. Navy had scouted every Army game. The cadets had never used the T formation. It had been installed just for the Navy game and it worked. In five running plays Army pushed the ball into the end zone. Navy blocked the extra point attempt, but the score inspired Army's defense, and just before halftime, Henry Romanek stripped the ball from the quarterback and had a clear field toward the end zone. Only a quick swipe by Navy's quarterback knocked the ball out of Romanek's grip and saved a touchdown. "Goddamn it, I should have scored," Romanek muttered as he trotted to the locker room at the half. "I should have scored." Maybe it would have made a difference.

Or maybe Coach Larson's rhetoric made the difference. During the halftime, Larson again used images of the impending war to fire up his players. "Boys, today is our last war together," he said. "We have a chance to win this war on this battlefield. Now listen, you boys are fine football players, and you will make even better officers. The nation will need you. . . . [L]et's show the nation what kind of football players you are and what kind of officers you will be."[35]

Navy's first team elected to receive the second-half kickoff. "This is why we play football, fellows, for moments like this," Busik told his teammates. "Let's do what we have to and win this game for coach." On eight of the first nine plays Busik called his own number, pounding into Army's line for unspectacular but consistent gains. On a fourth and 6 with the ball on Army's 16-yard line, he swept around the right end for a 15-yard gain, and on the next play Navy scored on a short plunge. The extra point gave Navy a 7–6 lead.[36]

Perhaps in the final analysis, however, Blaik made the biggest difference by being a whit too strategic for his own good. Navy's score did not diminish his belief that field position was the key to victory. By the rules of the day, the team that had been scored on had the choice of receiving the ball or kicking off. Rarely did the coach choose to kick off, but that was exactly what Blaik did. If Army kicked off and held Navy inside the 30, they could get the ball back in a better position to start a drive. Once again Navy returned the ball to their own 32-yard line, 68 yards from a touchdown. Once again "Barnacle" Bill Busik took control of the offense. The exhausted Army linemen, bloody and bruised from the brutal, smash-mouth line play, knew what was coming but were powerless to stop it. Busik saw that Olds's right arm was virtually useless and pounded power plays right at him. Time and again he was the focal point of double-team blocks, forced to combat two men with only one good arm. In twelve plays Navy marched down the field and scored a second 1-yard touchdown.

It was now 14–6. The two drives had taken almost the entire third quarter.

In the fourth quarter Army fought to get back in the game. But they just did not have the talent in the backfield to sustain drives against an outstanding defense. Army's last important drive ended when Busik intercepted one of Mazur's passes. By the midpoint of the fourth quarter the Army players were beat up, dead tired, and worn out. They could not dent the Navy defense, and they knew it. The game ended without another score.

After the final whistle, the two teams met in the center of the field. The Navy band played Army's alma mater, then the Army band played Navy's. In the stands, generals and admirals, as well as Eleanor Roosevelt and a hundred thousand other spectators, stood at attention in stone silence. Then, for the second time, the bands joined for the playing of the national anthem. "Cadets and middies stood close together, all of us singing our hearts out," Robin Olds recalled. His playing career was not over, but many of the other players had competed in their last game and would be commissioned officers in less than six months. There was a palpable sense that the boys in the middle of the field would soon be comrades in arms.[37]

After the game, Blaik met with a legion of sportswriters. He didn't exactly make excuses, but he did discuss several of the critical injuries. Navy just had "too much power and reserves for us," he emphasized. With their "Two-Ocean Navy" attack they had two backfields, two lines—two of everything. "I'm definitely not satisfied. I'm a bad loser," he said.[38]

Blaik knew what he needed. "If we had a few boys to stick in that backfield, we could have done better," he mused. Just a few good boys. Already he was planning for next year. He would get a few good ball carriers. In fact, he would get a few great ones.

3

* * *

A Few Good Boys

I bet football players, who don't know how to twist
their bodies and count one, two, three, four, still would
wipe out a lot of Japs.

— ILLINOIS COACH BOB ZUPPKE

SAN JOSE STATE college football coach Ben Winkelman,
his blond hair cropped short and his face red from the
intense sun, noticed a large geyser rise high in the air directly across the bay from his Waikiki hotel. It seemed as if God
had dropped a large lead football into the Pacific. It was about
eight o'clock, and he was eating breakfast at the Moana Hotel
dining room. Another geyser rose majestically from the turquoise
sea.[1]

Pointing toward the nearby naval base, he commented to his
waiter, "They must be having bombing practice this morning."
"Oh, no," the man replied as he poured another glass of papaya
juice. "[T]hat is a whale, or shark, or some big fish. They play
around there all the time." Winkelman watched several more
geysers erupt. He knew that whales were not that plentiful, but
thinking no more about it he finished his breakfast.

Gil Lieser, the student publicity director for Willamette University, was still in his room at eight o'clock when he heard the
sounds of bombs exploding out in the bay. He assumed it was

part of some "routine army and navy maneuvers" and, putting it out of his mind, walked to the dining room and ate breakfast. He was excited about the upcoming day's tour of the island, but the noise was distracting. When he wandered from the hotel lobby to the porch, he witnessed an authentic-looking military display: "Naval vessels were circling back and forth sending volleys of anti-aircraft fire into the air, and at frequent intervals water spouts would appear near some of the ships."

George Constable, a tackle on the Willamette squad, saw the same fireworks, recalling, "We were on the roof of the Moana, watching what we thought were some pretty realistic maneuvers. We heard shells, saw splashes, but were kind of oblivious. Ironically, I had a Kodak box camera in my room, but I wasn't about to go get it just to take snapshots of practice runs."[2]

It was December 7, 1941. Japan's attack on Pearl Harbor had begun.

Winkelman, Lieser, and Constable had come to Hawaii to play in several Shriners football games. They had arrived aboard the SS *Lurline* with the football teams of San Jose State and Willamette only four days earlier for a once-in-a-lifetime, two-week sports festival in paradise. After the ship docked, their hosts treated the players to an "aloha-style" welcome and escorted them on a tour of Honolulu, Pali Mountain, and the Punchbowl. On December 6 Willamette played the powerful University of Hawaii team, losing, 20–6; on December 13 San Jose State expected to get their shot at the once-beaten Warriors. In addition to playing football, plans called for the players to tour the islands, attend native festivities, relax on Waikiki Beach, and generally enjoy the weeks before Christmas. "We were up early on Sunday, the seventh, to take our scheduled bus tour of the island, the base at Pearl Harbor, and then a picnic on the north shore with a group of [University of Hawaii] coeds," one of the players recalled.[3]

By nine o'clock Winkelman heard a radio report confirming

that the Japanese had bombed Pearl Harbor. For Lieser, the "convincer" was "a small bomb crater" he visited a few blocks from the hotel. The players' reaction would soon be shared by almost every American. As one of his players told Winkelman, "If only I had a gun in my hands, I'd feel better."

Many soon had guns. Most of the San Jose State boys volunteered for temporary police duty, strapping on a Sam Browne belt and toting a riot gun. The Willamette players accepted assignments as guards, digging trenches, walking a perimeter, and looking for any signs of Fifth Column sabotage. During the few hours a day they were not working, they returned to Waikiki Beach for a dip in the Pacific.

On December 19 they finally packed into steerage of the luxury ocean liner SS *President Coolidge* and sailed back to San Francisco. During the six-day trip, they helped care for victims of the Japanese attack and lived in fear of an enemy submarine assault. Safe on the mainland, many promptly enlisted in the military. Coach Winkelman's team played a game against the Moffett Field team the day after Christmas, then disbanded before the New Year. The majority enlisted, and Winkelman himself became a captain in the Athletic and Recreation Office, Army Basic Flying School, Chino, California. San Jose State fielded another team in 1942, then discontinued football until 1946. Politicians, school administrators, and coaches across the nation debated: What role, if any, would football play in a nation at war? Could a violent game help win a deadly conflict?

Football is inevitably described with military metaphors. For Winkelman, it was time to turn the tables, as he tried to use the language of football to urge Americans to join in the war. "The enemy kicked off and we fumbled," he wrote. "They scored early on surprise tactics. They have still got the ball and are making a lot of first downs. But first downs don't count in the final score. It is going to be something else when we get the ball and start rolling. The last half of this game will tell the story and with our reserve material coming into action we will see consummated the toast of 'Bottoms Up' to the Japanese navy with the Rising Sun sinking." Others were not so sure. For the next four years, while servicemen fought and died in North Africa, Europe, and Asia, and as citizens on the home front struggled to make do with less of everything, the proper place of football aroused controversy.

In 1941, toward the end of his senior year in high school, sixteen-year-old Edgar Douglas "Doug" Kenna, Jr., thought he might like to attend West Point. His father, the head of an oil and gas association in Mississippi and Alabama, had a friend whose son was a football player at the Academy, and Doug liked the mystique of the place. He started the application process late and failed to receive an appointment, although he did obtain one to attend the Naval Academy. But he had no interest in being a sailor. "I was recruited by just about everyone," he recalled, "and my dad wanted me to stay close to home and go to Ole Miss, study law there, and stay in the state. So I accepted a football scholarship to go there."[4]

To suggest that Kenna was a fine athlete was like calling Seabiscuit a good horse. Kenna was a phenomenon, one of the most gifted high school athletes in the nation. In football he was a virtually unstoppable triple-threat tailback, the classic runner, passer, and kicker. He was an all-state basketball player and the state singles and double champion in tennis, ranked as one of the best three players in the Southeast. He hoped one day to compete in the decathlon in the Olympic Games. He was timed at 9.6 seconds in the 100-yard dash, long-jumped over 24 feet, and excelled at every event he tried.[5]

Kenna's Ole Miss freshman team was loaded with talent. Seven of the players would later make at least one All-American team, and several, including Charlie Conerly and Barney Poole, would have outstanding professional careers. But Kenna was the clear standout of the group of twenty-five freshman. The Mississippi varsity was also talented, ranked in the top fifteen teams in the nation toward the end of the season. During a mid-November bye week, Coach Harry Mehre commanded the varsity to play a full game against the freshmen. "We were sort of fodder for the varsity," Kenna remembered. "That year they had a great team. That was the Merle Hapes and Junie Hovious team. They were both All-American backs.

"We only had about eighteen players still ambulatory, the rest being injured in one way or another," Kenna said. "But we beat the varsity 49–36." Kenna's play had led to all 49 points. Walter Stewart, the lead sportswriter for the *Memphis Commercial Appeal*, was on hand to watch varsity legends Hovious and Hapes and assess their chances in the upcoming clash with Mississippi State. He left the game thinking only of Kenna. Kenna recalled that the headline on the next day's column was: "KENNA 49, OLE MISS 36."

Two days later Red Blaik called. He wanted Kenna and his dad to meet the Army coaches in New Orleans for the Sugar Bowl. In late December, the father and son made the drive from Jackson to New Orleans and sat in the rain watching Fordham and Missouri battle it out in the mud. In the first quarter Fordham blocked a punt, and the ball skidded through the end zone for a safety, the game's only scoring play. But Doug Kenna was more interested in what Blaik had to tell him than the action on the field. The coach assured Kenna that he would work out an appointment to West Point.

Had Kenna talked to Blaik a month earlier he might have stayed at Ole Miss. But December 7 changed everything. The day after the Japanese bombed Pearl Harbor, most of the Ole Miss football players enlisted in the Marine Corps. Kenna tried, but at sixteen he needed the permission of his parents, which was not forthcoming. When he returned to Ole Miss for the second semester, it was like a ghost town. "The campus was denuded," he said. "In the first semester there were something like 2,100 students on campus. After Christmas when we went back there were about 1,100—200 guys and 900 girls. And I was too young to appreciate that."

Blaik's staff arranged a deal. A Mississippi congressman made a trade with an Oklahoma congressman, appointing an Okie to the Naval Academy in return for Doug's appointment to West Point. Kenna's grades were so good that he did not have to take an entrance exam, only a physical; it was analogous to giving a drawing test to Leonardo. Kenna's class entered the Academy in June 1942. That first war class numbered over 800, more than twice as many as had been graduated that year. Congress had approved an enlargement of the Corps of Cadets from 1,960 to 2,496. Officers were suddenly in short supply.

The first war class brought Blaik's first recruits, and Kenna was the centerpiece of his efforts. He arrived two days early with Dale Hall, another superb football and basketball player, and stayed with the Blaiks in their house overlooking the Lusk Reservoir. "The second night the Old Man told us what was going to happen the next day," Kenna remembered. "We weren't sure we wanted to go through with that but by then we couldn't stop. Mrs. Blaik fed us well and treated us like her own children, but I had a pretty good idea that life was about to get a whole lot more uncomfortable."

The next day—R-Day or Reception Day—Kenna walked down to the massive granite Administration Building as a cadet candidate, the lowest of the low in the pecking order of the Academy. He received a tag with his name and company: Kenna, Edgar Douglas, Jr., F-2 Co. It had blank spaces labeled "waist," "shoulders," "inseam," and "shoes." He was then told to move to another area and wait for further instruction.[6]

An MP walked him and others past several buildings and lanes and then ordered them to stop and line up in single file. He said that he would motion them, one at a time, to come forward, turn to the left, and continue through a sally port until they saw a man in a gray coat and white pants with a red sash across his chest. Doug was to say: "Sir, Cadet Kenna reports to the man with the red sash." No more, no less.

Virtually no one reported correctly. Some said "candidate" instead of "cadet"; others forgot to say "Sir" or their own name. They all still carried the single suitcase of items that they had been instructed to bring to the Academy. Bill Jackomis, a football recruit in the later 1940s, recalled that the man in the red sash told him to drop his bag. He bent his knees and lowered his suitcase to the concrete. "I said drop that bag, mister! Now pick it up and drop it." This time Jackomis dropped it, but he still failed to satisfy the man in the red sash. "Mister Dumbjohn, I said drop that bag. When I say drop that bag I mean drop that bag. I don't mean ease it on down, I don't mean let it go, I don't mean bend down and let it go, I mean drop it! Now try that again, and this time you drop that bag so hard that it breaks the concrete you're standing on! Now DROP THAT BAG!"

Cadet candidates learned early that there was very little they could do correctly. Perfect obedience was everything. "Drop" meant "drop," not "lower down." Listen to what you were told and then do it—that was the first cardinal rule at West Point. And whatever else you do, don't ask questions. The man in the red sash was only too happy to explain: "From now on you will speak only when spoken to. There are only four things you are authorized to say. They are: 'Yes, sir.' 'No, sir.' 'No excuse, sir.' and 'Sir, I do not understand.'"

Listening to bags crash to the ground, Kenna knew he had entered another world. If the United States Military Academy at West Point was not so perfectly American, it would seem un-American. It's a hard place, plagued in the long winters with low, dark skies and bitter weather. The winds that come from Canada blow frigidly down the Hudson, attacking the Plain like a marauding army. It's a place of sally ports and gargoyles, of great Gothic facades and bastion corners with crenellated tops, of gray granite walls and prisonlike windows. The architecture defies exact description—part Gothic, part Tudor, and part Norman, with large doses of Beaux-Arts interiors—but the result is singularly uniform. Its form matches its function. Only soldiers, or perhaps Jesuit priests, could be trained at the Academy.

The most important buildings are enormous, as if they had been designed to crush any notion of individuality. The Administration Building, Taylor Hall, Thayer Hall, even the mess in Washington Hall and the Cadet Chapel, dwarf the individual, surrounding him with cold, gray granite. Stained glass windows depict cannons and bridges, medieval knights and scenes of battle. Carved stone friezes portray martial heroics, and statues of soldiers appear around each corner—every detail is a reminder of the purpose of a West Point education. The Cadet Chapel's stained glass features Sir Galahad and Lancelot, Joan of Arc and King Richard, and a triptych of "Duty," "Honor," and "Country." Courage and sacrifice are echoed in the Cadet Prayer: "O God. . . . Encourage us in our endeavor to live above the common level of life. Make us choose the harder right instead of the easier wrong, and never to be content with a half truth when the whole can be won. . . . Help us in our work and in our play to keep ourselves physically strong, mentally awake, and morally straight, that we may the better maintain the honor of the Corps untarnished and unsullied, and acquit ourselves like men in our effort to realize the ideals of West Point in doing our duty to Thee and to our country."[7]

A barber gave Kenna and his classmates high-and-tight two-minute haircuts. A tailor took their measurements for dress uniforms. A supply clerk issued them T-shirts, boxer shorts, handkerchiefs, black socks, robes, towels, and facecloths. After lunch in Washington Hall they received toiletries and other articles of clothing, including shoes, various uniforms, a pair of pressed white dress trousers, a gray wool long-sleeved overcoat, and a cotton belt with each cadet's name stamped on the back.

All day they were barked at and prodded from point to point, given instructions on how to stand, walk, dress, and march. The message was clear: there was only one way to do anything. One way to make a bed, one way to arrange a closet and a locker, one way to put on clothes, one way to walk down a flight of stairs, one way to stand at attention, one way to march, one way to serve a meal, one way to eat, one way to survive until the next day. "Theirs not to make reply, Theirs not to reason why, Theirs but to do and . . ."—they knew the end of the poem.

Robert Woods enrolled at the Academy on the same day as Doug Kenna, but he had attended Annapolis before West Point. "West Point was fundamentally different from Annapolis," he recalled. "Annapolis was not as severe, and there you encountered very different types. Some were tough on new midshipmen, others were laid back, even friendly. But at West Point all the upperclassmen were tough. Nobody was nice. I think the plan at West Point was to train soldiers in such a way that they would all respond the same in any given situation. And it worked. West Point produced extraordinarily disciplined officers."[8]

From the first day, cadets were taught even to stand and move alike. At Annapolis, Woods observed, marching and posture were not overly stressed. But they were critical at West Point. Almost seventy years later, Woods could still hear cadets shouting in his ear: "Rack in that neck, shoulders back, pop out that chest, suck up your gut, back end down, hips in." Woods, Kenna, and their classmates learned to march, and they would continue to march during the rest of their days at the Academy into their service careers. They would march to the same tempo, stand in the same rigid posture, and bark commands in the same accent.

The first day ended with a parade and the traditional swearing-in ceremony on the north end of the Plain at Trophy Point. High on the bluffs with a magnificent view of the Hudson River valley, it is the most majestic spot on the post. Dominated by the granite Battle Monument and surrounded by military hardware captured in battle and the names of West Point graduates who lost their lives for their country, Trophy Point has a solemnity unlike any other place at the Academy. Kenna swore the oath: "I, Edgar D. Kenna, do solemnly swear that I will support the Constitution of the United States and bear true allegiance to the national government; that I will maintain and defend the sovereignty of the United States, paramount to any and all allegiance, sovereignty, or fealty I may owe to any state or country whatsoever." In June 1942, with America at war in Europe and Asia, the words had a special note of urgency.

For the next eight weeks, Kenna experienced the nightmare of Beast Barracks. New cadets were pushed to their mental and physical limits. They were broken down so that they could be rebuilt as West Point cadets. Deprivation became a way of life. Cadets were awakened in the middle of the night to perform dress rituals and exercises; harassed at meals to a point where they could not consume enough food; and pushed physically beyond the point of exhaustion. Above all, they were taught to follow orders—immediately and without question.

One of the orders was to memorize all of the "cadet poop": useless, trivial information that they were expected to repeat verbatim. James Salter, a member of Kenna's class who would become a fighter pilot, novelist, and screenwriter, could after a half century still recall the poop. Asked to define leather, he repeated, "Leather: If the fresh skin of an animal, cleaned and divested of all hair, fat, and other extraneous matter, be immersed in a dilute solution of tannic acid, a chemical combination ensues; the gelatinous tissue of the skin is converted into a nonputrescible substance, impervious to and insoluble in water; this, sir, is leather."

West Point had its own language. A "bean head" was a plebe, a "brown bar" a second lieutenant, a "drag" a date, and a "wife" a roommate. A "cold max" in "dirt" was a cadet who did not miss a question on a geography exam; a "rock" in "juice" was a cadet fast sinking to the bottom of his electrical engineering class. Off post their language was incomprehensible; on post cadets were expected to have the poop at their fingertips and be able to recite it flawlessly under pressure in a blisteringly hot courtyard, in a driving rain, or during a raging blizzard. Kenna and his classmates knew there were 340 lights in Cullum Hall, 92.2 million gallons of water in Lusk Reservoir "when the water is flowing over the spillway," and 2,240 names on Battle Monument. They could answer to the question, "How is the cow?": "Sir, she walks, she talks, she's full of chalk, the lacteal fluid extracted from the female of the bovine species is highly prolific to the nth degree." And they could recite those creatures that they outranked: "Sir, the superintendent's dog, the commandant's cat, the waiters in the Mess Hall, the Hell cats, and all the admirals in the whole blamed Navy."[9]

The physical side of the hazing did not worry Kenna. "The rules," Joe Steffy, a contemporary football player, said, "were all very simple: 'You do this, you do that.'" His high school coach had given him excellent advice: "Listen, you don't have to worry about the hazing. Just treat it as a game you're playing. They're not going to physically hurt you. . . . They're going to yell at you and try to get you rattled and nervous and so forth." The point was just to take it. Kenna agreed. He was a football player. Opponents had punched him in the face and tried to stick fingers in his eyes in pile-ups; they had attempted to get him to lose his focus and think more about fighting them than winning the game. He knew how to maintain his composure. He had faced worse trials than having a third-year cadet berating him for not bracing his neck sufficiently.[10]

The only hazing that really upset Kenna, oddly enough, resulted from his athletic ability. From his first weeks on post, it was obvious that he was a terrific athlete. All new cadets are given West Point's Master of the Sword test, comprising the 300-yard run, dodge run, standing broad jump, vertical jump, bar vault, rope climb, chin-ups, parallel bar dips, softball throw, and sit-ups. In each of the ten events the cadet was given a score. The test seemed designed for Kenna's skills, and he scored higher than any previous cadet in the Academy's history. Blaik said he had "exceptional ability," strong words from a coach who measured out praise in teaspoons. When fall practice began, Blaik placed Kenna on the first squad at tailback, ahead of team captain Henry Mazur. Mazur was furious, and he aimed all his anger at Kenna.[11]

Mazur was in a difficult position. Like all first-year cadets, his West Point graduation had been advanced from June to January 1943, burdening him with an additional academic load. Furthermore, he had chosen the Army Air Corps, a decision that entailed enormous amounts of time on buses to and from Stewart Field and hundreds of hours in the air. Blaik recognized that the combination of academics, flight training, and football was simply too much for most of the first- and second-class players. They could not, he later wrote to MacArthur, "play football and at the same time have in reserve sufficient physical and particularly nervous energy to pursue their academic work and learn to pilot fast planes." After three weeks of practice, he dropped twenty of the twenty-four Army Air Corps men on the team, replacing them with a dozen plebes. Only Mazur, Robin Olds, and two quarterbacks remained "in order not to be bankrupt of experience."[12]

Mazur had difficulty with the herculean balancing act. As the season progressed his play became ragged, plagued by turnovers and erratic performances. Of the four fliers, only Olds seemed to be able to handle anything thrown his way. Mazur was not only the team's captain but also the passer and punter, two areas where inconsistent play was often disastrous. But more important to Blaik, Mazur's failings were one of the reasons the Army squad never developed a "team soul." Perhaps, he later mused, it was "a lack of leadership" or "a reluctance to accept responsibility," but whatever the cause, it was a serious problem. The class had played as yearlings during the terrible 1940 season, and Blaik, always the amateur psychologist, believed they had "formed subconscious habits of accepting defeats varying in degrees up to 45 points."[13]

Quite possibly Mazur resented the dismissal of his classmates and friends in the first- and second-year classes. And undoubtedly he realized that Blaik's confidence in him was razor thin, especially after the coach began to play Kenna with the first team. "Mazur was pissed," Kenna recalled. "I was a lot better than he was and he knew it. As the captain he should have thought about what was best for the team, but he went after me in the only way he could. He hazed me unmercifully—really gave it to me."

Kenna easily survived. But his football career faced one real threat in the summer of 1942. Should the sport continue in wartime? Government officials vigorously debated the role that football—and all sports—would or should play in the war effort. Football had many defenders. Like no other sport, it extolled teamwork and rugged masculine traits—the complex movements of a play, the specialization of all players, the clash of linemen, the dash of the runner toward the end zone, and the heady mixture of sweat, dirt, and blood. The violent appeal of the game was perfectly captured by a former player, the scholar Michael Oriard. Imagine, he asks, a perfect pass to a receiver streaking toward the end zone, the ball reaching his hands just as a defender hurls his body toward him. The receiver stretches for the ball in a graceful leap; the defender smashes into him in a violent thrust. It is the essence of football: "The receiver's balletic moves and catch would not impress us nearly as much if the possibility of annihilation were not real; the violence of the collision would be gratuitous, pointless, if it did not threaten something valuable and important. The violence, in fact, partially creates the art-istry: the simple act of catching a thrown ball becomes a marvel-ous achievement only in defiance of the brutal blow." Football is beautiful violence.[14]

Politicians and journalists drew parallels between football and the American character, celebrating the competitive, can-do spirit of the sport. The guiding dictum of football remained true to Theodore Roosevelt's summation: "In life, as in a football game, the principle to follow is: Hit the line hard; don't foul and don't shirk, but hit the line hard!" Football, TR maintained, taught boys to be "fine, straightforward, clean, brave and manly." It inculcated moral vigor and robust good health. It was not so much a sport as an ethos, an approach to any problem, a *Welt-anschauung*—tough, disciplined, fearless, unpitying, and, at bot-tom, ethical.[15]

A month before Pearl Harbor, Brooke Leman addressed the sport's virtues in "The Soul of Football":

> *I am the onrushing tide; the stern, tense, immutable spirit*
> *of progress.*
> *I am cooperation; I am teamwork;*
> *I am the breath of energy,*
> *The spirit of stamina and the supreme test of endurance . . .*
> *Who drive the enemy over the last line of resistance.*
> *For I am the tide of conquest and victory. . . .*
>
> *I brook no weaklings*
> *And my sons are strong men within whom is red running*
> *blood. . . .*
> *And the will to do or die—*
> *Such are my men. . . .*
>
> *I am the spirit of perfect machine.*
> *I am Art, for I am perfection of body,*

And clocklike coordination of brain.
I am the sport of gentlemen and the glory of young virile
manhood. . . .[16]

Even in wartime—especially in wartime—football's defenders could not imagine giving up the sport. Stephen Crane, in *The
Red Badge of Courage,* once commented that all his knowledge of
warfare came from watching football. "American football, quint-
essentially, is about war," the writer James Lawton explained. It
"has everything to thrill a military mind. It has the trench warfare
of the behemoths who crouch on the line of scrimmage, growl-
ing and cursing like infantrymen, hoping to win a little ground,
a little time. It has the outriders, the receiver, ghosting through
lines of defense. It has the running backs, who operate as armor,
punching holes in the cover, testing, probing, looking for a point
of breakthrough." It has assaults from the air and movements
into enemy territory, strategic game plans and tactical changes
in the heat of battle.[17]

But the challenging questions were obvious: Why would any
patriotic college athlete choose to play football rather than
enlist? And why would the government permit college football to continue when it kept healthy American boys from the
battlefront? Many college teams were already decimated by
volunteers in the weeks after Pearl Harbor. Fordham's team
enlisted en masse after their 1942 Sugar Bowl victory. Many
joined the Army Air Corps and trained at Floyd Bennett Field
on Long Island, earning the moniker the Flying Rams. There
were also the Flying Indians from Dartmouth, the Flying Cru-
saders from Holy Cross, and the Flying Eagles from Boston
College. Scores of colleges and universities dropped football
during all or part of World War II. Most of the schools that
dropped football for all or part of the war were small programs, but such traditional powers as Alabama, Arizona, Au-
burn, Baylor, Kentucky, Michigan State, Mississippi, Missis-

sippi State, Stanford, Tennessee, and Washington State took wartime hiatuses.[18]

Many Americans and some politicians argued that all mass spectator sports should be shelved for the duration of the war. At first, the debate was case by case. Should the New Year's Day Rose Bowl game be played in Pasadena only weeks after Pearl Harbor, when Californians were jittery over possible Japanese assaults on the West Coast? It was moved to Durham, North Carolina. Should the Indianapolis 500, the country's premier automobile race, be run when the country faced severe rubber and gasoline shortages? Indianapolis Speedway closed shop "for the duration."[19]

But soon the debate widened to all spectator sports everywhere. In April 1942 an American Institute of Public Opinion poll asked: "Do you think that professional sports should be continued during the war, or should they be stopped until after the war?" Some 66 percent of respondents said to play on; 24 percent said to stop. The commissioner of Major League Baseball, Judge Kenesaw Mountain Landis, fully and flatly agreed with the majority.[20]

All eyes looked to Washington, D.C., for direction from President Roosevelt. Antsy about the upcoming baseball season, Landis asked the chief executive, "What you have in mind whether baseball should continue to operate?" On January 15, Roosevelt responded: "I honestly feel that it would be best for the country to keep baseball going. There will be fewer people unemployed and everybody will work longer hours and harder than ever before. And that means that they ought to have a chance for recreation and for taking their minds off their work even more than before. . . . Here is another way of looking at it—if 300 teams use 5,000 or 6,000 players, these players are a definite recreational asset to at least 20,000,000 of the fellow citizens—and that in my judgment is thoroughly worthwhile." It was not a blanket statement for all sports, and it certainly did not protect any individual players of draft age, but it was interpreted as a green light for sports executives in baseball and football.[21]

But who would play? Thousands of college players had already enlisted. Thousands more were waiting for their draft notices. At the beginning of the war, males under twenty were below the draft age; Congress did not lower the age to eighteen until November 16, 1942. For the first wartime season, then, seventeen-, eighteen-, and nineteen-year-old players were still eligible, as were men with medical and other deferments. The demand for soldiers was not yet pressing. Compared to later in the war, few soldiers and Marines were fighting in the Pacific Theater, and almost none anyplace else. The North African campaign, America's first extended effort against the Germans, did not begin until November 1942.

But when it came to service academy football, Roosevelt was not the only decision maker. Leaders in the War Department and the Navy Department debated. Was football important in the training of troops? One faction asserted that the sport had as much to do with training soldiers as riding a horse had to do with driving a tank. The point man for this position was Commander James Joseph "Gene" Tunney, the boxer who had defeated Jack Dempsey for the heavyweight championship and served as the Navy's director of physical training during the war.

At first glance, a former professional fighter would seem an unlikely candidate to argue that physical contact sports did not contribute to the development of hardened sailors and soldiers. Tunney, after all, had emerged from a tough New York neighborhood, served in the Marine Corps during World War I, and earned fame and millions of dollars punching other fighters in the ring. But he took a hard line about military training.

"We have got to get down to the fact that we are at war," he said in an interview. "You can't train a man to be a fighter by having him play football and baseball. It has to be done the hard way—with special calisthenics and road work to build stamina and bayonet drill and handling of weapons to develop a warrior psychology." Playing football was nothing more than "athletic boondoggling. . . . It has no place in war or in preparing for war." He even went so far as to cast aspersions on the peacetime pursuits that had earned him, in one case, a million dollars for ten rounds of boxing. "You cannot win a war nor can you build warrior psychology by reviving the recreational sports of the 'era of wonderful nonsense.'"[22]

Commander Thomas J. Hamilton, the head of Navy's Preflight and Physical Training and former head football coach at Annapolis, disagreed with virtually everything Tunney said. Not only were sports—and especially football—an important tool in training pilots and other soldiers, it was the essential tool. Football, he asserted, was the "nearest thing to actual war," the closest approximation to the battlefield experience. War above all else was about competition—between nations, armies and navies, and individual soldiers and sailors. "Competition," Hamilton wrote, "is as old as the Navy itself and it is just as traditionally Navy as John Paul Jones. In peace time and in war time, the method the Navy has used to train crews is by competition." No form of competition steeled men for the difficult task of flying combat missions and defeating the enemy on land, sea, or in the skies as football.[23]

Early reports from the nation's selective service branches charged that Americans were weak and dispirited, a legacy of the pacifist 1930s generation. An alarming number flunked their draft physicals because of health and mental deficiencies. What the boys of the nation needed most, Hamilton believed, was a crash course in violent competition, the taste of blood in their mouths, and the look of blood in their eyes. They needed football.

Hamilton and Lou Little, the head coach of Columbia University, became the leading spokesmen for the importance of football in developing warrior traits. "Play football," Little wrote in 1942. "Play it hard and intensively with an even more savage will-to-win than in peace-time. Play intercollegiate football as much as the speeded-up educational programs which have accompanied the nation's war effort will permit." Play football and win the war. "There is no lesson football can teach the American college athlete that will not help him when and if he becomes an actual combatant in our fighting forces."[24]

Throughout the first six months of 1942, Tunney and Hamilton battled for the minds of the Navy brass in the press and naval bureaucracy. Gene Tunney never had a chance. Both former Navy Secretary Josephus Daniels and current Navy Secretary Frank Knox supported Hamilton's plan for training preflight troops. Knox maintained that there was a direct relationship between the "spirit which makes great football players and the spirit that makes great soldiers and sailors." For Hamilton, the holy trinity was: "Football! Navy! War! At no time in history have these words been more entwined and intermeshed than they now are." No one in the upper reaches of the Navy hierarchy disagreed.[25]

In 1942 a knockout victory by Hamilton was signaled by the creation of the V-5 Preflight Program. V-5 was the first step in a larger system of V-programs. There was a V-1 program for college freshmen and sophomores, a V-5 Preflight Program for aviation trainees, and a V-7 program for college juniors and seniors. The term of study initially ranged from eight months, for participants with seven college semesters under their belts, to two years, for those with no college experience. The goal of the V-programs was to educate and train junior officers to fight the war. It was not to become an "athletic boondoggle," as Tunney charged, or a government handout to colleges. As one authority on the program wrote, the V-programs were "not intended to protect young men from fighting, to save colleges from closing, or to achieve any of the other ends often ascribed to it by admirers and critics."[26]

But the V-5 Preflight Program, and others that followed, made college football a priority. Its regiment was established by three high-ranking Navy men: Undersecretary of the Navy James Forrestal, commander of aeronautics training Captain Arthur Redford, and director of flight training Lieutenant Commander Thomas J. Hamilton. In 1942 the Navy opened V-5 programs at the University of Georgia, the University of North Carolina, the University of Iowa, and St. Mary's College in California. Another one was opened in 1943, at the Del Monte Hotel in Monterey, California. Their goal was simple: use sports to train pilots. Along with a rigorous academic curriculum, which included mathematics, physics, celestial navigation, and aerology, and lessons in naval nomenclature and navigation signals, they hardened their bodies. Hamilton's plan called for the trainees to participate in a daily regimen of an hour and a half of running, swimming, chopping wood, calisthenics, and hard labor, in addition to another hour and a half of instruction in team and combative sports. Finally, the plan called for the men to play two hours of team sports a day. Football was the king of those sports, the sine qua non of the V-5 program. The best players, the ones with college football experience before the war, were on the varsity teams. The ones with limited prewar exposure played on intramural squads.[27]

Thousands of college football players entered the V programs. Unquestionably, Hamilton's and the Navy's initiatives "saved" college football during the first year of the war. For the work he accomplished in 1942, the National Collegiate Athletic Association chose Hamilton as football's "Man of the Year."[28]

The game, at least for another season, would go on.

4

★ ★ ★

Lost Teeth and Lost Chances

War is competition and the boys in this country grew
up on a background of competition. . . . We're not
content to play a game, we want to win that game. . . .
To lose is intolerable.

— JOHN KIERAN, *NEW YORK TIMES* SPORTSWRITER

RED BLAIK STILL needed a few more good men if he
hoped to beat Notre Dame or Navy. In February 1942,
Fats Ellinger traveled to Washington to work on several
congressmen, rounding up a few appointments for football recruits. He was staying in the home of Louisiana Congressman
Eddie Hebert and, according to his usual practice, paying no
attention to what he ate or drank or the hours he was keeping,
despite the severe heart problem that kept him out of uniform.
On the night of February 12, alone in his room, Fats suffered a
fatal heart attack. John Kieran of the *New York Times* wrote, "In
his heart—that bad heart he had been told about—he was the
Army officer that he never could be in fact. The thrill of his life
came when, with Red Blaik, he went back to West Point. He was,
by his own appointment, the Army's most devoted uncommis-
sioned officer." Ellinger was buried in the cemetery at West Point
on a cold day with a fresh blanket of snow on the ground. Blaik

mourned with his friends. "Such a friend and comrade is not replaced," he later wrote.[1]

Despite the loss, Blaik's recruiting efforts actually had an unusual wartime advantage over those of most schools. In most of the college programs, replacements were of immediate concern. But the football players at West Point and Annapolis were officers in training, and they would remain in school until they graduated.

Although the War Department reduced the course of study from four to three years in an effort to train more officers, cadets were not subject to the draft. They were already in the Army, though they would not receive their commissions until they graduated. This simple fact allowed Blaik to recruit effectively and plan accordingly. He knew, for example, that Doug Kenna and the other gifted cadets who entered the Academy in 1942 would be around for three seasons — that is, if they made their grades and were not busted out.

Or busted up. Injuries were always an incalculable factor for Blaik, the one thing he could not predict, chart, and integrate into his game plan. And in 1942 — as in 1941 — Army had talent, but it didn't run deep. Even with the addition of some gifted plebes, Army could not afford many serious injuries. As Olds commented, "In 1942 we had some fine players, some veterans and some plebes. But not quite enough. And many of the older guys had one eye on the war, and too many of the younger ones needed more beef on them and more experience."[2]

Blaik, however, needed some of the plebes to perform immediately. Like Kenna, some of them had played as freshmen at another school before transferring to West Point. Backs like Bob Woods, Tom Lombardo, Dale Hall, and George Troxell, and linemen like Ed Rafalko, Joe Stanowicz, and Bob St. Onge knew the game and understood what it took to play at an elite level. Blaik recognized that, of them all, Kenna was special. More than just a superb athlete, he was a ferocious competitor, a winner, and a natural leader. The number-one student in his high school class, a superior football, basketball, and tennis player, he seemed indomitable, ready, in Blaik's words, "to pay the price."

Kenna soon learned what the price would be. In one of the first full scrimmages he was hit and fell awkwardly. He knew something was wrong when he saw his left arm was "flipped back over" his shoulder and he couldn't move it. His arm was shattered, broken in seven different places from his elbow to his shoulder. At the post hospital, physicians set his arm and put it in a big L-shaped cast to immobilize his shoulder. Before it had even begun, Kenna's season appeared over.[3]

But Blaik wasn't so sure. For help in matters concerning the health and physical well-being of his players, he relied on Roland "the Beaver" Bevan, a garishly dressed trainer with a year-round tan who had been with Red since 1935. The two had similar ideas on conditioning. "Nowhere in his lexicon could be found the word 'coddle,'" Blaik wrote. "He did not drink or smoke, and he watched his weight assiduously." He watched his players less carefully. Some trainers drew a line between a player's being hurt and being injured; the Beaver drew his line between a player's being hurt and being dead. If a player was dead, he couldn't play. If he were merely injured, he could.[4]

Blaik claimed that Bevan had a nose for "malingering," a euphemism for a trainer's ability to tell when an injured player was being a trifle overdramatic. As an illustration, Blaik recounted the story of a West Point quarterback who was hit near the opposing team's sideline. Blaik believed he was injured, perhaps lost for the season. The Army physician rushed across the field as concerned teammates gathered around their quarterback. Bevan stood coldly, indifferently, beside Blaik, hardly glancing across the field.

Angered, Blaik uncharacteristically yelled, "What's the matter with you, Roland? Can't you see he may be badly hurt?"

"There is nothing the matter with him," Bevan responded,

sarcasm in his voice. "You ought to know him by now. You ought to know he's putting on an act."

"Never mind what you think or what I ought to know! You get the hell out there!"

Bevan sauntered casually across the field to the player. Gently he nudged his toe against the player's ribs, saying, "You can get up now. Everyone has seen you. You'll get applause and be the old school hero." With that, the player got up and walked to the center of the field, ready to resume the game.

As the player realized, Bevan had "made an ass" out of him. Blaik later wrote, "It was the last time . . . the quarterback ever indulged in histrionics, and he was a better player for it."[5]

But not all players were actors, and an arm broken in seven places, like Kenna's, was not a candidate for a quick fix. Almost seventy years later, Kenna could vividly recall Bevan's reaction: "Rollie didn't believe in injuries. I'm serious. He really didn't. If you had a broken leg he'd tell you to rub a little dirt on it and run it off. That was his idea of treatment." While Kenna was in the hospital, naturally depressed by the injury, Bevan came for a visit. "God damn it," he said, "you're going to start the Notre Dame game."

Two weeks later Bevan ordered Kenna's cast removed and began to treat the plebe with water and heat therapy. Bevan also had him eat a jar of calcium pills a day. "I ate handfuls at a time. I grew so much calcium in my arm that it is deformed," Kenna recalled. Although the pain remained and he had to struggle one-armed through a drafting class, Kenna was on the road to recovery.

Kenna had broken his arm in late September, only a few weeks before the first game of the season. The Notre Dame game was at Yankee Stadium on November 7. He had roughly six weeks to heal or, perhaps more accurately, find a way "to get out on the damn field." Fortunately for Army, their season was frontloaded with weaker teams.

The 1942 college season took place as scheduled, with some modifications. Most eligibility rules were scrapped, and freshmen, transfers, and virtually everyone else who could run, tackle, or kick was welcomed with open arms. Team travel was a mess. With rationing and travel restrictions going into effect, getting a team anywhere on buses or trains was often a logistical nightmare. But in 1942 and throughout the war, school administrators, coaches, and teams proved remarkably resilient. They made do with used equipment and improvised schedules and travel plans, but they kept the game going.

Army opened its season at Michie Stadium by defeating Lafayette College, 14–0, led by the running of Hank Mazur and Ralph Hill and the line play of Robin Olds. An Associated Press reporter wrote that Army "stumbled" to victory, noting that although the cadets dominated the play, they missed repeated chances to score.[6]

Like all college teams during the war, Army made mistakes because of erratic practice schedules. Army was not losing players to the draft, but the cadets' academic and training programs had been accelerated. For Robin Olds and the other pilots, the result was especially brutal. The summer before, Olds had learned to fly at the Spartan School of Aviation in Tulsa, Oklahoma. After only five and a half flight hours his instructor said, "OK, Olds, take her up and give me four good landings." Take her up—alone. Land her—alone. Olds survived, and during the next weeks he learned to loop and roll and spin, to dive toward a shack that he pretended was "full of Japs" and strafe it with imaginary bullets and bombs. Later he wrote, "Being alone in the immense sky, master of plane and self, was beyond anything I had imagined. Practicing what I'd been taught, and experimenting further into the envelope of possibilities, worked a magic I can only describe as ecstasy. It was total exuberance, surrender and mastery all at once."[7]

When Olds returned to the Academy, he was a pilot and a first-class cadet. "I was full of myself," he recalled. "Life was good." But the fall season quickly became punishing. He and the other Army Air Corps cadets went on an alternating day schedule. On the first day, Olds, Mazur, and the others were bused seventeen miles north to Stewart Field in Newburgh for flying instruction in the morning, bused back for their regular classes in the afternoon, and then they suited up for football practice. On the second day, it was academics, flight training, and football. They had to take the compressed two years of courses, complete their basic and advanced flight training, and still prepare for games. Like everyone else at West Point, they were tested every day in every class—no bell curves, no cream puff courses. Sometimes Olds had to return to Stewart Field after practice for night training. Often, after the nine-thirty lights-out, he went to a bathroom, sat on a john, turned on a flashlight, and studied late into the night. When he finally got to sleep he dreamed of flying.

Early in their plebe year all cadets learn to function without enough sleep. If they don't, they don't last at West Point. But for Olds and his group, sleep deprivation became a serious problem. In the air, mastering difficult maneuvers, any mistake could be deadly, especially in the mountains around Stewart Field. On October 29, 1942, Ernest Baker, Jr., and Louis Curcuru died in air accidents. Baker, the son of Colonel Ernest Baker, had attended Millard Prep with Olds. Baker and Curcuru were followed by Robert Horn on December 4 and Harold Young, Jr., on March 9, 1943. One crashed into a mountain, two lost control of their planes in spin-outs, and another miscalculated a landing. No one knew what role sheer, mind-numbing fatigue played in their deaths. It was not a subject anyone talked about.[8]

On the field, Olds took whatever he could get. "A 14–0 victory against Lafayette was a victory. Same as a 100–0 win. No style points. It was one down and on to the next." And so it went through most of October. Army rode roughshod over three Ivy League teams, defeating Cornell 28–8, Columbia 34–6, and

Harvard 14–0. Finally, on Halloween Day, they faced a strong Pennsylvania team. By then, East Coast sportswriters had pronounced that Blaik had worked a miracle on the Hudson. They were already writing about the following week's Army–Notre Dame game in the Bronx. "Army will probably come up to the Notre Dame game unbeaten," Shirley Povich predicted. Most likely, agreed Edward W. Cochrane, seeing that Red Blaik had "a powerful machine."[9]

The sportswriters' hype bothered Blaik. Interviewed in his office high in the South Gym, he was less interested in the past month than the next one. "Do you see that schedule hanging there on the wall?" he asked, pointing to the spot. "Do you see what's ahead? Pennsylvania on Saturday, then Notre Dame, Virginia Poly, Princeton and Navy. If I were inclined to be optimistic as a result of our past record, I'd be sobered by the contemplation of what's ahead." In the first four games, Blaik explained, Army had played teams in their own class. But now the "bed of roses" days were over. "Now we're stepping up, but not out, I hope." Thinking of Penn and Notre Dame, he added, "If we could only skip the next two games I'd feel a little better."[10]

After playing the first four games in small venues, Army now traveled to Philadelphia's Franklin Field, where nearly 60,000 fans held tickets for the Army-Penn game. Reporters described the atmosphere as "pre-war." For one afternoon the spectators seemed to forget the scarcity of meat, coffee, and butter; the ration cards for gas and the public drives for scrap metal, rubber, and cooking fat; the government's control over wages, rents, and labor disputes. On Saturday, the last day of October, with the leaves the color of fire and just a touch of winter in the air, it was all about boys who would soon be men. For one afternoon it was autumn, football, and a better time and place.

The game was a defensive struggle. Army's scouting report had emphasized the need to stop runner Bert Stiff. "Stiff Stiff," a scout had written. For two quarters the Cadets followed the script. The score was 0–0 at the end of the first half. In the second half Army began to make mistakes. In the third quarter, Hank Mazur threw an interception that a Penn back returned to the Army 4. Three plays later Stiff carried it in from the 1. In the fourth quarter, substitute back Bob "Woody" Woods ran to the left and threw a left-handed pass into the flat. Penn's Don Bitler intercepted the ball and returned it for a touchdown. A few minutes later Penn scored again. The final score was 19–0. Penn's best offense had been its defense. Army simply could not move the ball. They gained less than 150 yards and had to punt fourteen times.[11]

The game was bruising from beginning to end, and the Army injury list looked like an after-action report. Mazur and Ralph Hill were both hurt. Blaik said that he might have to start Woods and Carl Anderson in their place. Woods, a handsome, irrepressible character from Corning, New York, was unfazed by the prospect. He had played his freshman year in 1939 at Bucknell College and his next two years for Navy. A combination of youthful escapades and disastrous math grades resulted in his early departure from Annapolis. Fortunately, Blaik believed in second chances, especially for fast running backs, and he arranged an appointment through a Georgia congressman. There was only one problem: no one had sent Woods the official notice. He was almost twenty-two years old, and nonmilitary cadets had to take the oath before they reached twenty-two. Taking a chance that his papers had been sent to West Point, on the eve of his birthday Woods and his father borrowed gasoline from a neighbor, embarked on a 240-mile trip to West Point at five-thirty in the evening, ran into fog in the Hudson River valley, got stopped in Newburgh for speeding, explained their dilemma to a tolerant policeman, received a police escort to the gates of the Academy, and proceeded to the adjutant quarters. Eight minutes before midnight, Robert Woods took the oath as a cadet of the United States Military Academy.

After all that, the prospect of starting against the vaunted Notre Dame eleven did not cause Woods's stomach to churn. "I was smaller than most of the other boys but I never doubted my ability to play against anybody. It was just not anything I really considered. I knew that if I got an opening I could race toward the goal line about as fast as anyone else on the team," he said.[12]

After the lackluster performance of his backs against Penn, Blaik wanted even more firepower. He wanted Kenna, and Bevan assured him that the plebe was ready for action. If his arm wasn't completely mended, it was close enough. "Come Notre Dame time," Kenna said, "my arm was still in a cast, but now they had it in a cast with my hand tied to my belly. I could flip the hand out enough to take a handoff but I couldn't move the wrist. So I was ready to play the Notre Dame game with one good arm and one tied to my side. It didn't hurt too much. I just couldn't do much to the bad side."[13]

Blaik took his wounded cadets to New York the day before the game. Sportswriters accurately predicted more than 75,000 fans would turn out at Yankee Stadium, making it the year's largest crowd for any sports contest in the East. Even with wartime restrictions, New York was festive, with football the topic of the week. The Army–Notre Dame contest was just one of several games in the city. CCNY and Moravian would play at Lewisohn Stadium, Columbia and Colgate at Baker Field, and Fordham and LSU at the Polo Grounds. Football news was as inescapable, and even more reliably obtained, as war news. The night before the game, press, radio, stage, and screen stars appeared at the traditional Army–Notre Dame pregame rally at the Waldorf-Astoria Hotel, and the ball to be used in the game was auctioned off for the Army Emergency Relief Fund. More than 2,000 alumni attended the event, mingling with the stars of the day and military leaders from both war theaters.[14]

As the teams lined up for the two o'clock kickoff, the Notre

Dame players swaggered with confidence. Since tying Wisconsin in their opening game and dropping their second to Georgia Tech, the Irish had won four straight. Coach Frank Leahy had scrapped the traditional Notre Dame box for the recently developed T formation. Led by All-American quarterback Angelo Bertelli, they looked unbeatable. By comparison, Army looked banged up, dead tired, and thoroughly beatable. In addition, Notre Dame seemed to have Army's number: Army had not scored a point against them since 1938 and had not won a game since 1931.

When Bob Woods fumbled the ball in the opening series and Notre Dame recovered it on the Cadets' 31-yard line, the Irish stands erupted, anticipating another one-sided victory. But Army stiffened, fighting savagely to keep Notre Dame out of the end zone. Led by Olds, they stopped the Irish at their own 15 and 28 in the first quarter and at the 25, 30, and 31 in the second. While Olds roamed from end to end making tackles on the line, Army's defensive backs blanketed the Irish receivers, holding Bertelli to only four completions and 22 yards. Somehow, despite Army's offensive turnovers and miscues, the game was scoreless at the half.

In the middle of the third quarter Army runner Ralph Hill fumbled, giving the Irish the ball 35 yards from the end zone. By then Kenna was in the game. He recalled, "Our offense was, to say the least, anemic. Blaik put me in to see if I could get something going, and he kind of hid me at safety to keep me out of the action defensively. But Dick Creevy, a really good back, broke through the center of the line and took one look at my broken arm strapped to my side, and cut to that side. I lunged at him and tried to make a cross-armed tackle, but he went in for a touchdown." The quarter ended with Notre Dame holding a 7–0 lead.[15]

In the last quarter, Hank Mazur threw a long desperation pass that appeared to be tracking toward an Irish defensive back, but John Hennessey made a "miraculous catch," wrestling the ball from the safety's hands. The 41-yard completion moved the ball to the Irish 14. The 2,200 cadets at the game roared, their team finally in position to score. A pass advanced the ball to the 5, but an offside penalty moved it back to the 10. Three incomplete passes followed, ending Army's best offensive series. Notre Dame scored again in the last seconds of the game. Once again, the Irish had shut out Army.

Three games remained on the schedule, but now Blaik focused on getting his team well for the only one that mattered: Navy. In victories against Virginia Tech and Princeton, he substituted freely and gave the starters plenty of rest. Both Woods and plebe Tom Lombardo scored touchdowns against Virginia Tech. Princeton had always played well against Army—the Cadets had won only one of ten previous contests—but before the game, Blaik had the Army physician remove Kenna's cast, telling reporters that he would use Doug more as a passer. "The arm still didn't feel right, but I played—and I passed," Kenna recalled. In Army's second game of the season at Yankee Stadium, Kenna, dubbed "the new plebe of destiny" by the *New York Times,* passed for two touchdowns, Lombardo scored two, and Bob Woods ran for three. Army won, 40–7.[16]

Only Navy remained, but there were doubts that the game would take place. In the War Department in Washington, D.C., debate simmered over whether it was a good idea for Army and Navy to play a major football game during a war. A few military and civilian leaders thought that a hotly contested game between Army and Navy would send the wrong message at the very moment that the two branches were supposed to be working in concert. They noted that in 1917 and 1918, during the Great War, the service academies had canceled the game.

Even more important than the desire to show unity, however, was the need to reinforce the nation's rationing program. In an August 1942 memorandum to Chief of Staff George C.

Marshall, General Brehon Somervell, commander of the Army Service Forces and the central logistics officer, wrote, "We have been leaders in the movement to conserve rubber, in the interests of our future war needs, by rationing of gas and by the elimination of all pleasure and other needless driving. In doing so we have pressed for effective action on the part of the many government and state agencies concerned. . . . To play the Army-Navy game this fall would negate our whole effort." Staging the game, Somervell maintained, would "violate all the arguments" the Army had advanced for rationing and "prove us unworthy of the leadership we have assumed."[17]

Football to Somervell was not a "morale factor." It was simply a "mass spectacle" that encouraged Americans to clog the highways and railways. A thorough, hard-driving engineer who was overseeing the construction of the Pentagon, he adhered ruthlessly to a wartime standard. In his cost-benefit analysis, the Army-Navy game hurt more than it helped.

Throughout the summer and fall, new West Point Superintendent Major General Francis B. Wilby lobbied continuously for Army's football program. He wrote to General Marshall that football was crucial to the Academy's well-being; he told the director of the Army Emergency Relief Fund that the broadcast rights for the Army-Navy game would permit the Army Athletic Association to contribute $50,000 to the fund; and he pulled every string in and around the White House that he could reach. By early October, his tireless letter writing and meddling had yielded results. The game would take place, but not in Philadelphia's cavernous Municipal Stadium. It would be a smaller affair, at Thompson Stadium in Annapolis.[18]

General Joseph T. McNarney, deputy chief of staff and one of Wilby's inside operators, reported that the game was discussed at the October 2 Cabinet meeting. Secretary of War Henry Stimson told the president that he was against holding the game in Annapolis and would not attend. He thought the press would jump on any news of Army and Navy officers driving government and private automobiles from Washington to Annapolis. Roosevelt admitted that he had not considered that point and thought he might place additional restrictions on attendance, but he insisted that the most important national game on the football calendar would take place.[19]

Slowly, fact by fact, the details of the Army-Navy game reached the public. For the first time since 1893 the contest would take place in Annapolis, and except in a few special cases, no one residing more than ten miles from 20,000-seat Thompson Stadium would be permitted to attend the game. That included the entire Corps of Cadets. In place of the loyal, vocal Corps, two of Navy's four battalions of midshipmen were assigned to the Army sideline and commanded to cheer for the Cadets. Wilby dispatched a cheerleader to Annapolis to teach the midshipmen the "text and timing" of Army's cheers and songs. But even with the scaled-down proceedings, more than 40 million Americans in the United States and on bases throughout the world would listen to the WIP, MBS, NBC, and CBS broadcasts of the game. It was the largest listening audience in the history of the contest.[20]

For Coach Blaik, the game took the shape of a "nightmare." He wrote to General MacArthur that the travel restrictions ensured that almost all of the spectators would be midshipmen and Navy supporters. Even the Army officers from Fort Meade, thirteen miles from the stadium, were not permitted to attend. As a consequence, the official party of six Army officers who accompanied the team "were quite conspicuous in the background of blue."[21]

The day of the game lacked the usual big-game tension. Bob Woods noticed it as the team ate breakfast at the Lord Baltimore Hotel. "The team was too casual, almost as if it was going to play just another game. But Navy was not just another team. For Navy, Army was by far the most important game of the season. I've always thought that Army wanted to beat Notre Dame more than any other team. But Navy's goal was always to defeat Army."[22]

Woods was only a plebe, but he had played for Navy in 1941, and no one on the Army team knew the Navy players better. "I know what I wanted to do," Woods said. "I wanted to go up to Coach Blaik and say, 'Sir, I know this Navy team, and they're going to come out roaring. I think you should speak to the team and fire them up.'" But Woods kept silent.

Everything about the day was eerie. Blaik sensed it, too. It "was so devoid of the usual game excitement," he wrote, "as to seem unreal." It was as if, due to some national emergency, the country had been ordered indoors. "On the trip from Baltimore to Annapolis we didn't pass twenty-five cars, and when we entered the Naval Academy grounds there was not a Corporal's guard to be seen." The bus driver even got lost several times looking for the stadium. When they finally found it, "there were less than twenty-five people in the stands." Everything seemed muffled. "The pre-game warm up before the small crowd took on the form of the fantastic, when the Middies on the so-called Army side gave our team the Corps cheers."[23]

As the midshipmen took their places and local spectators found their seats, the unique reality of the game became clear. A few people outside Annapolis were permitted to come. Some of the Middies' dates were trucked in from Washington, which struck one reporter as "reminiscent of a scene from a Russian movie." Most major sporting events bring together movie stars, stage personalities, captains of industry, military brass, political leaders, and millionaires. The 1942 Army-Navy game became famous for who wasn't there, which was close to everybody. Eleanor Roosevelt, who loved the pageantry of the game, lived outside the ten-mile radius and stayed away. There wasn't much gold braid on the military uniforms or gold stars on shoulders. Except for Maryland's Governor Herbert R. O'Conor, Navy's

superintendent Rear Admiral J. R. Beardall, and Army superintendent Major General Francis B. Wilby, the stands were VIP-
free.[24]

Army was a 3–1 favorite to win the contest, but their record
in important games had been terrible since Hitler had invaded
Poland. It was painful for the Academy's faithful to contemplate:
Pennsylvania, 0-3; Notre Dame, 0-3-1; Navy, 0-3. But its players were healthier than they had been since the beginning of the
season, and Navy had never beaten Army four straight.

Even if half of the 3,200 midshipmen at the game were cheering for Army, the atmosphere tilted toward Navy. Midway in the
first quarter, the game settled into a pattern best described as
"too much Navy and almost no Army." The pace of the game
was furious. Allison Danzig commented, "The crowd was in
bedlam and the action was so fast that there wasn't time to light
a cigarette in the press box." The midshipmen behind Navy's
bench cheered with delight, joined in the celebration by the middies in the "Army" rooting section, who forgot their assignment
during the frenetic action.[25]

Time after time, Navy drove deep into Army territory. In the
second quarter, Navy had drives that stalled on the Army 6-inch,
6-yard, and 12-yard lines. Meanwhile, on three consecutive series Mazur had to punt from his own end zone. On the third
kick, Gordon Studer returned the ball to the Army 4. A few plays
later, plebe substitute Joe Sullivan plunged across the goal line
from the 1.

Navy dominated the line play, holding Army to 35 yards of
offense in the first half. "Those guys used every trick you could
imagine," recalled Olds. "Held, tripped, clipped, kicked—everything, the dirty bastards. And the referees were blind. Didn't see
a thing." On one play early in the second quarter Olds broke
through the line, his eyes on Hal Hamberg, who was dropping
back to pass. Shifting to pick off Olds, a Navy blocker took aim
and slammed a violent forearm into the tackle's mouth, knock-

ing out his two front teeth and breaking off pieces of several others. His teeth had ripped open a gash in his lower lip and cut his tongue. Olds dropped to the ground, screaming, instinctively beginning to look for his teeth. Francis Merritt, the other tackle, bent close and asked what he was doing.[26]

"I think I lost some teeth," Olds said. "Help me find them."

Merritt was shocked. Olds was spitting out blood as he talked, and his lip was gashed open. There was too much blood to tell how bad his teeth were, but one thing was clear: Olds was done. "You need to get out of here, Robin. You're in really bad shape. You need a doctor right now."

"But I got to find my teeth," he insisted.

"Why?"

"I don't know, I just do," Olds said as he continued to comb the grass for them.

Olds left the game, replaced by his close friend Henry Romanek, who had seen what had happened to Olds. Enraged, he played like a wild man, punching, hitting after the whistle, and trying in whatever way he could to even the score. "I was out of control," he recalled. "It was no longer a game for me." He soon drew a penalty, and Blaik pulled him out of the game.

Back in the locker room, team doctor Captain Ollie Neiss cleaned Olds's mouth and sewed thirty-two stitches in his lip. One of the best-looking cadets on the team, Olds now looked as if he had been knocked through the front window of a car. He had cotton stuffed in his mouth and nose, a bandage covering his lower jaw, and a uniform covered with blood.

With his mouth and tongue swollen, Olds communicated to Blaik through sign language: he wanted to get back in the game. Blaik asked Neiss, who answered, "He'll be all right if he can stand it." With a wave, Blaik sent him into action.

It did not take him long to even the score. During a pass play, Olds saw his Navy nemesis miss a block and fall to the ground. Before he could rise to his feet, Olds crashed into him, breaking several of his ribs. "It was the only time in my entire career that I intentionally tried to hurt anyone. But I was determined to get that little sonofabitch," he remembered. As the Navy player lay on the ground, rolling back and forth in pain, Olds got close to his ear and said, "You sonofabitch, remember that. Your ribs will heal. I'll never get my teeth back."

At the half Navy had 7 points, Army none. If the Cadets needed any inspiration greater than the performance of Olds, they were not likely to find it, and in the second half they needed it.

Inspiration is a poor substitute for execution and smart play. In Army's first series in the second half substitute back Carl Anderson fumbled the ball away, and in the third series Mazur threw an interception. Navy returned the ball to the Army 35, and scored two plays later. 14–0. Army still had not shown even an inkling of an offense.

Army's next series went nowhere. Adding to the humiliation, Mazur's punt went off the side of his foot and only moved the ball 1 yard forward. Blaik had seen enough. Although it was Mazur's final game—he would graduate in January 1943 and fly in the war by the spring—Blaik pulled him and sent in Kenna.

With his arm more or less healed, Kenna demonstrated the full range of his talents. "The final quarter belonged pretty much to Army," a reporter wrote. More accurately, it belonged to Kenna. Passing and running, he twice drove Army down the field. In one series he moved the ball 76 yards to the Navy 6; in another he moved it 53 yards to the Navy 3. But neither drive pushed the ball into Navy's end zone. Final score: Navy 14, Army 0.

It was a cold, uncomfortable Army locker room. Olds remembered that "those cheap bastards" had provided neither hot water nor enough towels. Blaik, normally quiet in defeat, said little. He did approach Olds, whose performance he later described as "one of the most magnificent demonstrations of fortitude and determination I ever saw on a football field."

"Robin, I am sorry about your losing your teeth," he said.

"That's all right. I always wondered how I'd look without them," Olds answered, trying to force a smile. Almost sixty years later he could still smile about the Navy game and his last football season, writing, "For some reason, my performance during our 6-3 season earned me All-American honors, but I never did get my goddamn teeth back."[27]

It had been a disappointing year. In a letter to MacArthur, Coach Blaik—now Colonel Blaik—ignored the team's successes and agonized over its failures. He had built the Army offense around Mazur's running, passing, and kicking, but as the season progressed and Hank came closer to graduating and going off to the war, his production lagged. In justice to Mazur, Blaik recognized that he "did not have the time nor the absorbing interest so essential to positive accomplishment. [His] first love had to be [his] career and to graduate in January with wings dictated [his] every thought." Still, Blaik felt let down by many of the third- and fourth-year cadets: "[W]e failed to meet our possibilities and my personal disappointment comes from the realization that the football contribution to a rejuvenated Corps spirit is not complete."

The future looked brighter, however. Of the twenty-two letter winners, seven were plebes and eight yearlings. Kenna had ended the season as he had begun it. And Tom Lombardo, George Troxell, Bob Woods, Ed Rafalko, Dale Hall, and Joe Stanowicz had shown promise. More important, Blaik had looked into Army's Promised Land. On Wednesday, November 4, 1942, just three days before the Army–Notre Dame game, he had his plebe team scrimmage against the varsity. The Irish had made the transition to the T formation, and the plebes spent a few days trying to master its complexities; they consistently broke through the varsity line and made long gains. After the practice Blaik asked an assistant, "If our plebes, with that little experience, can make the T go that way, what would an experienced varsity do with it?"[28]

The idea of the T—with its emphasis on speed, deception, and, especially, discipline—appealed to Blaik's Scottish soul. No matter what modifications coaches devised, at its core the single wing was about power. It trafficked in runs between the tackles and physical man-on-man confrontations. It was an infantryman's idea of football. The T was more of a cavalry, or armor, offensive, the sort of attack that emphasized the general's tactics more than the soldiers' guts. It was an offense made for Colonel Earl Blaik. All he needed was a few more swift backs and a legion of smart, undersized, quick, and powerful linemen. With the T, and a few more recruits, he could turn Army football into one of the first modern teams. And he could take charge as never before.

5

★ ★ ★

"God Gave Me That"

The hocus-pocus which is called the T-Formation
made 90,000 spectator converts and seemed definitely
to signal the arrival of a new era in college football.
The day of the tug-of-war is out—Clark Shaughnessy
and his Stanford Indians have definitely killed it.

— CURLEY GRIEVE, *SAN FRANCISCO EXAMINER*

CHIEF OF STAFF General George C. Marshall liked football—he really did. In his final year at Virginia Military Institute he went out for the team, something of a terror at 145 pounds on a scale that weighed heavy. He would have tried out earlier, but he promised his mother to stay away from the game during his first two years, and VMI's team was disbanded because of an outbreak of typhoid fever his third year. But he made his last year count. His tenacious defense helped VMI tie Virginia and defeat their archrival, Virginia Polytechnic Institute. Of Marshall's play in the VPI game, the *Rockbridge County News* commented that "the tackling of G. Marshall in backing up the interference was of the highest order."[1]

Over the years, he even grew to respect the football program at the United States Military Academy—he did not love it like Dwight Eisenhower and Omar Bradley and Douglas MacArthur did, but he liked it well enough for a nongraduate. It was Marshall, after all, who reportedly said during World War II, "I want an officer for a secret and dangerous mission. I want a West Point football player." Therefore it must have been difficult for him to sit in his Washington, D.C., office in 1942 and write a crushing letter to General Francis B. Wilby, the new superintendent at the Academy.

"I regret that the War Department cannot approve your recent request for the movement of the Corps of Cadets from West Point to New York, Cambridge and Philadelphia to attend six football games now scheduled to be played this fall," he wrote. Hence that odd Navy game. As for the 1943 season, Marshall had grave reservations: "As much as we recognize its morale value, it certainly is not essential to a people at war. There seems to be no compromise to the acceptance of our full responsibility for leadership in this matter. We must not only practice what we preach, but we must guide others to similar positive action."

His logic marched relentlessly toward its inevitable conclusion: "I therefore direct that the United States Military Academy football schedule for 1943 be cancelled as a measure to conserve transportation to serve the war needs."[2]

On the other side of the country a young boy began his last high school football season. "He had history written all over him," one of his teammates later observed. But he looked more like a choirboy than a football player. Handsome, with rosy cheeks and an ever-present smile, he was the boy next door, the one who was always delivering newspapers, mowing lawns, and raking leaves in his hometown of La Verne, California. He was small, "a skimpy scamp scaling but 160," wrote the *Los Angeles Times*. And he probably was not even 160. But when he touched a football he became pure speed and grace, shifting gears, avoiding tacklers, and darting from one side of the field to the other. Everyone who watched him play knew he was special. In 1942 one sportswriter, who had followed the high school scene for decades, wrote that the kid was "perhaps the outstanding prep athlete developed in the Southland since Jackie Robinson."[3]

His name was Glenn Davis. His high school football coach claimed that Glenn began showing signs of exceptional athletic talent when he was ten, for "he could pass as well as any boy on the varsity team!" Many accounts of his talent verge on the mythical. Al Wolf, a sports columnist for the *Los Angeles Times,* gushed, "His speed is natural. Without seriously training Glenn placed in the Southern California 100 and 220 finals in 1942 and 1943." Even Davis himself was mystified about the source of his most distinguishing trait, his unnatural speed. "God gave me that," he said toward the end of his life. "I didn't have to work for it."[4]

Davis set league and Southern California scoring records during his sophomore and junior seasons, but during his senior year he was virtually unstoppable. "The thing about Glenn," his Army teammate Doug Kenna noted, "is that he had three forward gears that no one else had. He was also the best cutback runner I ever saw—always looking to get out the other way. And when he got a half step on anybody—I mean anybody—he was gone. No one could catch him." He might have been the fastest football player ever at that time, faster than Carlisle's Jim Thorpe, Army's Elmer Oliphant, Notre Dame's George Gipp, Illinois's Red Grange, Michigan's Tom Harmon—faster, in fact, than any of the legendary runners. During that last prep year his team, Bonita High School, finished 9–0 and won the Class A Southern California Championship. Davis scored a state record 237 points, an average of 26.5 points per game. In the championship game, a 39–6 victory, he scored 32 points on five touchdowns and two extra points, and he passed for the other touchdown. He scored on runs of 4, 6, 12, 59, and 78 yards, on dashes up the middle and sprints around the ends, and on long punt returns.[5]

With his All-American speed and All-American smile, with his phenomenal success on the football field, baseball field, basketball court, and cinder track, Davis might have formed a lofty opinion of himself. But he was quiet, soft-spoken, and shy. The son of a banker, he had the modest comportment of his father's profession in that era. His best friend was his twin brother, Ralph. He was raised by Southern-born parents to say "Yes, sir" and "No, sir," to respect others, and to take only what he had earned. He had earned an athletic scholarship.

Glenn considered going into the Navy V-12 program at the University of Southern California, but before he made the decision he began to hear from Earl Blaik. "I didn't know anything about West Coast football," Blaik recalled. But he had a friend, the head of the Dramatics Department at Dartmouth, who had ties to the Los Angeles area and knew about Davis. "This is a great, great, great prospect," he said. Better yet, the boy wanted to go to a service school. Blaik made several more inquiries. Everyone said the same thing—the kid, though small, was in a class by himself. The only problem was that Glenn and Ralph wanted to go to the same school. It had to be a package deal, which was easier done at a place like USC than Army. But Blaik and Wilby had pull. Glenn got an appointment from Congressman Jerry Voorhis in the 12th District in Los Angeles County, and Ralph got a presidential appointment. By the middle of the summer, they had packed their bags and boarded a cross-country train to West Point, where they stayed with the Blaik family while they studied for their entrance exams.[6]

Davis's manners and seriousness impressed Blaik, and his athleticism soon became apparent. In the Master of the Sword physical fitness test, Davis blew away Kenna's record. A perfect score was 1,000 points; the average for all cadets was about 550 points. Kenna had scored 901½; Davis finished with 962½. No examiner at the Academy had ever seen such a combination of speed, strength, explosiveness, and nearly perfect coordination. Blaik tried to put Davis's athletic ability into words: "[Y]ou're talking about Ted Williams, you're talking about the greats, Ty Cobb, when you're talking about Glenn." Comparing Davis and Doc Blanchard, Army's two great backs, Bill Yeoman, a teammate of both players and a longtime Division I-A coach, said, "There are words to describe how good an athlete Doc Blanchard was. But there aren't words to describe how good Glenn Davis was."[7]

After a week of practice, any of Blaik's doubts about Davis's size had disappeared. But there were doubts about the 1943 season. George Marshall never signed or sent his letter canceling it, yet he remained doubtful. The Navy V-5 Preflight Program helped, but it trained pilots at only three universities, one college, and one training center. Most of the men who enlisted or were drafted into the military became soldiers in the Army. And as the 1942 season ended, General Marshall and the War Department still had not taken a stand on the immediate future of football.

In November 1942 the Selective Service lowered the draft age from twenty to eighteen, signaling a crisis. As college men at all levels left the nation's campuses and headed for induction centers, sports programs began to disappear. School officials eliminated many baseball and track programs, and spring football practices resembled a party for few guests. In 1942, for example, more than one hundred players had turned out for the University of Oklahoma spring football practice; in 1943 only thirty-six showed up, and most of them did not plan to be in school in the fall. With American offensives in North Africa and the Pacific demanding soldiers, the prospects for college athletics were more dire than ever.[8]

Marshall and Secretary of War Henry Stimson were content to write off college sports as war casualties. On February 12, 1943, the War Department announced that students in its college-administered Army Specialized Training Program (ASTP) were prohibited from playing intercollegiate sports. Varsity sports, including football, consumed too much time and energy. ASTP would now be lean and focused, an accelerated, no-frills effort to train officers and get them out in the field. The announcement, a United Press reporter observed, "was interpreted generally as a knockout blow to college football."[9]

College administrators expected that the Navy would follow the Army's lead, and they anticipated declining enrollment, reduced revenues, and slow death by economic strangulation. Dr. Edward S. Elliott, Columbia's director of athletics, admitted that "things look pretty dark," and Lew Andreas, Syracuse's director of athletics, noted that austerity would have a "disastrous effect" on college sports. Some maintained a stiff upper lip. Major John L. Griffith, the influential commissioner of the Western Conference — the Big Ten — asserted, "The caliber of the performers will not be so high as what we've had in the past, but we do not intend to quit as long as there are eleven boys who wish to play football, nine who are interested in baseball, and five who like to play basketball." But his words seemed to echo like pennies dropped into the coffers of his Big Ten universities.[10]

For the second time in two years the Navy sailed to the rescue. The week after the Army's decision, the Navy announced its officer and technical education plan. The college students enrolled in its V-12 program were permitted to be, well, college students. That is to say, they could join fraternities, date coeds, have a burger and fries at the malt shop, and, if they had the inclination, energy, and passing grades, play college football. "Students under the V-12 program," read the announcement, "will be required to maintain the Navy's standard of discipline, although military activities will be kept at a minimum and subordinated to academic training." Navy officials seemed to be saying, "Study hard but have some good, clean college fun."[11]

The V-12 program effectively consolidated the V-1, V-7, and V-5 programs to funnel qualified students into reserve midshipmen's schools and produce commissioned officers. It began on July 1, 1943, in time for the fall season. Thousands of college players entered the program. Some 372 colleges eventually participated in the Navy or the Army college training scheme — 241 Army and 131 Navy. The boom in government-funded students permitted many schools to remain open during the war, field varsity teams, and generate revenue from sports. Throughout the war, the schools with V-12 programs dominated the national rankings. Many of the finest coaches in the country enrolled in the V-5 and V-12 programs. Bernie Bierman of Minnesota was the dean of wartime coaches, and his peers included Woody Hayes, Bud Wilkinson, Bear Bryant, George Halas, Paul Brown, James Crowley, Matty Bell, and former University of Michigan standout player and future president of the United States Gerald Ford.

The Navy V-12 program was the single most important factor in the survival of the game for the remainder of the war, but several others contributed as well. Under the V-12 program, trainees were freely moved from one school to the next. A football player who had starred at Minnesota, for instance, might enter the V-12 program and be sent to USC, Notre Dame, Purdue, or any one of a hundred or so other schools. As a result, schools dropped all pretense of eligibility rules. Not only could freshmen play immediately, but so could all transfers. Eligibility rules stipulating number of hours, grades, and residency disappeared. In the Big Ten, nonstudents could even play the opening games of the season if they planned to enroll in the November V-12 semester.

The result of the different Army and Navy approaches toward education and sports created a whacky college football scene. Because Secretary of War Stimson refused to alter his edict of no varsity sports, colleges and universities with ASTPs had no chance to compete and normally disbanded their teams for the duration. Those with V-12 Navy and Coast Guard programs remained viable and competitive. But those with V-12 Marine programs, which attracted the most aggressive and talented athletes, were poised to dominate. Such Marine-rich institutions as

Notre Dame, College of the Pacific, Duke, Northwestern, Georgia Tech, Michigan, North Carolina, and Purdue, as well as such smaller schools as Franklin & Marshall, Rochester, and Colorado College, experienced unusual gridiron success during the war. Of course, as the war progressed and increasing numbers of Marines were needed to storm Pacific beaches, a number of college teams suffered a rapid reversal of fortune.[12]

While the Navy planned to save the free world and college football, Colonel Blaik, alone or with an assistant or two, imagined stratagems to defeat Navy. In 1941 Navy had been the favorite—and won. In 1942 Navy had been the underdog—and won. There had to be a way—there was always a way, he thought—to win. He would arrive at his office earlier, stay later, drive his staff harder, prepare his players better, give just a little bit more. "Blaik hated losing," Doug Kenna said. "It ate at him like a cancer. And losing to Navy was intolerable."[13]

The team needed new blood, and Blaik's first important adjustment was on the coaching staff. He had to replace the late Fats Ellinger as head line coach. At the top of his list of candidates was Herman Hickman. Herman was built along the general lines of a prolate spheroid, wide in the middle and blunted on the ends, more like a rugby ball than a football. Blaik likened him to a "gigantic iron beach ball." There really was no one quite like him in the game. Dubbed "the Poet Laureate of the Little Smokies," the son and grandson of Tennessee lawyers, he could outtalk, outdebate, outrecite, outplay, outwrestle, outeat, and outlaugh virtually everyone inside and outside the game. Certainly no one in the world had his résumé. It was almost as if the dour Blaik had searched America for the football coach most unlike himself.[14]

The legend of Herman Hickman began on the football field, where he played guard for Coach Robert Neyland's University of Tennessee Volunteers. In Hickman's three seasons (1929–1931), the Vols went 27-1-2, dominating southern football and forging a national reputation. In Hickman's final college game, against New York University in Yankee Stadium, he totally dominated the line of scrimmage and NYU's huge tackle Galahad Grant. Toward the end of the game, the NYU coach removed Grant to save him further embarrassment, asking only what it was like to play against Hickman. Grant replied, "Coach, that big Southerner just called me a Yankee sonofabitch and I didn't even answer him back—that's how good he is."[15]

Watching the game that day was the legendary sportswriter Grantland Rice, a Tennessean with a soft spot for colorful Rebels. Rice hailed from Murfreesboro and Hickman from Johnson City, neither too far from Knoxville, so they had once practically been neighbors, and they both loved English poetry and spirited conversation. Rice placed him on his 1932 All-American team and in the 1950s named him to his All-Time College Football team as a guard alongside the immortal Pudge Heffelfinger (Yale, 1902).[16]

Hickman's lifestyle was easy copy for any scribe. As Herman once wrote to sportswriter Tim Cohane, he believed that "if you go to bed early, don't overeat, save your money, and arise early, you will live longer—or at least it will seem a helluva lot longer." After college Hickman became an All-Pro guard for the Brooklyn Dodgers in the National Football League, as well as a popular professional wrestler. He ballooned to over 300 pounds, constantly smoked cigars, and quivered with laughter at the slightest provocation. He had been an orator in preparatory school and college and he had a talent for memorization, which he used to master an impressive literary canon. Although Alfred Lord Tennyson, Robert Browning, Rudyard Kipling, and Edgar Lee Masters were some of his favorites, his range was diverse. At the slightest prompting, he would break into a verse on whatever topic was under consideration.[17]

No single story could fully capture Herman's charm, but Rice

told one that came close. Around 1946, just after the greatest
Army teams had graduated, Rice and Pete Dolan of the *New
York Sun* fell into conversation with Hickman in a private dining car. The Navy game was two weeks off. Rice inquired about
Army's chances: were the Cadets still the Cadets of recent yore?
"Granny," Hickman began, "the best way I can put it is this"—
and, Rice remembered, "he immediately broke into a string of
verse, delivered with meticulous inflection in a trained, vibrant
voice. On and on he went, building up to the climax:

> *"Though much is taken, much abides; and though*
> *We are not now that strength which in old days*
> *Moved earth and heaven, that which we are, we are,—*
> *One equal temper of heroic hearts,*
> *Made weak by time and fate, but strong in will*
> *To strive, to seek, to find, and not to yield."*

Years later Rice remained stunned by the performance, writing,
"Estimate the number of people in the world who, without a moment of warning or preparation, could deliver letter perfect, and
fitting the moment and discussion, the last 16 lines of Tennyson's
'Ulysses.'"[18]

Blaik first interviewed Hickman for a coaching job in New
York at the Vanderbilt Hotel. The man's "kinfolk" stories and off-
hand observations cracked a smile even on Blaik's face. "Colonel," he said, "I have three loves: my wife, football and my belly.
And I don't rightfully know which I love the most." But when
the conversation turned to coaching, Hickman's humor faded
and his face turned serious. Later, after the two had driven from
the Vanderbilt to Blaik's office in the South Gym, Hickman gave
a chalk talk to the colonel and assistant coach Andy Gustafson,
outlining his ideas on line play and blocking techniques.[19]

It was typical of Blaik to ask detailed questions about the
proper way to throw a block, the most effective way to teach

it to the players, and the best way to practice and prepare for games. "Sometimes Blaik didn't ask questions so much as interrogate," one of his assistant coaches observed. He wanted to test the temper of the man as well as the depth of his knowledge. Less than a decade later, when he was looking for another line coach, he asked a candidate named Vincent Lombardi such questions as: What pulling technique do you teach your offensive guards? What technique do you teach guards for turning up into a hole? On defense do you favor a forearm shiver or a forearm left? What technique do you teach for downfield blocks? Blaik expected full, specific answers. There was an exam every day with the colonel.[20]

Blaik recalled that the day was "blistering hot," and his office at the top of the South Gym was right under the roof. There was no air conditioning or fan and no escape from the heat. And the office itself was intimidating—walnut paneling, mahogany desk, West Point coat-of-arms, a large framed picture of General Douglas MacArthur. It was enough to give pause to anyone who walked in.

The atmosphere certainly registered on Hickman. With so many college programs suspended during the war, coaching jobs were becoming scarcer, and Herman was broke. He needed the position at Army. A large man, 290 or so pounds on a generous scale, he was nervous under Blaik's relentless grilling, and he began "to perspire so profusely at the blackboard that actual pools of water formed at his feet." Blaik, thoughtful in his own intense way, observed his discomfort and generously asked if he would like to remove his shirt and pants and continue in his skivvies. Herman said, "Yes," and the interview went on with him stripped to his underwear. Finally, the colonel had heard or seen enough. The near-naked Herman got the job.[21]

Hickman found lodging for his wife, Helen, and their Chihuahua, Tiny, at Jack Martin's Bear Mountain Inn, and in the summer of 1943 went to work with the rest of the football staff, developing a plan to beat Navy. Although Hickman insisted that

mealtime was his, the rest of the day—and night—belonged to
Blaik. When you went to work for the colonel, Doug Kenna remarked, "you signed a lifetime contract with him." If he couldn't
sleep and wanted to go to his office to work, he expected that
someone on his staff would want to join him. "If he called, you
went," Kenna said. "No questions. Just, 'I'll be ready in ten minutes.'" When Hickman took the job at the Academy, he became
part of Blaik's gravitational pull. The work was unrelenting, but
the rewards were enormous.[22]

It was the summer of the new offense. All his career Blaik, and
virtually every other coach in football, had been, in one variation
or another, a single-wing man. It was *the* offense of the 1920s and
1930s, the formation of such featured tailbacks as Jim Thorpe,
Red Grange, Bronko Nagurski, Sammy Baugh, Tommy Harmon,
and Charlie "Choo-Choo" Justice. Its strength was its power.
The offense, especially when deployed with an unbalanced line,
was able to muster a heavy concentration of manpower at the
critical point. It was designed to get double-team blocks at the
point of attack and to knock defenders on their asses.

A play normally began with the center snapping the ball to
the tailback lined up 4 or 5 yards behind the line of scrimmage.
The tailback could then pound the ball up the middle, sweep
either end, pass, or quick-kick in an attempt to alter his team's
field position. Or he could also run the more deceptive spin series—where, with his back to the line of scrimmage and the ball
hidden close to his body, he would hand off to one of two or
three players moving past him in different directions. The offense
normally had a wingback who blocked, went out for passes, and
occasionally ran; a blocking back (or quarterback) who almost
always just blocked; a fullback who occasionally took the snap
and handed off or ran up the middle; and, of course, the classic runner, passer, kicker tailback. The theory behind the single
wing was Napoleonic—movement and concentration of mass at

the enemy's weakest point. The problems with the single wing were that it lacked deception, was ineffective to the weak side of the line, gave very little room for wide-open play, and was not a particularly good passing or kicking formation. The best coaches tinkered with it and added imaginative wrinkles; the worst coaches just used its bone-crunching mass power. Generally speaking, it produced low-scoring, often dull, plodding games.

Then in 1940 in California a football revolution took place when an unsuccessful coach joined a losing team and manufactured magic. In 1939 Stanford finished 1-7-1 and fired its coach. In came Clark Shaughnessy, a coach with a reputation for theoretical brilliance but no real accomplishments to back it up. That year he had coached at the University of Chicago, and his team had been awful. After losing a close game to open the season and then defeating a hapless Wabash squad in the second game, they demonstrated an athletic futility seldom matched in college football. They were trounced by Harvard 0–61, Michigan 0–85, Virginia 0–47, Ohio State 0–61, and Illinois 0–46. A November victory against tiny Oberlin salvaged nothing. Football, thought Chicago's President Robert Maynard Hutchins, did not belong in any serious university. Stealing a line from the economist Thorstein Veblen, Hutchins said, "Football has the same relation to education that bull fighting has to agriculture." He wanted no part of it, and at the end of the season the Board of Trustees gave him his wish and voted to discontinue the program.[23]

Chicago's decision made some sense. Stanford's made none, unless by hiring Shaughnessy school officials hoped to kill football there, too. They certainly weren't getting any PR benefits. The coach was as ascetic as the most devout monk. He didn't smoke, drink alcohol, nor abide those who did. Bob Zuppke, Illinois's most successful coach, claimed, "The world lost a great undertaker when Clark Shaughnessy decided on football coaching." Shaughnessy lived in a world of Xs and Os, where diagrams of plays on a blackboard were more important than players. He was the sort of coach who rarely forgot a number and seldom remembered a name. But he had a vision of a new way to play the game, and at Stanford he discovered a team that could give it flesh.[24]

Reviewing Stanford's 1939 game films, he believed that the team had the right combination of talent for his new, dynamic offense. Before the 1940 season, Fielding Yost, Michigan's most famous coach, had remarked, "There is only one formation that's any good and it's the single wing." At that very moment Shaughnessy was tinkering with one that was better. Although the idea of the T formation was not new, no coach had fully exploited its potential, and at the end of the 1930s it was seldom used. If the tailback was the crucial position in the single wing, the quarterback was the heart of the T. In the T the quarterback lined up directly behind the center, who was in the middle of a balanced line. The fullback lined up about 5 yards behind the center, two halfbacks about 4½ yards behind the tackles. It was the position of the quarterback and the three other backs that gave the offense its characteristic T look. The balance of the formation made it impossible for the defense to anticipate the point of attack.

The quarterback, his hands under the center's rump, took the snap and could drop back to pass, hand off to a back on a quick opener, pitch to one of his backs for an end sweep, or run some sort of play-action pass or misdirection counter. The line play was also different in the T formation. Instead of the single wing's characteristic double-team blocks, T linemen used more man-on-man blocking, especially trap, brush, and influence blocks. The key to the formation was timing. If a play was properly executed, a lineman would have to hold a block for only a second. By that time the back was through the hole and headed into the secondary.

The T was a heady mixture of speed and deception, and

Shaughnessy added yet another ingredient to the mixture—a man in motion. By sending one of his halfbacks into motion, the mad scientist of coaches further opened up the game. It was as if the playing field had suddenly widened and each defender had to cover more space. If executed correctly, the T was a game-changer, as revolutionary an offense as had been seen in any sport anywhere.

From the grandstands, the change was easy to see—or, more precisely, easy not to see. Single-wing snaps were long—4 or 5 yards from the center to the back. The ball was momentarily visible between the two points. But with the quarterback's hands under the center to take the snap in the T, that crucial opening prelude to a play became virtually invisible. Suddenly the quarterback had the ball and things started to happen. He moved to his right or left, he spun around, and he dropped back. Hiding the ball as much as possible as the running backs moved past him in different directions, a skilled quarterback faked some handoffs and made others like a sleight-of-hand card shark.

Shaughnessy's quarterback, Frankie Albert, a slender player who took to the T like a duck to water, was one of the best. In Stanford's first game of the 1940 season he mystified the University of San Francisco defense. "You could tell by the holes we had that somebody was confused," one of his teammates recalled. "We were running right by people who didn't know we had the ball." "This type of football is different," wrote a reporter the next day. "Why, some of those Stanford kids running away from the play actually had defenders chasing them harder than other defenders were chasing the ball carrier." The USF coach was described as "a man who had just seen a ghost." Shaughnessy's new offense seemed like an unseen presence lurking on the field, disturbing the repose of the defenders of the single-wing faith.[25]

Stanford added new words to the vocabulary of football, from "quick openers" and "ball handling" to "handoffs" and "bootlegs." Dubbed "the Wow Boys," Stanford finished the regular season undefeated, then knocked off Nebraska in the Rose Bowl. Shaughnessy also helped install some of his T designs into the Chicago Bears offense in time for their 1940 National Football League title game against the Washington Redskins. Like Albert, Bears quarterback Sid Luckman proved adept at ball handling and running the offense. Chicago drilled Washington, 73–0. By the end of the 1940 season, coaches across the country had seen the future—one that had a man in motion and a backfield shaped like a T. By 1950, 250 of roughly 350 college teams had converted to the T.

Everything about the T formation appealed to Blaik. The offense featured relatively small, light linemen and quick, smart backs; it depended on discipline and clocklike precision. At Stanford Shaughnessy had converted several backs into linemen, announcing to coaches everywhere that powerful behemoth beef-eaters were not necessary to win football games. Although Blaik had never been one of football's great innovative thinkers, he knew that Shaughnessy's offense promised to neutralize the power advantage of Notre Dame and Navy. And he had Doug Kenna and Glenn Davis, the fastest man he had ever seen. With those two and the T formation, 1943 would be the first season of modern football at West Point.

6

★ ★ ★

Making the Grade

You take Thorpe. I'll take Davis.
— Earl "Red" Blaik

PAUL BUNKER WAS DEAD. Class of 1903, he had been West Point's first great football player, chosen by Walter Camp for his All-American team in 1901 as a tackle and in 1902 as a halfback. In his last season he was arguably the finest player in the country. Raw-boned, blond, and ruggedly handsome, he bulled his way across the line of scrimmage in an age when the game had little finesse or elegance. He was famous for playing hurt and sticking it out. During the 1900, 1901, and 1902 seasons, he played every down.

He had stuck it out to the end in the Philippines, retreating to Bataan with his classmate Douglas MacArthur and moving down to Corregidor with Jonathan Wainwright. On May 6, 1942, when Wainwright surrendered his forces, he ordered Bunker to lower the American flag and burn it; he refused to allow it to fall into Japanese hands. Bunker did as he was ordered, keeping only a small piece of the flag, which he hid under a patch in his khaki shirt.

There the piece of the flag stayed for the next ten months as Bunker slowly starved to death in a Japanese POW camp. Close to the end, committed to a hospital with blood poisoning and infected blisters on his feet, knowing he was going to die, he gave half of his piece of the flag to Colonel Delbert Ausmus, instructing him to give it to the Secretary of War when the conflict ended. Soon after, on March 16, 1943, Bunker died. He had served more than forty years in the Army. The Japanese burned his body—but not before Ausmus removed the other piece of the flag to return to American soil.[1]

As a football player, Casimir Myslinski reminded Red Blaik of Bunker. A plebe quarterback whom Blaik had switched to center, Myslinski was the prototype for the new Army team. Tough, quick, and relentless, he had been elected captain by his teammates for the 1943 season, and he returned to the Academy in the late summer after spending time on maneuvers with the New Jersey National Guard. He arrived in ideal condition, the picture of ruddy good health. "Did you ever see a finer or more clean-cut group of boys in all your life?" Blaik asked a *New York Times* sportswriter. "He was proud of them," the journalist wrote. "Any American could not help but be proud of them, too."[2]

If the reporters' tone toward Army's team and the Academy was not precisely new in 1943, it was more intense than ever before. Before the war, reporters criticized West Point for being elitist and anachronistic. But since then the Academy had gone martial—less marching and riding horses and more 155mm field pieces and fighter planes. "The parade ground at West Point is deserted," journalist Wayne Whittaker wrote in 1943. "The full dress uniforms repose on hangers in cadet barracks and the plumed headgear—dubbed 'tarbucket'—is packed away on a shelf." Echoing through the hills were the low rumble of field artillery pieces and the sharp rat-a-tat-tat of machine guns, and "thousands of feet above the gray stone towers of the academy buildings [was] the silver flash of training planes flying in formation, their wing tips almost touching." The massive fortress above the Hudson now commanded awe. Arthur Daley of the *New York Times* wrote that it was "inspiring to walk among those majestic and architecturally beautiful buildings this year and to mingle with the gray-clad hosts who are our generals of the future."[3]

By 1943 journalists had transformed Army's team from a squad of football players to representatives of the country's first line of defense. They were America's soldier-players, commanded by Colonel Blaik and adored by General MacArthur. Navy's players struggled to erase their image of elitism, but the men in long gray coats were as All-American as the G.I. Joes slogging up the gut of Italy.

West Point became America's team in 1943 in part because of the War Department. Marshall's decision not to allow its ASTP trainees to play college football meant that West Point was the only Army team playing a college schedule. A cornucopia of college teams represented the Navy. If Annapolis fell short, Americans with nautical leanings could cheer for Great Lakes, Sampson, or Lakehurst Naval Center; they all fielded powerful teams that played college schedules. Or they could support any one of more than a hundred naval V-12 or V-5 college teams. But West Point stood alone. "With the soldiers," wrote Allison Danzig before the first game, "it's different. If the West Points don't stand up for them, the season is just a lot of spinach."[4]

The backfield, deep in fast players, inspired hope. The normally phlegmatic Blaik especially praised Doug Kenna, "the best back Army has had since Chris Cagle," the gold standard of Army runners. "A great back," agreed backfield coach Andy Gustafson. "That boy can really turn it on, and try to bring him down. He can kick right well, too, and he can pass and he's one of the smartest." With Kenna as the anchor, Blaik planned to use Tom Lombardo as the quarterback and Carl Anderson, George Maxon, Bob Woods, and Bud Troxell as complementary runners.[5]

Yet the line caused concern. Except for a few players, it was small, light, and inexperienced. Everyone on the team was new to the T offense, and blocking techniques in the T were much more difficult to master than running assignments. For linemen accustomed to double-team blocking and "manhood" power plays, brush and influence blocking seemed to be on a different planet. Blaik could hope only that the team would mature and improve as the season progressed.

Then, in a preseason scrimmage, Kenna ran the ball left, saw an opening to the right, cut hard, and collapsed without being touched. He had torn the ligaments in his right knee. Sportswriters said that he had simply twisted the knee and would be out for only a few games. In truth, he had ruined it, blown it out in an age when there was not much that could be done about it medically or surgically. One of the most gifted cutback runners ever to enroll at West Point had lost his gift.

Replacing Kenna was the new kid, the one his teammates had begun to call "Junior," the fresh-faced one from sunny California. Until the end of September Blaik had rarely mentioned Glenn Davis, and his name had not appeared in many newspaper columns. That changed with the first game of the season, against Villanova.

Villanova was a small school whose enrollment barely reached a thousand, and in most years it would not have been much of a match for West Point. But 1943 was not most years, and with the aid of a V-12 program, the Catholic school was unusually blessed with talent. Each member of the squad was a naval or Marine trainee, and almost all had college football experience. One had been an All-American at the University of Miami; another, one of the best centers in the South at the University of Florida. Still others had starred at Georgetown and Boston College. If Villanova wasn't exactly an all-star team, it was a fine group of football players.[6]

Glenn Davis was the one who performed like a star. He scored

Army's first touchdown of the season, broke loose for several long runs, and set up the final score with a pass interception and a 40-yard run to the Villanova 2. Army totally dominated the game, substituting freely and winning, 27–0.[7]

By the second game, a 42–0 drubbing of Colgate, Davis had moved from inside the newspaper stories to the headlines. "DAVIS, PLEBE, IS STAR FOR WEST POINT," announced the *Washington Post*. Colgate was confused by the T offense, prompting Allison Danzig to write that the traditional power football team from upstate New York was "utterly at the mercy of the blitz, baffled by its fakery and rooted to the ground by its speed." They had few answers for anything Army tried and none whatsoever for Davis, who scored touchdowns on two long runs and threw for another one. He threw four passes, completed all of them, caught two passes, carried the ball eleven times for 147 yards, ran back kicks, and intercepted a pass. "For a substitute for Kenna, it was a fair day's work," a reporter dryly observed.[8]

Two games were enough to convince Blaik that the T offense fit his team's talent perfectly. The T was still something of a novelty in the East, and Villanova and Colgate had trouble predicting patterns and reacting to the ball—or even, in some cases, knowing where the ball was. All Davis needed was a split second of indecision by defensive players to embark on a long run. But Army also had problems with the new offense. Occasionally it was too fast for the Cadets as well, leading to an inordinate number of fumbles and offside penalties. Army fumbled six times against Villanova (losing just one) and nine times against Colgate (losing three). In fact, Army fumbles and penalties stopped more drives than the defenses.

In the third game, Army faced Temple, a team with no V-program players that was limited to freshmen under eighteen and 4-Fs, males with physical deferments. Temple made do with kids—only three players were upperclassmen, and only one had played college football.[9]

Army scored early and often, and by the fourth quarter Blaik became concerned by the unseemly score. He didn't want to embarrass Temple, so he told his players to stop trying. "I don't want another touchdown scored against that team," he emphasized. "Not one. If anybody scores they will have to deal with me." But late in the game Chuck Sampson, a lineman playing in his first game of the season, intercepted a pass with no one between him and the goal. Slowly, but at his top speed, he lumbered toward the end zone. "At about the ten," Doug Kenna remembered, "you could see his mind sorta begin to work, and he slowed down even more. At about the five what Blaik had said must have kicked in, because he looked like he was moving at a slow walk, and for no apparent reason he cut toward the middle of the field." Clearly, Sampson had decided that orders from his superior trumped personal glory. As the Associated Press reporter wrote, he stopped running and "placed the ball in front of the goal posts on the 1-inch line."[10]

The crucial question was what to do next. In an age when coaches rarely sent in plays, the signal caller on the field had to make the decision. Any regular offensive play would surely result in a touchdown, and just to down the ball four straight times would look suspicious. There was no really good choice, but the quarterback made a quick, Solomon-like decision. Sampson had got Army into the fix, and he could get them out. The quarterback called for a first-down field goal attempt. Sampson, who was not a kicker, was given the job. "Somehow he made it without falling on his ass," said Kenna. "But kicking a field goal on the first down was a worse embarrassment than scoring a defensive touchdown." Fortunately, it was the last score in the 51–0 shutout.

The week after the Temple game Army was ranked third in the country, behind only Notre Dame and Michigan. In three games Army had scored 120 points and had yet to be scored against. Their next opponent, Lou Little's Columbia team, had scored two touchdowns and lost two contests. Ticket sales for Baker Field in the Bronx were brisk. New Yorkers were in a good mood. The American Army was moving toward Naples, Italy had switched sides and declared war against Germany, the Yankees had just defeated the Cardinals in the World Series, and B-17 Flying Fortresses were raining destruction on Hitler's Reich.[11]

Despite threatening weather—it was gray and overcast, spitting rain on and off—the crowd numbered close to 25,000. Army started the game in a fog, fumbling early and looking dazed. "Unable to credit their eyes," Allison Danzig wrote, "the spectators had a vision of one of the most shocking reversals of all time." Then, in a snap and a flash, it was over. Max Minor, a gifted plebe who had played under Dana Bible of Texas the year before, went in motion to the right, drawing a slight shift in the defense, and quarterback Tom Lombardo pitched the ball to Junior Davis, who raced toward the left sideline. He picked up a few blocks, shifted into a higher gear, and sprinted 82 yards down the sideline.[12]

The Corps of Cadets exploded with cheers while an "ominous silence fell upon the Columbia stands," observed Danzig. Davis's performance was so spectacular that even when the game was not out of reach it seemed so. He scored two more times, on an 18-yard pass from Lombardo and a beautiful, sweeping 36-yard run. In the second half, Army scored so often and so fast that Blaik ordered his team to punt on first down rather than run an offensive play. For the fourth straight game the Cadets did not yield a point. As a result of the 52–0 victory, Army moved up to second in the polls.

Next up was Yale, which by the fall of 1943 resembled a united armed forces academy. In 1942 its enrollment had been cut significantly by the war. As they had done during World War I, Elis answered the call of service without hesitation. But in 1943 the Army and Navy commandeered most of the college's facilities. Between the Army Air Force's Technical Training School and the

Navy's V-1, V-5, and V-7 programs, most of the students at Yale wore Army, Navy, or Marine uniforms. "In short," Roy Hoffman of *The Pointer* wrote, "Yale today is molded to the desires of the War and Navy Departments."[13]

What was good for the war was also good for the Yale football program. Its 38-man squad contained 10 Navy men, 19 Marines, 2 naval ROTC, and only 7 civilians. Led by transfers from other schools, Yale had beaten several good teams and had lost badly only to fourth-ranked Pennsylvania. Running what Coach Howard Odell called "the war system"—an offense based on deception, man-on-man blocking, and passing—the game promised to test the strength of Army's T attack.[14]

In the second half, Yale finally pushed across the "heretofore inviolate" Army goal line. Fans in the Yale Bowl cheered as if the Elis had just won the game. Army was leading, 26–0, at the time. The game was never close, ending in a 39–7 Army victory and capping off the first half of the season: five victories and 211 points to their opponents' 7. Only Notre Dame, with its power-house Marine V-12 squad, ranked ahead of Army. Right behind the Cadets were Navy, the V-12-loaded Purdue, and Pennsylvania—Army's recent nemesis and next opponent.[15]

Junior Davis was in trouble. What no opposing defense could do, Army's academic curriculum could—stop him in his tracks. Plebe mathematics covered a range of topics, from advanced college algebra and solid geometry to plane and solid analytical geometry and plane and spherical trigonometry. None of those "ometrys" were to Davis's liking. It was not for lack of study. After every away football game, when his teammates had an evening to relax, Colonel Francis "Buck" Pohl drove Davis back to West Point for a late Saturday night tutoring session. "Many a night," Blaik later wrote, "Glenn set his alarm for a 4:00 a.m. bout with the books." Everyone on the team knew that Junior's problem was not his work ethic. It was his aptitude.[16]

Between early morning studying, evening tutoring sessions, days full of academics, afternoons devoted to football practice, and games on Saturday, he was bone-weary and seriously worried. "It wasn't easy for me academically," Davis recalled of those painful days. "I had one hell of a time. I was competing with kids that had already graduated from college! Some of 'em had actually graduated from college. Others had two or three years of college. Going in there from a little old school, 350 kids here in . . . LaVerne, 18 years old, never studied hardly in my life because it wasn't that difficult—[I] really [wasn't] prepared for that kind of shock."[17]

Joe Steffy, a later teammate of Davis, sympathized with him. "Practically everybody at that day and time went to either prep school or college before they went to West Point. They did not go from high school to West Point. The academic transition was just too great." But Glenn was "literally taken out of high school and put in there," Steffy continued. "He was expected to perform academically and athletically. I'm sure none of the coaches imagined that he would be so good so fast. Maybe they thought that he would have time to get used to the place. But it turned out that he was all-everything right away. That's a lot of pressure to carry around with you."[18]

At West Point Davis faced an unforgiving system. As he recalled, "We had five classes a day to study for. We were graded every day in every subject. Every third day you have an exam over the past three days. Counts double. And you got to be proficient to play. Or to stay. If you flunk a course, one course, and it can be a physical deficiency—you flunk, you're out. You leave West Point. And so, everybody else was getting out of class at 3:30 every afternoon, and they'd study from 3:30 to call to quarters, call for dinner. Well, I'm out there practicing football. . . . Then I come in dead tired and I've got five classes to study for the next day."

Davis's academic troubles were all the more pressing because of West Point's ranking procedures. Every Thursday cadets received their grades for the previous week. Class averages were calculated on a regular basis. West Pointers always knew precisely where they stood in every subject and where they ranked overall. The knowledge gnawed at Davis. Doug Kenna remembered him sitting tensely in the locker room before a game and telling him to relax: "You don't have anything to worry about. You'll play great." Glenn replied, "You know, I don't think I did very well on that last math test." "Can you imagine?" said Kenna. "It's moments before kickoff and he's thinking about how he did on an exam. He's not worried about the game. He's worried about flunking out."[19]

Perhaps Davis's academic troubles, combined with the upcoming games with Penn and Notre Dame, motivated Blaik to push Kenna back into action. The knee had not healed, but Roland Bevan was giving it one treatment after another, sure that Kenna could play through the pain. The week before the Pennsylvania game Doug was back at practice, throwing passes and limping through plays. He didn't look good, but he looked good enough for Blaik, who told reporters that he expected Kenna would play a portion of the game.[20]

Army could have used a healthy Kenna. Penn was an impressive team that seemed to save its best game for Army. The teams had played four previous contests—Army had won the first in 1901, in the early months of Theodore Roosevelt's presidency, but Penn had taken the games in 1940, 1941, and 1942. In 1943 the Quakers looked just as strong. Led by quarterback Bob Odell, the brother of Yale's head coach, the team had an array of experienced V-8 and V-12 players who had transferred from other institutions. Their squad was deeper and better balanced than Army's on both sides of the line. Adding to Penn's chances was the weather. The week before the contest, rain turned Franklin Field into a soggy mess. "Our forte is speed," Blaik told reporters the day before the game. On a muddy track, Davis's and the Army T's advantages would be diminished.[21]

More than 70,000 spectators, including 200 veterans from the Valley Forge Hospital, crowded into Franklin Field, the largest sports gathering in Philadelphia since Pearl Harbor. At times the game seemed as messy as the field. William Richardson wrote that Army played "spasmodically," one moment looking like "a million dollars" and the next resembling "a punctured penny." Davis played his worst game of the season, scoring no touchdowns and fumbling once to set up a score for Penn. A hampered Kenna did little better, throwing an interception that ended a promising drive. Army's pass defense was dreadful. Time and again Penn's receivers got behind the Army defenders, though it was difficult to pass the wet ball accurately. Still, Army had its chances. It led, 7–6, at the end of the half, 13–6 at end of the third quarter. But in the final quarter Odell made a beautiful leaping catch between two defenders and outraced the Army defensive backs 40 yards to the end zone. The game ended in a 13–13 tie.[22]

The first week of November, supporters of both Notre Dame and Army were worried. Some of their countrymen fretted over the landing of American troops in Bougainville in the Solomon Islands; others, the strikes in the country's coal fields. Some enjoyed worrying about the end of a movie: Ingrid Bergman didn't get on the plane with Humphrey Bogart at the end of *Casablanca*. The Solomon landings proved successful. The strikes ended. *Casablanca* became the top-grossing film of the year.

But at Notre Dame everyone had a local worry: life after Angelo Bertelli. In 1941 the secular gods in the nation's capital had rained munificent blessings on Notre Dame, the college with the golden dome. The second-highest number of Navy V-12 trainees — 1,851 — had been assigned there, including an unusually large complement of Marines. Most of Notre Dame's returning

In 1941 Earl "Red" Blaik returned to West Point to revive the football team. The recently appointed superintendent of the Academy rejected the "concept of graceful losing." Blaik's duty was to produce a winner.

Blaik demanded complete commitment to winning and attention to detail. "You have to pay the price," he told his players. Here he addressed the 1942 team.

The Army coaching staff, 1946

Felix "Doc" Blanchard enrolled at West Point in 1944. "I've just seen Superman," an opposing coach said after watching him play.

(Army Athletic Communications, USMA)

By the time he graduated from West Point, Blanchard was recognized as one of the greatest college football players in the history of the game.

Glenn Davis never looked like the image of a rugged football player, but he was perhaps the most gifted athlete ever to attend West Point. "There aren't words to describe how good Glenn Davis was," a teammate recalled.

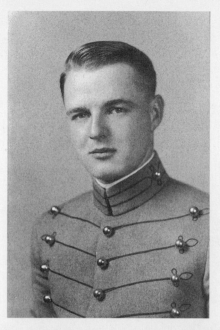

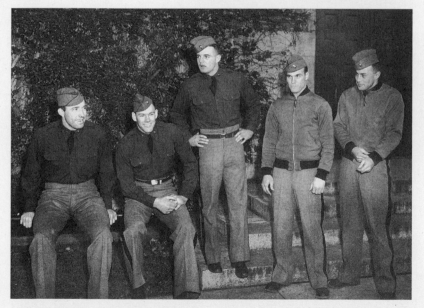

Blaik called the squads of 1944, 1945, and 1946 his "storybook teams." Some of the players that carried them to victory were (left to right) ends Barney Poole and Hank Foldberg, and backs Glenn Davis, Young Arnold Tucker, and Doc Blanchard. *(Army Athletic Communications, USMA)*

DeWitt "Tex" Coulter
(Army Athletic Communications, USMA)

Edmund "Rafe" Rafalko

Herschel "Ug" Fuson

Edgar Douglas "Doug" Kenna

Tom Lombardo

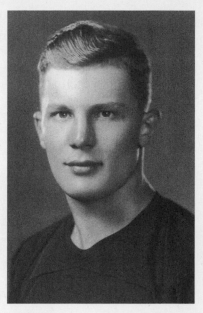

Robin Olds

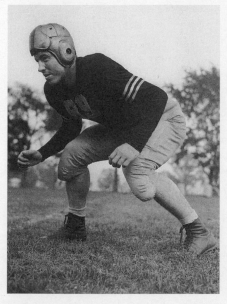

Barney Poole

Robert Woods

Doc Blanchard and Glenn Davis, Mr. Inside and Mr. Outside, dominated college football in the mid-1940s. Here Blanchard helps Davis suit up for another victory.

(Army Athletic Communications, USMA)

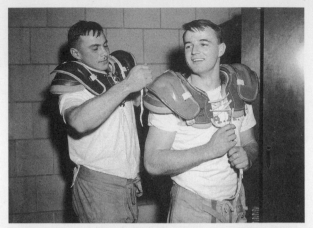

"No one in the game had as much speed and as many gears as Davis," a teammate said. "He could be surrounded one moment and gone for a touchdown the next."

(Army Athletic Communications, USMA)

Blanchard (35) had size, power, and speed. Sometimes, sportswriters thought, he played like a man among boys.

(Army Athletic Communications, USMA)

On November 11, 1944, as American troops battled in Western Europe and the Pacific, Army played Notre Dame in Yankee Stadium. The game shocked everyone in sports. *(Army Athletic Communications, USMA)*

On December 2, 1944, the Army-Navy game returned to the big stage, this time Baltimore's Municipal Stadium. First Captain Bob Woods said, "It was the greatest game I've ever seen." Here General George C. Marshall autographs programs before the game. *(Baltimore Sun)*

Less than three weeks before the beginning of the Battle of the Bulge, Army officers and men of the 2nd Infantry Division, at 1st U.S. Army headquarters in St. Vith, Belgium, follow the play-by-play action of the game. Across the globe, other soldiers and sailors were doing the same. For a few hours the war seemed to stop. *(National Archives)*

players as well as a significant number of transfers were part of the Marine contingent. The accumulation of such bountiful raw, aggressive football talent with the school's football tradition and coaching superiority almost guaranteed that it would be the finest team in the nation, ranked number one since the very first week in the season, when they opened with a 35–12 victory over second-ranked Michigan.[23]

Until the Army game, the Irish had been led by Bertelli, that season's Heisman Trophy winner. Sportswriters bestowed on him various nicknames—"The Springfield Rifle," "The Arm," and "Mr. Accuracy." A three-year starter, he had been runner-up for the Heisman as a sophomore and an All-American as a junior. In six games in 1943 he had completed 25 of 36 passes for 511 yards and 11 touchdowns.

But the V-12 program's first semester ran from the beginning of July to the end of October, and on November 1 the reserves were subject to call-ups. Bertelli had turned twenty-two in June and was in the older Marine V-12 age group. Unknown to him and the others in the program, the Marines were on the cusp of a manpower shortage. Toward the end of November, Marines from the 2nd Division assaulted the beaches of the Tarawa atoll in the Gilbert Islands. After three days of intense fighting they had killed virtually all of the Japanese defenders, but not before suffering more than 3,000 casualties, including 1,009 deaths. "Bloody Tarawa" was a hard lesson about warfare in the Pacific Islands. From the Gilberts to the Marshalls to the Marianas to the Bonins to the Ryukyus—from Tarawa and Kwajalein, Saipan and Tinian, Iwo Jima and Okinawa, and all the other islands along the way—the U.S. Marine Corps would be the shock troops of the Pacific, the first in and the first to die in battle.

The week before the Notre Dame–Navy game, the Marines sent down the call to Notre Dame for about 90 of its 140 trainees. Angelo Bertelli was ordered to report for basic training at Parris Island.[24]

He played his last college game in Cleveland against Navy, the third-ranked team in the country, undefeated, absolutely loaded with talent. After a close first half "the Arm" went to work, shredding the Midshipmen's pass defense. On a fine, summery afternoon, more than 82,000 people in Municipal Stadium watched him throw three touchdown passes, perfectly run the T offense, and leave the game with a smile and a wave. Then he was off to catch a train to South Carolina.[25]

West Point had a parallel concern. About the time that Bertelli arrived at Parris Island, the Athletic Board was convening to decide the fate of Cadet Davis. As a result of a deficiency in mathematics, the board decided that he should be dropped from the "Football 'A' Squad" effective Monday, November 8. The board also recommended that on the same day he also be "picked up" as a member of the Off-Season Track Squad, which had practices on Monday and Friday. Then, in a slick twist of bureaucratic maneuvering, the board further decreed that he should be excused from track drills and permitted to attend "conferences, critiques and light work-outs for the Football Squad prior to his attendance at extra academic instruction." He could also continue to eat at the football training table.[26]

It was the best Blaik could make of a difficult situation. The decision allowed Davis to fully prepare for and play in the Notre Dame game on November 6 and remain on the team to practice in the weeks before the Navy game. But if he failed to improve his grades, he would not be permitted to play against Navy. Bob Woods, his teammate in the backfield, recalled Davis's studying every free moment he could find: "If we were going to a game on a bus, or returning from one, Glenn was in the back with his nose in a book."[27]

Army–Notre Dame was the national game of the year between the two top teams. The sheer level of clamor was deafening. Blaik was his normal laconic self, saying little and giving away less. Frank Leahy, by contrast, in his third year as the Irish coach, played the underdog and talked to the press continuously. The legendary Knute Rockne, who used to wail as if he was at a wake before any big game, was not in the same league as Leahy when it came to the expectations game. Leahy had advanced negative talking, if not thinking, to a stratospheric level, making him the Arthur Schopenhauer of the coaching fraternity. The week before the Army game he tried valiantly, if unsuccessfully, to convince sportswriters that without Bertelli Notre Dame did not stand a chance against the mighty Army eleven. They would have to make do with the eighteen-year-old substitute Johnny Lujack.[28]

Army had not beaten Notre Dame since before FDR was elected president or scored on them since war broke out in Europe. And Lujack started quickly, completing his first three passes for 110 yards and leading his team down the field for the game's first score.[29]

Notre Dame's linemen and running backs were clearly more powerful. Yet Army kept the game close until midway through the third quarter. Series after series they conceded yardage to the Irish runners but kept them out of the end zone. Then the Cadets mounted three drives of their own—the first ended with a Carl Anderson fumble, the second with a Davis fumble, the third with a Kenna interception. Davis, in particular, struggled throughout the contest, fumbling several times, throwing an interception, and never able to break loose for one of his breathtaking dashes. Final score: Notre Dame 26, Army 0. Davis studied math on the bus ride back to the Academy.

In the next two weeks Army won its sixth and seventh games of the season, defeating a very good Sampson Naval Training Station team, 16–7, and a weaker Brown squad, 59–0. But the failure to score against Notre Dame and the 13–0 loss to Navy in Michie Stadium destroyed any feeling of pleasure in the season. By the last national poll of the season, Army had dropped out of the top ten. Soldiers in Italy and the Pacific were looking for an

Army team to bolster their spirits, a squad they could cheer on to victory over Navy. Army's losing streak against its rival remained intact. It was a lot for Red Blaik to bear.

So was the sight of Glenn Davis leaving West Point the winter after he busted out.

7

Historic Hours

> In my dreams I hear again the crash of guns, the
> rattle of musketry, the strange mournful mutter of the
> battlefield. But in the evening of my memory, I come
> back to West Point. . . . [W]hen I cross the river, my
> last conscious thoughts will be of the Corps, and the
> Corps, and the Corps.
> — GENERAL DOUGLAS MACARTHUR

STANDING BEFORE THE 474 graduates of the 1944 Class of West Point, as well as their fellow cadets, family, and friends, General Brehon B. Somervell looked cold and unapproachable. His gray hair might have been parted with a razor, his mustache trimmed with the aid of a magnifying glass. He was a general who got things done. Graduating sixth in the 1914 class, he had chased the desperado Pancho Villa in Mexico and won a medal for gallantry in the Meuse-Argonne offensive in World War I. As the head of the Works Progress Administration in New York he had overseen the construction of La Guardia Airport, and as the commander of the Army's Construction Division he had been in charge of building the Pentagon. In 1942 he took command of the Army Service Forces, the main logistical arm for American forces in World War II. The delivery of the tanks, planes, bombs, guns, and ammunition needed to win the war was under his control.[1]

His 1944 commencement address focused on the leadership challenges that the new officers faced. It won't be long, he told them, before the "citizen soldiers" under their command, and the officers above them, say "He has it" or "He hasn't it." In a long, thoughtful address studded with quotes from great leaders, he expounded on the characteristics officers need to lead troops into battle, ranging from a sense of mission and personal responsibility to technical knowledge, good judgment, a solid work ethic, and basic humanity. It all amounted to character, what Abraham Lincoln and Theodore Roosevelt had and what most men lacked. "In this graduating class," Somervell predicted, would be men, steeled in "the acid test of war," who will "achieve international fame as leaders of men. There will be others whose accomplishments will be few and whose names will be concealed in the War Department files."

The 8,000 people in the massive field house listened with more than polite respect. Among the graduates were some famous names—Donald Alfred Gruenther, a son of Major General Alfred M. Gruenther, chief of staff of the Fifth Army which had recently taken Rome; George E. Pickett IV, a great-grandson of the Confederate general who had charged the Union line at Gettysburg; and John Sheldon Doud Eisenhower, the son of Dwight D. Eisenhower, the supreme commander of the invasion of Europe, whose duties forced him to miss the ceremony. John Sheldon's father had sent a message to the graduates—a promise, really—that tough days lay ahead for them and America, but that he had full confidence in their "soldierly qualities of devotion to duty, character and skill."

Somervell also had some news to announce. "This is a historic hour," he said, pausing and looking across the rows of cadets. "Today these walls, these hills, the very shadows of Battle Monument take on a new meaning and a deeper significance. Only a few hours ago the mightiest undertaking ever attempted by our Army was launched against the enemy entrenched along the shores of France. Today our forces began that grim, tough and bloody march from the shores of the Atlantic to Berlin. Many of you will join in that march. Many of you will become part of the sweep in the Pacific which will lead eventually to the destruction of Japan. How much it will take to achieve victory no one can predict. Of one fact and one only may we be sure. We *are* going to win." A roar of applause and cheering rose to the girders of the field house. It was June 6, 1944.

When Somervell had finished, Superintendent Major General Francis B. Wilby called each new officer to the stage in the general order of merit in recognition of their accomplishment. Somervell shook the hand of each of the 474 men. Throughout the proceeding the applause grew, reaching a crescendo when the last name, that of class "goat" William Benjamin Tuttle, Jr., was read. The cheer added humor to the solemn occasion. But character was not learned in books or conferred in class rank. Tuttle would go on to lead troops against the Siegfried Line in World War II, behind communist lines in Korea, and against Vietcong in Vietnam, winning three Combat Infantry Badges.[2]

Some 5,500 miles away, a few hours earlier, Lieutenant Henry Romanek, West Point Class of 1943, prepared the forty-five men in his platoon of the 149th Engineer Combat Battalion with a much shorter speech. "History will be made by what we do here today," he told his young men, not much more than boys, mostly from farms in the Midwest. Like him, they were loaded to the gills with equipment—steel helmets, itchy wool uniforms, thick jumpshoes, heavy field bags with toiletry articles and eating utensils, loaded rifles, and ammunition for the day ahead. Unlike his men, Romanek wore his heavy black onyx West Point ring. He had graduated high in his class, played as a reserve on the line for the football team, and revered the Academy. Romanek was a model of strong, thoughtful, quiet leadership. Sitting with his men in the damp darkness on the deck of the USS *Garfield*, a transport ship surrounded by thousands of other Allied vessels in the English Channel, he tried to prepare his men to face an entrenched enemy. "Now let's do our job and make our country proud," he said.[3]

At 2:00 a.m. Romanek and half of his platoon scrambled down rope nets into an LCM (Landing Craft, Mechanized) and grouped behind a platoon of infantrymen. The LCM pitched back and forth like a flat board on the open sea, and as it crawled toward the beach of Normandy almost every man aboard vomited. For over four hours the men were left with their own fearful thoughts. They hoped what they had been told was true—that the Navy guns and the bombers would destroy enemy positions before the first wave hit the beach. Some entertained thoughts of meeting only token opposition once the coxswain lowered the ramp of the LCM. Others, more experienced with the darkness between what the Army brass said would happen and what actually would happen, prepared for the worst.

First light came at 5:45 a.m., as did the Allied bombers—waves of B-17 Flying Fortresses, B-24 Liberators, and B-26 Marauders attempting to drop 500-pound bombs on the beaches. The thin shreds of eastern light were speckled with antiaircraft fire. German 88mm flak and automatic antiaircraft guns streaked toward bombers, most of which dropped their payloads miles from the beaches. The men in the LCM could also hear the large German coastal guns, some of them huge mounted naval canons, firing at the Allied armada miles off the coast. The Navy guns responded, pounding the German positions and gouging massive craters into the earth. The men in the LCM could feel the great thuds of the big guns in their chests. "It was like a pounding inside of you," Romanek recalled. "Like the world was being destroyed."

At 5:50 a.m. American soldiers began landing in the waters off Omaha Beach. The first were the men in the LCTs (Landing Craft Tanks) with their Duplex Drive (DD) tanks. The DDs, dubbed Donald Duck tanks, were amphibious assault vehicles, outfitted with canvas buoyancy skirts and intended to be launched two miles offshore in order to float to the beaches and attack land fortifications. The tanks' job was to destroy the enemy positions in the bluffs that escaped the air assault. That was the plan. But virtually all of the DD tanks were swamped and sank in the choppy waters. Looking out of his LCM, Romanek saw the tanks disappear, their crews struggling, mostly unsuccessfully, to escape their Donald Duck coffins.

By 6:30 the first wave of LCMs arrived at the drop-off zones. In front of them was a perfect beach for an invasion, a fact not lost on the Germans. It was a flat, crescent-shaped strip of firm sand flanked on either side by steep cliffs. Keeping watch over the beach were high, grass-covered bluffs. Commanding the bluffs, and dug into them, were the German defenders, equipped to rain death on any attackers. They had positioned thirty antitank and field guns, six mortars, and eighty-five machine guns there. Omaha Beach was a killing field, an open shooting arcade. The Germans had also mined the beach heavily, stringing concertina wire and linking land mines together. They had loaded the beach with antitank and antivehicle obstacles, made mostly of steel and wood. The defensive network was trenched, interconnecting, and designed to deliver direct, plunging, and grazing fire. The entire purpose of the demonic defenses was to kill any invader who stepped onto the beach—or, better yet, to kill him before he even reached the dry ground.

Gazing over the top of his LCM, looking through the smoke and bursts of fireworks, Romanek spotted the first landing crafts reaching the beach and saw everything that had gone wrong. The bombers and Navy guns had not destroyed the enemy's positions, and there would be no tanks to shield his men. Belches of artillery fire from the bluffs obliterated entire landing crafts. Bursts of machine-gun fire cut through the American soldiers wading through the surf. Beginning about a hundred yards from the beach, the water was a patchwork of gray and dark blue and crimson. On the beach some soldiers lay motionless, face down; others had been blown to pieces.

Machine-gun fire began to hit Romanek's landing craft. *Ping, ping, ping.* And artillery shells landed to the right and left, splashing water high into the air. "Everybody stay focused on what we need to do," Romanek shouted to his men. "Let's do our jobs and everything else will take care of itself." For many of his men he had become a surrogate brother, father, and confessor, a friend who they counted on now above all. He no longer wondered if some would die. The only question was how many. "What was going to happen? I didn't know. But it was going to be bad," he recalled.

Within minutes the coxswain stopped the LCM and moved to the rear to release the clamps holding up the ramp. Exposed to enemy fire, he was killed in seconds. When the ramp dropped, German fire raked across the men in the front portion of the craft. A mist of blood filled the air. Bullets ripped through flesh. Pushing from the rear, the engineers struggled to get out. Moments earlier, their landing craft had provided safety. Now, "we had to get out or die," Romanek said. Already more than half the men in the LCM were dead or dying. "Get the hell out of here," he ordered his men.

In a few seconds — fraught and endless — Romanek scrambled over the dead bodies and shoved his way to the front. He jumped. A bullet ripped into his chest before he hit the water. He felt a burning pain and slipped almost peacefully into shock. His mind wandered. As he recalled, for some reason he thought of his time at West Point and the 1941 game against Navy, just a week and a day before Pearl Harbor. America was still at peace, and an Army-Navy game was the most important event in the fall. Life had been so simple then.

Thoughts of West Point and football caused him to look at his left hand, where his West Point ring was still on his finger. "I can't lose my ring," he thought. "I can't lose it. And I don't want to die here today." The thought of dying focused his mind, ending its dreamlike path toward death. Struggling to breathe and to keep his head above water, he began to strip off excess baggage. Backpack, gas mask container, ammunition—none of those mattered anymore. He did not need toiletries or candy bars or eating utensils. His feet gripped the sand under the channel and he pushed forward.

In a glance he saw that many of his men were dead, floating on the choppy water and sinking below the surface. "Who's going to show them where to go? Who's going to help them survive?" he thought. He struggled to do something, to say something. But his mind was again losing focus. He felt numb, almost as if he had been shot full of Novocain. He couldn't save anyone, not even himself. "Oh God, I *am* going to die here."

A strong hand grabbed Romanek. He looked. A Navy corpsman with a high school sophomore's face and wild and fearful eyes wrapped an arm around him and dragged him to the beach. Slowly, moving from one steel obstacle to another, they made their way across the killing field to a patch of rust-colored shingles beside a seawall on the western extreme of the beach, which provided some relief from the German positions on the bluffs. Grass fires caused by the naval bombardment accorded some cover. But the black smoke drifting across the beach made it even more difficult to breathe.

His strength was drained. Romanek lay there, his blood seeping out of holes in his chest and back, listening to the men's frantic cries, seeing fresh horrors wherever his eyes moved. This was war. Not the kind he had read about in novels and textbooks. This was an inferno—a war stripped of humanity, structure, and sense. Several times Romanek shut his eyes. The easiest thing for him to do at that moment was just to go to sleep and never wake up.

"I played football at Army," Romanek told the corpsman. They were the first words he spoke to the man who saved his life. "I played in two Army-Navy games, and I never knew Navy guys could be as nice as you. Thanks." In seconds Romanek stopped talking and began to shake, then he began to convulse and swallow his tongue. He had gone into shock. The corpsman stuck his finger in Romanek's mouth, preventing him from swallowing his tongue, and hugged him. He knew he had to give him the warmth of his body.

The corpsman administered basic first aid. After giving Romanek a shot of morphine, he cleaned and disinfected the wounds with water and sulfa powder, the most widely used antibiotic during the war. He stopped the bleeding. He also gave Romanek twelve sulfa pills, with precise instructions to take one every 4 hours. The idea that Romanek would survive for 4 minutes, let alone 48 hours, would later strike him as a trifle optimistic, and he downed all the pills in one shot in a preemptive strike against the bacteria. Meanwhile, he thanked the corpsman and asked his name and where he was from. Smitty from North Carolina answered, then went off to treat other soldiers.

Romanek relaxed. He had no place to go—couldn't get there if he did. The job he had been trained to do—plant markers pointing out an exit route from one section of the beach—would have to be done by other soldiers, perhaps the men in his platoon who had survived the landing. All he could do was recline on the hard, smooth, golf-ball-size rocks and wait and watch. With a worm's-eye view of the battle, he watched more and more men storm out of landing crafts, many falling dead. He felt the breeze on his face, smelled the smoke from grass fires and the discharge of weapons, heard the sounds of more than a dozen different weapons. Sometimes, during a lull, he heard the Germans speaking on the bluffs, but mostly the sounds were of battle—guns and screams and oaths. He didn't sleep. He was afraid if he did he would die.

Occasionally Romanek looked up at the slate sky, where American fighter planes buzzed back and forth along the beach. One of his best friends from West Point, a cadet with whom he had prepped and played football, was among them. Robin Olds, the handsomest, toughest, meanest player on the 1941 and 1942 teams, was hundreds of feet above him, pissed off at the world.[4]

Olds was a pilot in the 479th Fighter Group, a unit that had spent most of its time in England "sitting on its collective asses and not doing much of anything." Finally, on June 5, the pilots had been routed out of their bunks and sent to the briefing room, where a colonel had announced, "Gentlemen, this is it!" "We were whooping and hollering, pumping our fists in the air, slapping one another on the back, punching the guys next to us, jumping on the chairs, clapping and whistling," Olds later wrote. "It was an incredible scene!"

From the briefing room Olds moved to his P-38 fighter, painted with black and white invasion zebra stripes. "The poor plane looked like hell, but we were told it would keep our own people from firing at us," he said. The mission of the 479th was to escort the invasion fleet across the channel, keeping it safe from Luftwaffe attack. The winds were high and the heavy clouds low as Olds and the others flew toward the fleet. He wondered briefly how Ike was going to assault the beaches with seasick soldiers, but he was soon struck almost numb by the scene below him. He saw a ship, then another, then hundreds, then thousands, later writing, "I remember chills cascading down my spine, a feeling of awe and the soulful realization that we were part of what would become one of history's most unforgettable events."

Never seeing an enemy plane, he returned to base shortly after dusk. The next day, June 6, he was in the first group of the 479th to fly to the beaches of Omaha. His mission was the same as it had been the day before: fly top cover for the Allied landing forces and protect the fleet from Luftwaffe attacks. He flew through columns of black smoke caused by burning ships and watched small boats bob in the water as they advanced toward the beaches. Occasionally one of the landing crafts took a direct hit, belching flames and disappearing "quickly in the roiling water." "My stomach churned knowing that brave men were dying even before reaching land."

But Olds kept focused, searching the horizon for enemy fighters and bombers. He expected a day of dogfights and action. But there were no German planes. "I had been ordered to fire only at German planes—no exceptions," Olds recalled years later. "I really didn't question the order. It seemed perfectly sensible. Keep control of the beaches. Made perfect sense." He was sure that other fighter groups had orders to attack German land positions. The people who had planned such a massive invasion must have thought of everything, and if he decided to ad hoc change his orders, he would undoubtedly get shot down by friendly fire or gum up someone else's job. So he flew and from his ringside seat watched "one of the greatest events in history."

Only later did he realize that his well-conceived assignment left no room for contingencies. He was flying a Lockheed P-38 Lightning, a heavy fighter armed with a fixed forward-firing 20mm cannon and four fixed forward-firing 0.5in machine guns, in addition to external bomb and rocket loads. It was made for aerial combat, but it could have been used to strafe the ground. Flying at 500 feet, through the smoke of grass fires, watching hundreds of men die, he knew he could have attacked the pillboxes and machine-gun nests on the bluffs—but West Point men did not disobey orders.

"Our boys are getting killed down there, and we're doing nothing, not a god damn thing," he told another pilot over the radio. It wasn't his assignment, the pilot answered. "I know, but those are our boys down there." When Olds had been frustrated on the football field he had attacked, lashing out at any opponent he could reach. Once, in a Notre Dame game, he even threatened to knock out his own quarterback if he insisted on calling a particularly stupid end-around play. Red Blaik had once called him a "perfect player" because of his relentless, aggressive style. Now there was no one to hit and knock down. More than a half century later, he could still recall his exasperation. He was in the biggest American action in the war so far and couldn't fire his guns.

Romanek was equally powerless, another spectator on the day of days. All that morning and afternoon he witnessed the human drama swirling around him. By evening, the sheer number of Americans landing on the beach had overwhelmed the Germans. GIs had attacked the pillboxes with grenades and flame-throwers, discovered angles of fire to kill the machine-gunners, and bravely did what they had to do to take the bluffs. The sound and fury of the day subsided during the night, and the sound of surf washing ashore was heard once again, broken occasionally by the report of a sniper's rifle or a moan or sharp cry from someone on the beach.

Romanek's eyes remained open. He saw matches flicker as wounded soldiers lit cigarettes and fireflies of light as they dragged deeply. Everywhere he saw the detritus of battle—abandoned rifles and ammunition belts, burned-out tanks, used-up medical supplies, headless helmets, stray limbs—things large and small, significant and insignificant. The Allies had let slip the dogs of war and this was the result. He had seen it all, from sunrise to sunset and through the moonlit night.

Many wounded soldiers died on Omaha Beach that night, killed by snipers or succumbing to their injuries. Finally, roughly twenty-four hours after Romanek had jumped toward the channel, his company commander found him. "You're still alive. Excellent work, soldier," he said. It was like a compliment from Red Blaik—"Good tackle, Romanek."

Medics carried him to a field medical center, and he was then transported back to England. He would never be quite the same.

More than 2,000 American soldiers were killed, wounded, or missing by the end of a day that saw 34,200 troops land on Omaha Beach. As casualty figures go, the losses at Omaha were not out of proportion with those of other days of the Normandy campaign. The shock was that the casualties occurred so fast and that the first wave suffered so grievously.

Journalists and military leaders wondered: How much should Americans know? The American-led Allies had landed, attacked, and finally overcome the enemy. How much needed to be said?

In the sanitized conventions of the period, it was easier to use football analogies than graphic descriptions of the wounded and killed. General Eisenhower was portrayed as a college football coach, and his football background was often mentioned. In the days before D-Day journalists reported that Ike was nervous, rubbing a lucky coin between his fingers, consulting with his "battle teams." His fateful meeting with his key advisers sounded like a coaching staff conference—the "quiet, stocky" Admiral Ramsay; the "cool, incisive" Air Chief Marshal Leigh-Mallory; the puckish, intent General Montgomery; and Eisenhower, calm, controlled, weighing all the factors, reviewing them one by one. "In view of all these factors," he said, "I think we had better go ahead." A *Time* correspondent wrote, "With one characteristically casual sentence General Eisenhower loosed the fateful lightning that will stab and flicker over Europe until Nazi Germany is down." The very cadence of the language, the use of imagery and metaphor, echoed Grantland Rice. It sounds like the description of the second Joe Louis–Max Schmeling fight or a Notre Dame–Army football game.[5]

The iconic images of D-Day—the shots of *Life* photographer Robert Capa—are famously grainy and gray. The story of how a lab technician dried the images too quickly and destroyed most of the pictures, saving only ten badly blurred frames, is well known. But the effect was to bleed out the grisly details. In the magazine, the accompanying text again echoed the Rice school of journalism: "Rain soaked the streets of the lovely old city of Caen, capital of the Norman empire, and splashed against the gray walls of the cathedral at Bayeux. Along the beaches from Cherbourg to Le Havre God blew in with the west wind."[6]

Eisenhower made the analogy explicit. "Football has often been likened to war," he said in 1945 — "the razzle-dazzle passes to the air forces, the end sweeps to racing armored columns and the busting through the middle to bone shattering infantry attack." And a successful military operation like D-Day was like the contest on the gridiron, where coaches planned and prepared for success. "This thing is a good deal like a football game," Ike noted. "It takes thorough training, planning and tremendous hitting power to push the ball across the goal."[7]

Eisenhower was certain that the athletes of America, and especially the football players, were uniquely equipped and trained to fight in the war. He would later write, "I noted with real satisfaction how well ex-footballers seemed to have leadership qualifications. . . . I believe that football, perhaps more than any other sport, tends to instill in men the feeling that victory comes through hard — almost slavish — work, team play, self-confidence, and an enthusiasm that amounts to dedication."[8]

For West Point, and the Army as a whole, June 6 marked the commencement of a new phase of the war, with greater demands for manpower. Casimir Myslinski and his class graduated with second lieutenant's commissions and were sent overseas to battle. The two classes remaining at the Academy and the third plebe class that would report on July 1 continued to prepare for war. Over the summer, they were dispatched to bases and camps across the country, receiving instruction in the latest military weapons and tactics.[9]

The incoming plebes faced a sharp learning curve. During Beast Barracks, the "Beast Detail" included new twists. They learned to throw a grenade and fight with a bayonet, scout an enemy and patrol a perimeter, set up a camp and shoot a rifle, and defend against a gas, air, or mechanized attack. And, of course, they mastered dismounted and extended order drill. In mid-August, after Beast Barracks, the new cadets joined the corps for field maneuvers.

The third-class cadets—those in their second year—spent the summer firing weapons and learning battlefield tactics. They concentrated on marksmanship, firing rifles, light and heavy machine guns, carbines, mortars, and antitank weapons in field conditions. Instructors from the various branches—infantry, cavalry, field and coast artillery, engineering, and signal corps—met with the third-class cadets to explain the basics of their jobs. At Lake Popolopen, just off the Academy grounds, the sound of .37mm antitank guns and .50-caliber machine guns echoed through the woods as the cadets practiced blitz attacks. They also learned to man assault boats, build pontoon bridges, and fight in urban environments.

The first-class cadets, including Doug Kenna, Tom Lombardo, and Ed Rafalko, went in different directions. Those who had selected the Army Air Corps headed off to one of the Army's bases for primary flight training. The ground cadets received additional training at Lake Popolopen as well as branch instruction. Some traveled to Armored Force School at Fort Knox, Kentucky, others to Fort Benning, Georgia; Fort Bragg, North Carolina; or Camp Davis, North Carolina, to engage in maneuvers with regular tactical units.

Each cadet moved one step closer to the war. During the day they trained for combat. In the evening they discussed it. At night they dreamed about it. The conflict, they were certain, was closer to the middle than the end. America was going to win, they were sure, but they would be needed before it was over.

8

★ ★ ★

"I've Just Seen Superman"

As a matter of interest our squad was predominately
southern and I must confess a partiality for the
southern boy.

— RED BLAIK TO DOUGLAS MACARTHUR

THAT SUMMER, a new kind of cadet began to show
up at the Academy by train, bus, and automobile. Big
strapping boys, mostly from the South, they challenged
the men in the cadet store to supply properly fitting uniforms.
Traditionally, when the tailor measured each plebe for a pair of
tight dress pants, he asked if he "dressed right or dressed left,"
referring politely to the leg of his pants in which he preferred to
house his genitals. But some of the latest batch of boys had legs
as thick as middle-aged trees, deeply muscled and bulging in the
thighs and calves. The tailor needed unprecedented lengths of
measuring tape.

Thomas "Shorty" McWilliams recalled meeting Felix "Doc"
Blanchard: "You can't believe the size of his legs. I know his thighs
were better than 28 inches. . . . He'd have to split his uniform
pants to get them over his legs, they were so big." A writer for the
Saturday Evening Post claimed that Blanchard's thighs were only
25 inches, 8 inches larger than Scarlett O'Hara's corseted waist.
Doc was a running back, not one of the new enormous tackles.

Under the old height and weight restrictions, no one so large could have been admitted to the Academy.[1]

Nor did they act like normal peach down–cheeked newbies. They radiated confidence and maturity. And power. They were not fresh out of high school, seventeen- and eighteen-year-old boys. Most had spent a year or more at another university; some had already served a year or more in uniform. They were twenty- and twenty-one-year-old men, many loud, fun-loving types who had been recruited to the Academy more for what they could do on the playing field than the battlefield.

They were not the most academically distinguished cadets in the Academy's history. Barney Poole, a big Mississippian, recalled that he could keep his ears above water in most of the subjects, but there was no way he was going to master that "damn Spanish." For DeWitt Coulter, an even bigger player out of Texas, it was mathematics. "I wasn't that good in academics," he later admitted. Solid geometry and spherical trigonometry were as mysterious to him as alchemy.[2]

Coulter's struggles stayed with him for the rest of his life, many years later still giving him nightmares. "I have dreams now about West Point," he said in the late 1980s, when he was working in a home for mentally handicapped men. "I'm back at West Point and I'm having a hard time with my math work . . . trying to get through the course. And I'm there with some of the [mentally handicapped] guys, and they're just breezing through the course, and I just can't figure it out, why I'm having such a hard time and they are not."[3]

The new big men had come to play football for Colonel Blaik. They might or might not make it to Europe or the Pacific before the war ended. Meanwhile, they would inspire the men in battle by running, passing, and kicking a strangely shaped brown ball.

In the fall of 1944 George Barney Poole arrived at West Point from just southwest of nowhere, Mississippi. The game programs would list his hometown as Gloster, but he hailed from somewhere in the Homochitto Forest of Amite County, down where Mississippi snuggles close to Louisiana. In his neck of the piney woods, there were so many football-, basketball-, and baseball-playing Pooles that even astute Mississippians like Doug Kenna got confused over which one was which. "There were probably about six hundred people in Gloster, and five hundred of them must have been Pooles," Kenna said. "It was right out of *Deliverance*. But they could all play sports, that's for sure."

Barney was the ninth and youngest child in his family. "My dad died when I was fourteen months old, or we might have had a big family," he later recalled. He had two older brothers, James Eugene, whom everyone called "Buster," and Ray Smith, who, oddly enough, just went by Ray. Of course, he had several dozen aunts and uncles and heaps of cousins. "My dad was one of, I think, five or six boys with two sisters. My mother [Emily Berryhill] was one of six girls with one brother. Those two were the dominant families in this one rural community. Three of the girls married three of the brothers. It was nine in our family, I think eight in another one, and maybe six in the other, double first cousins. There were five of us my age and within a couple years, [who] went through high school [and] played football, basketball, and baseball." As far as Barney was concerned, Kenna—who played on several teams with Barney at Ole Miss—had no excuse for confusion over the exact relationships of the Poole clan.[4]

Tales of the physical prowess of the Poole family extended back for generations. "The story goes that great-granddaddy Flemin Poole was a huge man with arms that reached down to his knees," noted Ray Poole. "He come from South Carolina and I've been told he stopped when he got to the Mississippi because he couldn't get across the river." A preacher and a prizefighter who did a little farming as well, Flemin could lift mules over fences, quote whole passages from the Good Book, and box the ears of everyone in the county. His son Will A. Poole was similarly big and powerful. "Papa was a big, strong, tough man," remembered Buster, the only one of his sons with clear memories of his father. But one day down at the sawmill Will developed a stomach ache. Two weeks later, on December 29, 1924, he died of appendicitis.[5]

The wider athletic fame of the Poole family began with Buster. In the early 1930s in Mississippi, few students actually stayed in school long enough to graduate, and the Homochitto high school was little more than a one-room log cabin. Because of financial trouble, its students went through only the eleventh grade, after which the academically thirsty had to drink elsewhere. Being more athletically than academically endowed, Buster left Homochitto for the fields of semipro baseball. "He was quite a hit," Barney recalled. "There he was, 6-2 or so, 212, and could run like a deer." And he still had a year of high school eligibility. The high school coaches "flipped over him," but he had to live in the district where he was going to play, and his only family lived in an eleven-grade town.

A sheriff in Natchez, a distant relative, had room in his jail. If Buster did not mind bedding down in a cell next to drunks and an odd criminal or two, he could become a legal resident of the school district. Barney later insisted that Buster "actually lived [in the cell] for the better part of a year in order to get to high school." Buster said he resided in the jail only for the football season and then moved into a one-room apartment above the drugstore. Reporters covered the story, and college scouts took note of Buster's skill on the field. By the time he graduated from high school, he had accepted a scholarship to Mississippi State, a logical choice given his farming background. "He was all set to go, and then along come the recruiter from Ole Miss who later became the Athletic Director at Ole Miss. He came by at the proper time for him to go to school, so [Buster] loaded in and went with him," Barney recalled. "A lot of the State people said, 'Hell, he thought he was going to Starkville 'til they drove up to Oxford and he really didn't know the difference then.'" True enough, Buster affirmed. "If someone from State had come by first, I would have gone there."[6]

Buster stayed and matriculated at Ole Miss, where he lettered in football, basketball, and baseball. He then became the National Football League Rookie of the Year and a three-time All-Pro end for the New York Giants before eventually becoming a fixture on John Vaught's coaching staff at his alma mater.

Ray Poole followed Buster to Ole Miss and kept the Poole name on the sports pages in the South. Like Buster, Ray was a three-sport athlete — an end on the football team, one of the leading scorers on the basketball team, and a pitcher on the baseball team. His two stints at Ole Miss (1941–1942; 1947–1948) were interrupted by wartime service in the Marines. He was an All-Conference and All-American football player who went on to an outstanding professional career with the New York Giants and the Montreal Alouettes.

When it was time for Barney to choose a college, he followed the new family tradition. As a sophomore at Ole Miss he played on the 1942 football team, which had been all but gutted by players who had enlisted after Pearl Harbor. The team struggled to a 2-7 record, with victories over only Kentucky Teachers College and Memphis. The next year the Mississippi Board of Trustees abolished football in state institutions. Barney's local football career was over.[7]

Barney took his game on the road. Like more than 100,000 other American boys of draft age, he enrolled in the V-12 Navy College Training Program. For more than a year Barney was permitted to stay and participate in sports at Ole Miss. He began to feel a trifle "self-conscious with everyone getting drafted" around him. Finally, he said, the government did "pull [me] off the street and put [me] at North Carolina with that V-12 program." He received orders to report to the university on July 1, 1943, for Marine Corps reserve training. It just happened that his orders coincided with the beginning of summer practice for the football season. As far as Barney was concerned, football seemed an ideal way to get in shape for the battlefield.

In 1943 North Carolina was loaded with V-12 trainee football talent. Barney was joined on the team by his brother Ray, several "double first" or "just plain old vanilla first" cousins, and All-American quality players from throughout the South. Coached by Tom Young, UNC rolled over such traditional rivals as North Carolina State, South Carolina, and Virginia, but had more trouble with schools similarly stocked with V-12 or V-5 preflight training talent. Wake Forest beat UNC early in the season, and Duke beat them twice. But for Barney it was a memorable time of sunshine and family togetherness, a final season before Ray went off to war. Ray was voted onto the All-South team and third-team All-American by *Look* magazine and United Press International, and Barney was chosen honorable mention All-American. "A beautiful place," he reminisced. "I can remember football practice down in Kenan Stadium or over on the practice area. I remember particularly when right up over us the chimes started to ring. . . . I'm a little partial to institutions with bells." But Ray was called into the Marines during basketball season, and the world became a little more frightening.

By that winter of 1943–1944, the Marines had been fighting and dying for more than a year in the Pacific. In the Atlantic Theater the United States and the Allies had engaged the Axis forces in North Africa, Sicily, and Italy; D-Day was still six months off.

In the spring of 1944 Herman Hickman, the slow-talking, laugh-inducing charmer, came south looking for football players. He knew his way around North Carolina. Before working on Blaik's staff, he had been an assistant coach at Wake Forest and North Carolina State. In Winston-Salem he huddled with the Demon Deacons' legendary coach and his longtime friend D. C. "Peahead" Walker. Peahead was famous for two qualities. No one fashioned better nicknames than he. He dubbed a for-

getful player "Amoeba Brain," an academically challenged Penn-
sylvanian "Anthracite Head," a long-jawed one "Hogjaw," and
anyone in the Wake Forest divinity school "Preacher." He was
also a brilliant judge of football talent.

Army needed better players to defeat Navy, Herman said, and
he wanted the names of the finest V-12 and V-5 players. "I'm not
interested in ordinary athletes," he emphasized. "I want some
good athletes [to] play on a national championship–type team."
Peahead offered a few names; he was more than happy to shepherd a few away from rivals Duke and North Carolina. One of
the players he singled out was Barney Poole.

Hickman went to find Barney. His recruiting approach combined patriotic appeals with athletic sweet talk. "He tells us that
the impetus to put [a championship] team together didn't just
come from Red Blaik, but from General Eisenhower and General MacArthur, and the people that was in the war over there,"
Barney said. "Herman was a great teller of stories and entertained us royally. He said that they had—and I heard Peahead
make this comment too—that [the generals] had decided they
had shifted too much to the brain and a little too much away
from the physical on the military officers they had to start the
war with."

"'Course that caught my ear 'cause I had spent a lifetime in
athletics and was a fair to middling student on just the happen-
so, 'cause I didn't work on it like I could have," Barney recalled.
And he never doubted Hickman's sales pitch. "I think what was
being said wasn't made up by Herman Hickman, even though he
was very capable of making up a good story. It seems that that
was a tone that had gotten something from the top, and I heard
the names MacArthur and Eisenhower mentioned because they
was the top cheeses right at the moment."

Hickman then turned from the patriotic to the personal. "We'll
make an All-American out of you," he promised Barney. "I don't
know, maybe that was more important than it should have been,"

Poole recalled decades later. "I make no apologies for the feeling, because I think that's what it takes to get someone there." He had seen Bruiser Kinard win All-American honors in the mid-1930s and his brothers Buster and Ray get close to the very top, and he wanted some of that glory.

Part of what Herman Hickman said was reinforced by his brother Ray. Induction into the Marines had impressed on him that war was a deadly business and leading men into combat was a serious job. "They say we're ready to go across [the Pacific] and go to war," Barney remembers Ray telling him after completing his V-12 training. "I guess we are, but we moved mighty fast, and if you've got a chance to go to the Academy, they say that's the best training you can get. You damn well better take the best training you can get." You see, Barney said, Ray "thought he'd been pushed mighty fast to lead men into battle. That weighed very heavy on my decision to take the appointment."

Barney was sold. He was going to West Point.

Backfield coach Andy Gustafson picked him up in New York and drove him to the Academy. Barney was almost twenty-one years old, a shade over 6-3, 220 pounds, with enormous pass-catching hands, a shock of dark uncombed hair, and a friendly smile. He had an open, likable expression, and Gustafson had to ponder how he would fare during Beast Barracks. He suggested that Barney might not be cut out for the Academy. "He says just very coyly that I might not be able to take the harassment, that I was a pretty mature individual. I might not like to put up with that childish type of hazing," Barney recalled, but he accepted the challenge. "You couldn't have pulled me out with a bulldozer 'til I finished that plebe year."

But Gustafson was at least partly right. Barney Poole never fully bought into the West Point program. When he walked through the sally port, he was not even aware of the four-year military commitment after graduation, and he regarded many of the most venerated formalities and traditions of the Academy almost as jokes. He was not exactly a rebel, driven to break all the rules, but he chose to bend some of them when it tickled his fancy. The longer he stayed at the Academy, the bolder he became.

Morris Herbert remembered fondly that when he became a plebe, Barney Poole was already an established character on and off the field. Herbert recalled the joy of watching Barney at mess during his Beast Barracks summer. It was a stressful time for all plebes, and mess was a time of particularly high anxiety when new cadets barely had time to gobble a few mouthfuls of food. Three times a day the entire Corps of Cadets dined together on linen-covered tables in Washington Hall. Mess involved so many rituals that it was impossible for a young cadet not to break a few. Plebes removed their hats at the foot of the mess hall steps, double-timed to their tables, and stood at attention until an upperclassman ordered, "Take seats!" Then, as one observer wrote, they "sat braced on the forward three inches of their chairs, eyes locked on the helmet of Pallas Athena embossed upon each plate." And that was only the beginning. Different cadets were assigned to cut food into precisely equal portions, serve coffee or water, and make sure that the table was adequately supplied with silverware, dishes, and food. During the brief meals upperclassmen peppered plebes with questions about weather reports, the schedule for the day (or week or month or year), the movie playing at the post theater, or any poop trivia they were expected to know. Joy and mirth were generally excluded from the plebe diet.[8]

But Herbert remembered furtively scrutinizing Poole as he went out of Washington Hall. "Barney Poole would leave the mess hall with the rest of the first class . . . ahead of the plebes. We would watch him leave the mess hall, and as he left it [he] walked out through the area called the 'poop deck' where the officer in charge sits. [When he] was no longer in view of the officer in charge, Barney had a trick of taking his hat and flipping it in the air. It would do a complete somersault and land right side up on his head. Of course, you're not allowed to wear your hat in the mess hall and he was still in the mess hall. All of the plebes used to wait for Barney to do this. . . . It was done with a great deal of aplomb and élan, and we thought it was great."[9]

Another of Barney's favorite tricks involved creating a bit of havoc outside the barracks. After meal formation, plebes would mill around their barracks, waiting for instructions from the company commander and first sergeant. If Barney saw a company without a commander or first sergeant close by, he would occasionally shout, "In battery!" It was an order that ran contrary to a plebe's existence. The order new cadets in Beast Barracks heard more than any other was "Rack that neck in!" It was an order to "brace"—to push his chin so deep into his neck that it seemed to disappear into his Adam's apple. Except when they were in their rooms or showers, plebes were expected to "brace" at all times, and if they did not do so with sufficient violence, some upperclassman would assuredly scream, "Rack your neck in, dumbjohn! I want to see six wrinkles in that neck." The theory behind bracing is that it imparts the proper chest-out, shoulders-back, eyes-forward military posture, but in reality it was a form of hazing.

The order "In battery!" by contrast, was the physical opposite. An eighteenth-century naval term, it refers to when ships of the line would move their guns forward to fire at an enemy and then pull them back in to reload. "In battery" meant firing position; "heave" meant loading position. At West Point "In battery!" signaled a cadet to thrust his chin as far forward as possible, stretching out his neck like a turkey searching the ground for something to eat. The companion order of "Heave!" normally followed, signaling the cadet to resume his proper brace.

Barney was delighted to give the "In battery!" order but was not so keen on the "Heave!" follow-up. Herbert recalled Poole walking by a group of plebes at attention and commanding, "In battery!" Out went the chins. "And then he'd leave us there and go to his own company. So our upperclassmen would come back and find us all with our chins stuck out, waiting for the second command. I know very well that the seniors, the first classmen, in our company were always upset about that. And they knew who did it; there was no question in anybody's mind. Barney was not the most serious cadet that we ever ran into."

At first there was even some question about how good a football player he was. Doug Kenna recalled that one day in the spring Coach Blaik called him into his office and told him, "We just got your friend Poole to come up here." Kenna thought he meant Ray Poole. "Ray was just a ferocious player, and one of the greatest blockers I ever saw. The last thing you ever wanted was to get blocked by Ray, because he'd come at you all elbows and knees and hurt you. He really would. So I told Coach Blaik, 'Holy Gosh, Ray Poole's going to be the best player you ever saw.'"[10]

Blaik looked at him and said, "No, not Ray, we got Barney Poole."

"You got the wrong Poole!" Kenna responded. He recalled Barney from the freshman team at Ole Miss. "He was sixteen years old and about 230 pounds, 200 of it was blubber. He was slow and couldn't move and I was sure Ole Miss gave him a scholarship on the assumption that since he was a Poole he was bound to be great. But he wasn't much then."

But once practice began, Kenna's doubts faded faster than the dew under the early morning summer sun. Barney Poole was a remarkable end. "I don't know what happened," Kenna said, "but now he was 230 and all muscle. Still wasn't fast, but really athletic, and had wonderful soft hands. He could catch anything." Like his two brothers, he was big, aggressive, and "loved to knock people down." He enjoyed the pure, physical aspect of football, the collision of body on body, the test of power, technique, and will. Barney had a fine sense of humor and an easy country charm, but buried just beneath the surface was a competitive desire to be the best and to win. He just hated losing, and on the practice or game field he never gave less than his best.

In most outward respects he was not at all like Glenn Davis, but they were kindred souls when it came to playing a game. Barney cherished his memories of playing with the Californian. On occasional Sunday afternoons during Gloom Period, that seemingly sunless stretch of time between November and March when West Point is gray and cold and dreary, Poole and Davis would wander down to the gymnasium. "[You] couldn't do anything else much, in the winter time, I guess. We'd eat lunch, [and] we'd wind up at the gymnasium to start a marathon basketball game. We'd just pick up a team. . . . We'd have a pretty good basketball game, and the score got something like 275 to 270. It was about to be time to quit and go get showered for the night meal. I remember Ug Fuson and one other boy. . . . They let a little bit of horseplay slip into the basketball game. We were dead serious, playing as best we could. They started horsing around a little bit and let someone break away, and they didn't even chase to try to head him off. Glenn Davis got fighting mad. His eyes got red. He says, 'If you're going to play, you ought to play the best you possibly can! If you're not going [to play] the best you can, dammit you ought not to even suit up to play.'" Barney thought, "There's a guy that can put in words what I think."

Although Barney was sometimes mystified by all the rules and regulations at the Academy, it did not take him long on the football field to realize that he was at the right place, surrounded by his kind of athletes. Davis, he said, "had a determination that I never saw. I played with some great athletes, and I grew up with some in my family. They don't get much better athletes than my brothers Ray and Buster and some of my cousins." But Davis? "A total absence of anything except dead seriousness and the eye on the goal—he never took it off." Even better, Doug Kenna and the other leading players on the 1944 team were not far behind Davis and Poole.

DeWitt "Tex" Coulter thought a great deal more about hitting than he did about shining his shoes. His knack of striking fear into opponents made him a considerable asset to Army's football team, though at times a liability in practices. But his forgetfulness about uniform regulations and his sheer pigheadedness concerning the polish of his shoes made him a target for any upperclassman who glanced at his oversized feet.

Barney Poole credited himself for keeping DeWitt in the Academy. He and DeWitt were about the same size, and since in 1944 cadets were still placed in companies according to size, the two football players were roommates. Poole noticed on a regular basis that DeWitt had a less than regulation shine on his shoes. They would be standing out in morning formation, Poole remembered, and "some little guy" from "way down the ranks" would dart purposefully toward DeWitt. "Here they'd come, and they'd get up and chew old Tex out something unmercifully." And DeWitt would get a little steamed. As the upperclassman continued down the line DeWitt, talking out of the corner of his mouth, would say, "I wonder how far I could knock that little son of a bitch if I decided to hit him." "Cool it, Tex, we've got Notre Dame this week. We can't win without you," Barney would reply in his most charming, calming Mississippi accent.[11]

Life had taught DeWitt to strike back. The road from a shack just east of Red Springs, Texas, to the Academy had not been smooth. He was the youngest of four children whose father died from tuberculosis when DeWitt was four. It was right before the Great Depression, but in Texas times were already hard and his mother had no means to support her children. To make matters worse, the day their daddy was buried, a paternal uncle showed up and took their only possession, a cow. A West Point teammate remembered that when DeWitt recalled the incident, his fingers gripped a desk so hard that they were sheet white. DeWitt said, "Boy, if I could ever get ahold of him, I'd. . . ." His voice trailed off. "[H]e could have pulled him apart, he was such a strong, well-coordinated (man)."[12]

DeWitt's father had been a Mason, so his mother, with the encouragement of the uncle, arranged for the children to go to the Masonic Home in Fort Worth. "That was my home from first grade through the eleventh grade. In effect, we were orphans," DeWitt recalled.[13]

"The Home," as it was known, had opened its doors just before the beginning of the twentieth century, welcoming any child between the ages of five and thirteen whose father had died a Freemason in good standing. It was built on soft ground, causing buildings to crumble before their time and waterlines to collapse and break. "It was a grim place where misbehaving kids were lashed with straps and locked up in closets," wrote a journalist. Any infraction of its rules resulted in severe punishment, including beatings with rubber hoses. The children were called "inmates" rather than orphans, and the surrounding community made them feel like second-class citizens.[14]

All his life DeWitt remembered the emotional pain of entering the Home. "That first night at the orphanage, well, I don't have a word that fits it," he said. "They put me in Dorm One, my brother Ray in Dorm Two, and my sisters L.E. and Ima, God knows where. I thought I would never see them again." All that he could do was cry and shiver with fear and wait for sunrise.[15]

In the late 1920s Rusty Russell, a thin, quiet man whose eyesight had never fully recovered from a gas attack on the Western Front during the Great War, brought football to the Home. When he accepted a position to teach science and coach football, the Home had a rocky, briar patch football field, not enough helmets for even eleven players, worn hand-me-down uniforms, and an old Dodge truck that belched smoke and provided the team's only transportation. But with surprising speed Russell transformed his football team into a powerhouse. Competing against the leading high school teams in the state—schools with the best uniforms and up-to-date facilities—the Home earned a unique place in Texas football lore.

At the Home boys began to play football young, starting on the 65-pound team and working up to the 80-pound, 110-pound, and high school teams. They learned to play a particularly intense, smash-mouth football, channeling their rage against their fortune in life. As DeWitt recalled, "We couldn't make what we called the 'city guys' admire us for our situation, but we could make them fear us. You know, a good healthy fear. So we played a very tough brand of football. The ball is snapped; you continued to hit people until the referee blew the whistle." Sometimes the hitting continued after the whistle. And woe to the opponent who acted as if he were not in a particular play. If DeWitt or his teammate Hardy Brown spied some guy looking across the field whose head was not on a swivel—well, either of the two would lay him out cold. "You made him know that he had to look out for you; he had to look out for you and not other people," DeWitt said. Life can come at you hard. A man needed to pay attention.

The Home hitting technique was developed by the Brown boys, Hardy and his older brother Jeff. Jeff Brown introduced an unusual block that he dubbed "the Humper." Using his shoulder like a fist, he crouched low with his back straight and leaped and rotated his shoulder in the same movement, concentrating on hitting his opponent in the middle of the face. He later told a reporter that he envisioned the best way to topple a fence post: "Hit it low and the fence post might not budge. But hit it high and the fence post would topple over." In an age before face masks, the well-delivered Humper would break a nose, split a lip, or loosen a few teeth. A perfect Humper would knock a player unconscious. The Texas coaches howled to referees about the block, but at that time it was not illegal.[16]

Hardy Brown transformed his brother's blocking technique into a tackling one. Hardy was a tough kid, even by the standards of the Home. As a young boy, he had witnessed his moonshining father gunned down by two rivals; a pair of shotgun shells had ripped off part of his back and side. When Hardy told his mother the news, she "looked like she had seen a ghost," then ran off, deserting her children. Understandably, Hardy grew up angrier and more confrontational than the other boys. He was handsome and had a winning smile, but he also possessed a mean streak that festered over the years. At the end of his life he confessed to DeWitt that he hated "everybody in the world."[17]

"It's like a boxer," Hardy later said of his tackling style. "Take one step forward, keep your back straight, keep your eyes open, and SHOOT." He would hit a player on the chest, chin, and helmet, knocking it off, all in one shot. It was "like a Jack Dempsey punch," former San Francisco 49ers player Red Hickey said. "It didn't need but six inches. That's all it needed and you went to sleep." "He learned to put that hump into you and he could hit," recalled another professional player. After his own professional career was over, Hardy was asked if anyone hit as hard as he had. "Nobody. NOBODY," he answered. "I really mean that. Unless it would have been some one of my teammates back at the Home."[18]

DeWitt learned to block and tackle like the Brown brothers. Stories about hard-hitting high school football players are common, and most contain a strong dose of exaggeration. But everyone who saw Coulter and Brown in a game agreed that they played with an unusual ferocity, a brand of attack that bordered on street fighting. Doc Blanchard, no stranger to violent collisions, smiled when he recalled playing linebacker behind Coulter. "You know, it was a lot of fun . . . because it was really easy. . . . Tex only knew how to play football one way—and that was wide open, all the time." In the early 1950s *Sport* magazine ran an article on the toughest men who ever played football. The select list included Coulter and Hardy Brown.[19]

Most of the players on the Home team were scrawny kids, normally 20 or 30 pounds lighter than the boys they lined up against. DeWitt was different. With a round baby face, slits for eyes, and a snubbed, flat nose, he looked like a young Babe Ruth. He was also a tall, big-boned boy, 6-4 and well over 200 pounds without any fat on his body. "You know, that guy, you could see his backbone when he played for us," said Goble Bryant, who played against DeWitt in high school and with him at Army. "He didn't have any meat on him at all, but he could do a front circle-up on a high bar. He could do a split-away on the rings. Now, he didn't look like one of these Olympic athletes, but I'm telling you that he did it correctly. . . . He was [a] championship boxer, wrestler. Broke the Academy record in the shot put." Another Army teammate, Joe Steffy, agreed. He said Coulter played at "237, and he was nothing but skin and bones at 237. You could count his ribs."[20]

DeWitt's personality, however, was smaller than his body. When not playing football, he said little and stayed in the background. He was always a bit odd, Steffy recalled, with "a loner-like personality." That wasn't exactly right, but his teammates had a hard time finding the right word. "I can't describe it the way I feel it. He had a little difference there. Super guy, but a very quiet man, didn't say much. . . . [H]e didn't talk." Bryant thought that off the field DeWitt was as "gentle a man as you'd ever see. . . . He'd be hard to rile. . . ." But always he kept his distance—from classmates, teammates, and family. Even at the Home there was an invisible wall between him and the others, as if he were afraid to get close to anyone.[21]

The emotion he expressed on the field was anger. "On the

football field he was just all aggression," remarked Bill Webb, who played across the line from DeWitt at the Academy. Virtually all his teammates at Army agreed. Albert Joy recalled a scrimmage on the Plain when he successfully hooked DeWitt with a block, resulting in a good gain. A few downs later the same play was called, with similar results. Angered, Coach Blaik said, "Run that play again!" "All I can think of was, there's going to be Tex waiting for me to come around again," remembered Joy. "I'd gotten him twice. So I figured I'd better do something. I came around and hooked him a little differently, and got him. It made him so mad he kicked my hand, and left that. . ." He held up a hand with a permanently dislocated finger. Was DeWitt tough? "Yes, on the field he was. In fact, I think some people might even refer to him as being slightly dirty."[22]

There was no need for the modifier. He was slightly more than slightly dirty. Joe Steffy was more direct: "Oh, DeWitt was the essence of the [phrase] 'mean streak.' Compared with DeWitt, everybody was a Sunday school boy." More than a half century after playing with DeWitt at West Point, Steffy said, "There was an anger in Tex that he kept bottled inside. A rage really, that you never saw off the field. You only saw it when he was playing football—and then it was just something wild and uncontrollable. He didn't care about plays or penalties. Sure he wanted to win, I guess. But I'm not sure he thought about winning in terms of the score board." Winning for DeWitt was laying someone out. Cold.[23]

After earning All-State honors for three consecutive years playing for the Home, as well as winning a national championship in the shot put, DeWitt accepted a football scholarship from Texas A&M. But he received a draft notice before he reached College Station and went instead to basic training in Mineral Wells, Texas. From there he was supposed to go to Shepherd Field in

Wichita Falls to be trained as an airplane mechanic. He never got there. Someone discovered that he was an accomplished football player and shipped him to a physical education school for non-coms in Miami Beach.

Soon the Army returned DeWitt to Shepherd Field. He was resting in his barracks when he heard a commotion. In charged the company commander, asking, "Where is DeWitt Coulter?" DeWitt thought, "Oh my goodness, what have I done?" Or, more likely, "What is it that I didn't do that I was supposed to have done?" It turned out that he had done nothing wrong; he had merely flattened other Texas high school football players for three years.

"Private Coulter, how would you like to go to West Point?" the officer asked.

"Me sir?" DeWitt answered, followed by a quick, "Boy, I'd like that."

Later DeWitt learned that he had been singled out by a West Point birddog scout in Texas. Senator Tom Connally of Texas, chair of the Senate Committee on Foreign Relations, was only too happy to proffer an appointment, and before long DeWitt was on a train to New York. First he went to Cornell to prep for the entrance exam. After passing it, he traveled to West Point.

He arrived on July 1, a big, sweating boy with oversized hands, high-water pants, and serious academic deficiencies. "I was over-awed, actually, because I wasn't that good in academics, because of that Masonic Home high school. We got a very good education in things like English, but not math," he remembered. But his country needed him to break a few noses and ribs.

The Davis boys were going back to West Point—Ralph for his second year, Glenn for another plebe year. After busting out, Glenn had passed a deficiency test in math and been readmitted, but by the rules of the Academy that meant repeating his entire first year. Once again, the boys' mother packed lunch bags full of fried chicken for the long cross-country train ride from San Bernardino, California.

The twins sat and talked, occasionally looking at 1944 America as the train rolled across the country. Always intense, always a worrier, Glenn talked about his need to improve his grades and the pressures of studying, Academy life, and football. No matter where the conversations began, they kept returning to football—their teammates, the T formation, Army's chances in 1944. They observed a man sitting across from them, tall and straight, his hair brushed back like steel spikes, listening intently to their discussions. Eventually he introduced himself. "My name is Shaughnessy," he said. "Clark Shaughnessy."[24]

The coaching legend who brought the T formation and a Rose Bowl victory to Stanford was now the coach at the University of Pittsburgh, and his team was scheduled to play Army on October 14. He was not a spy, hoping to get some inside skinny, just a football coach with several thousand miles of track in front of him. He explained that Colonel Blaik was one of his friends and that he had even alerted him to the son of a fullback he had coached at Tulane University during the Great War. The dad was a big, tough fullback who went on to medical school. The son was also a fullback, as large and as rugged as his old man.

"You'll be seeing him this fall," Shaughnessy said. "Remember the name: Felix Blanchard."[25]

Nobody called him Felix. His dad was "Doc," and as the boy reached his teens he became "Little Doc." By the time he reached West Point, his father had died and nothing about him was little. He was massively built, incredibly fast, and crushingly powerful. He was Doc Blanchard. As a youth he enjoyed reading comic books about superheroes, and he looked like a comic book rendition of a football player. Andy Bershak, one of his college coaches, told another member of the staff, "I know some folks would rather see a pretty girl with a lovely figure than anything else. Personally, I'd rather look at Blanchard getting dressed for a game than any pretty girl I've ever seen! What a build!" After Notre Dame coach Ed McKeever scouted Doc and watched him carry a football, he wired the other coaches in South Bend: "I've just seen Superman in the flesh. He wears number 35 and he goes by the name Blanchard."[26]

Going to West Point was not a dream for Blanchard. He was a southern boy from Louisiana French stock, with no roots in the military. His father had raised him to tote a football, not a rifle. When the child was one day old, a cousin recalled, "His dad put a football in his crib for luck." By the time he was two, his father was teaching him how to kick and carry a ball. Apart from football, Little Doc enjoyed a typical southern boyhood in Bishopville, South Carolina. He played mumble-the-peg and hooky from school, batted around baseballs and tennis balls, worked for Boy Scout badges and delivered groceries for spending money, and enjoyed swimming and diving in Lake Delano on hot summer days. But always there was football. Little Doc carried a ball, tucked firmly into the pocket between his bicep and hand, nearly wherever he went.[27]

Little Doc had the body to fulfill his father's fantasies. He weighed 159 pounds when he was thirteen and 180 a year later. A standard story about his early football career maintained that the first time he was sent into a game, a rival fullback ran over him for a touchdown. Embarrassed, he considered quitting the team, but his father talked him out of it. That play may have been his last football setback. His father sent him to high school at St. Stanislaus, a highly regarded Christian Brothers prep school and athletic power in Bay St. Louis, Mississippi. There he made the All-Gulf-Coast-Region Class A team. Twice he played on teams in the New Orleans Toy Bowl, the high school curtain-raiser for the Sugar Bowl.[28]

By his senior year, he was one of the premier players in the country. West Point recruiters tried to sell their program to Blanchard. "I really wasn't very interested," he later admitted. He considered Tulane, where his father had played, but he really wanted to go somewhere near his home. His father's health was declining, and he wanted to be close to his family. Jim Tatum, his first cousin, coached the freshman football squad at the University of North Carolina. After spending a few days in Chapel Hill, he signed on, leading the Tar Babies to the 1942 state title.[29]

By the end of his freshman year he was eighteen and military service loomed ahead. He attempted to enroll in a Navy V-12 program but was rejected for deficient eyesight and—ironically—for obesity, at least according to the Navy's height and weight standards. Instead, he was drafted into the Army and sent to Miami Beach for basic training. From there he was ordered to Clovis, New Mexico, for Air Corps training in chemical warfare. The idea of his son engaged in chemical warfare did not sit well with his father, who moved him in another direction. "My father was interested in me going somewhere [else] and kept pushing that," he recalled. "I guess Colonel Blaik and the staff had remembered me along with all the other people they had tried to recruit to . . . play ball" at the Academy. "Really, it was through my dad." Through his dad's work and an appointment from Senator Ellison "Cotton Ed" Smith—who was legendary for announcing, "Cotton is king and white is supreme"—Doc won a spot at the Academy. A few weeks before he began Beast Barracks, his father died.[30]

Doc's arrival at West Point on July 1, 1944, made an immediate impression. Jim Tatum, who had tried without success to help Blanchard sweat off pounds before his Navy V-12 physical, said that Doc was "all muscle and concrete." The adjectives his teammates most used to describe him were "massive," "heavily muscled," and "thick." Blaik judged Blanchard "the best-built athlete I ever saw; six feet and 208 pounds at his peak, not a suspicion of fat on him, with a slim waist, Atlas shoulders, colossal legs." Olympic track coach Lawson Robertson was equally impressed, observing that anyone who saw Doc in a track suit would never forget the size of his thighs. Leo Novak, Army's track coach, agreed, observing, "If that boy pulled a muscle, he wouldn't even know it." "Doc's body looked indestructible," said Doug Kenna. "I think it could have survived a bomb blast."[31]

Doc was also exceptionally fast. Shorty McWilliams, who played in the backfield with Doc in 1945, recalled that both he and Glenn Davis were sub-10-second sprinters for the 100-yard dash, but Blanchard could beat both of them in a 60-yard race. "He exploded out of those blocks like Buddy Young," the diminutive world-record-holding sprinter and professional football player of the 1950s.[32]

John Sauer, another teammate, recalled his first impressions of the southern running back. Before Doc entered the Academy, when he was still prepping at Lafayette College, he visited the post and went swimming at Delafield Pond, which had a high tower that the cadets used as a diving platform. "I was one year older than him," he said. "But I was watching him from the sand beach and he got up on a 30-foot tower and did the most beautiful two-and-a-half-pike dive I ever saw in my life, and when they told me that big horse played football, I said, 'We've got something here, because this fellow can do everything.' And he could; he was a great athlete."[33]

And he knew it. Like Barney Poole, Doc had a fun-loving, down-country appeal, engaging and friendly but also confident. A reporter for *Time* magazine described it as an "impish, hillbillyish charm," with an easy, wide-mouthed laugh and a drawl "that could pass for Amos & Andy's Kingfish." He was one of the few players—perhaps the only one—who was at ease around Blaik. The first time the coach ever saw Blanchard, it was the year before Doc entered the Academy and the team was practicing in the field house. "He'd been standing there watching," Blaik remembered. When the practice ended, Blaik strolled over and said, "What do you think?" Doc thought for a second and replied, "Not so hot." "That's typical of Doc," Blaik added. He was not easily impressed and quick with an opinion.[34]

Even Tex Coulter was attracted to Doc, perhaps because he had the same alpha-dog nature as Hardy Brown. He didn't pull a punch on or off the field. "He was just a lot of fun," Coulter said. "I remember Colonel Blaik asking each of us before our first practice if we drank. Well, most of us dodged that one, but Doc just said, 'Oh, sure.' And he did not sign the abstinence pledge during his years at the Academy. If there was some harmless fun to be had at West Point, Doc would be somewhere near the mix."[35]

Herman Hickman and Andy Gustafson had enjoyed the athletic fruits of war in the summer of 1944, arranging for some of the finest players in the nation to come to West Point. Before the war they had participated in America's premier football programs. Joining Barney, Tex, and Doc, the other 1944 plebes for Beast Barracks included Arthur Gerometta (University of Illinois), Young Arnold Tucker (University of Miami), Herschel "Ug" Fuson (U.S. Naval Training Station), Thomas Hayes (University of Nebraska), Harold Tavzel (Miami University of Ohio), Dean Sensanbaugher (Ohio State University), Shelton Biles (Vanderbilt University), and William West (Dartmouth College). Henry Foldberg, Milton Routt, and Joe Starnes had, like Coulter, gone directly from high school into the service. Many had been through the rigors of basic training and played for a service team. Now they had come together for another mission: to give Army soldiers around the world a team to follow, a team that would represent the greatness and the power of the United States Army. The new players were a wartime windfall, to be sure, but they didn't guarantee a championship—and Navy was getting stronger with the same windfall. The '44 season promised to be special.

9

★ ★ ★

Warm-Up

Ashes to ashes, dust to dust.
If Blanchard don't get you, then Davis must.

THOUGHTS OF LOSING again to Navy had haunted Blaik in the months after the 1943 game. They woke him up in the middle of the night, pushed him into his office, and nagged at him every crowded minute of the day. Three seasons he had coached Army. Three seasons his cadets had charged out of the gates, won their first four or five games, and looked like world-beaters. Each year, the second half of the season had tested them. Track coaches claim that sometimes a runner has "to run off the edge of the cliff," go beyond where he has ever been and see if he has something left inside—something that hard work and talent had put in reserve—that will propel him to victory. Blaik's Army teams had failed each year's test.

In 1941 and 1942, for the most part, he had not taken the field with players he had recruited. Doug Kenna, his first stand-out player, would have helped in 1942, but he broke his arm. In 1943 Blaik had more of his own boys. They had looked terrific in the first five games, but once again they couldn't go the distance. Three years and the same thing—not one win against Penn, Notre Dame, or Navy.

On New Year's Day 1944, at eight in the morning, Blaik convened a staff meeting. Wearing his brown business tweeds, he looked ready for work. Andy Gustafson and Herman Hickman, his two hard-drinking assistants, struggled with painful hangovers. Gustafson wore dark glasses. Hickman sported a "weary smile." Blaik wanted to make a point. As he later put it, "I wanted to impress on my assistants that this was the first day of the year in which we were going to beat Navy and we must get to the job without delay."[1]

Blaik's job, the staff's job, boiled down to this: no more mistakes. That spring on the North Field close to the Hudson or, when cold weather blew down the river, in the nearby field house, Blaik honed and refined his T offense. In 1943 Army had fumbled too often, a result more often than not of poor timing and bad handoffs than crushing hits. The backs had to take better care of the ball. So over and over again they ran plays—end runs, a fake to a halfback, and a pitch to the fullback; straight buck, a halfback plunge through the tackle hole; cross buck, a halfback run off the opposite tackle; split buck, a fake cross buck and a handoff to the fullback going in the opposite direction; off tackle; reverse off tackle; and traps.[2]

Everyone had to be on board with the program, from the War Department and the superintendent on down to the coaches, players, and the cadets cheering for their team. In May, well before the start of the 1944 season, Blaik had written a private letter to General Wilby because he had "doubts as to the propriety of dispatching the information" through official channels. He began by informing the superintendent that Navy would have another powerful team. Grantland Rice, Blaik noted, adding underlined emphasis, had recently written: "To the South Pacific: From all appearances the Navy team will be football's 1944 standout. . . . Army will be good, but hardly up to Navy class. . . . It would not be surprising to see Navy the *best team* in the *country, college* or *professional.*"[3]

Army needed better athletes and secure congressional appointments. "Oddly enough," Blaik wrote, "it has been more difficult to secure the prospects than the appointments. This is due in main to the fact that the Navy and Marine Corps have cornered the market of good athletes as most athletes are enrolled in the V-12, V-5, or Marine Corps Units." Army had attracted a few outstanding players who were borderline students. In a list he sent to Wilby, Blaik rated his recruits' talent and commented on their academic abilities. His football scale was:

5 — excellent; will be on varsity squad this fall.
4 — above average.
3 — average.

The list of 5s included Poole ("Fair Student"), Blanchard ("Fair Student"), and Foldberg ("Fair Student"). Some needed additional support in getting through the Academy.

In September, after several weeks of preseason practice, Blaik wrote to Wilby again to reinforce his earlier message. He thought Navy had an unfair advantage over Army. They started their semester later, scrimmaged against good teams that used the Army T offense, and had less rigorous eligibility standards. But he was not making excuses. "I wish to assure you," he stressed, "that the coaching staff has no such feeling as we have dedicated our entire thoughts since last fall to [the] winning of the '44 game." But — and here is where he needed Wilby's help — "every consideration compatible with West Point tradition should be used to encourage these plebes so that they will be available for training the entire season."[4]

Blaik did not want a repeat of the previous year, when Davis's academic trouble crippled him before the Notre Dame and Navy games. What exactly Blaik was asking for was not made explicit. He did not come right out and ask for the standards of the Academy to be changed or his athletes to be given anything. It was just that some of the players needed careful academic guidance.

The next day Wilby wrote a response to Blaik stamped Confidential, agreeing, "[T]he game on December 2d [Navy] takes priority over almost anything else here at the Academy this year," and he was willing to "make every concession possible to the men on the football team, so that they would feel that . . . I [am in] back of them 100% in doing everything possible to win that game." He recommended careful monitoring of grades, for there was "no excuse for losing any players on account of academic ineligibility." He closed as he had begun: "The winning of that game on December 2d is the only thing that counts in my opinion."[5]

Not all of his players needed academic help. In the stellar 1944 crop that Hickman recruited to West Point—and that Blaik sought to protect—was a center from the University of Tennessee named Herschel "Ug" Fuson, whom Blaik rated as an "Excellent Student." Ug was a broken-field scatback trapped in a lineman's body—or at least that was how he liked to see himself. In high school in Middlesboro, Kentucky, he had won a Reader's Digest Award as an outstanding student and graduated valedictorian in his class. He had accepted a scholarship to Tennessee, played there in 1942, and then enrolled in a program at a U.S. Naval Training Station. But Hickman, a Tennessee grad himself, learned of Ug's prodigious talents on the gridiron and in the classroom and just naturally concluded that he belonged at West Point.[6]

Fuson had a little of Hickman in him. He had an aw-shucks charm and a quick wit. Thomas "Shorty" McWilliams, one of his later southern teammates, never forgot Ug's rendition of songs from the Tennessee hills, and Doug Kenna thought he was "just a wonderful guy—and really smart." Joe Steffy believed that Ug was one of those cadets who had been "earmarked" to return to the Academy to teach. "He was first in his class in French," Steffy said, destined to be sent to "all the right schools," and go on to get a master's degree. "Back then, [the Army would] draw a line; if you were above a certain level academically, you were listed to go to other schools. If you were not, then you stayed in line outfits and carried your gun."[7]

But Ug was sold on combat. He had come to West Point to study, play football, and serve his country. Steffy described him in tones of deep respect: "In a group of very fine people, he was a little above. First place, he played center, played halfback, played tackle, played end. . . . He could go in and do it all." And beyond that, "Ug was the perfect teammate. If you needed something, he was there for you. We came from all over the country, but Ug made us feel like a family."

Another player who signed on for the mission and provided stability for the team was Edmund "Rafe" Rafalko, a son of Polish Catholic parents who had immigrated to America from the region north of the Pripet Marshes. An honors student and standout athlete in football, basketball, and baseball in Stoughton, Massachusetts, he was recruited by Tennessee, Brown, Columbia, and Cornell, among other schools, and was set to go to Columbia when he heard from West Point. The Academy was filled with rural Protestant boys from military backgrounds, not his type. But his parents wanted him to go to West Point, and he agreed, rushing to the Academy just in time to be sworn in on July 15, 1942. "I was only eighteen and my parents probably wanted to keep me away from the war for a few years," Rafe recalled. "But I went in with my eyes open — and they opened wider that first day."[8]

Rafe was a solid student and excelled on the football field. In 1942 he was one of eight plebes who made the traveling squad and played in most of the games. He saw even more action in 1943, gaining a reputation as a clutch player and a quick wit. In an oration before taking the field against Yale, Blaik turned to Rafe and asked, "What are we going to do in the Yale Bowl today?" The safe answer would have been, "Win, sir." But Rafe instantly replied, "Shit in it, Colonel."[9]

Fuson's and Rafalko's names seldom made the sports page in the months before the season. The standard word on Army was great backs, no line. In August the *Washington Post* ran the headline: WANTED: LINEMEN WITH BRAINS; APPLY TO ARMY COACH BLAIK. "We'll probably get a fair line out of the new candidates, but then you never know how many of them are going to stay eligible," Blaik pleaded. "You know, it's a tough grind up here at the Point these days from a scholastic standpoint." Some reporters questioned his lamentations. Tim Cohane, one of his favorite sportswriter friends, wrote: "Col. Earl Blaik and Herman Hickman have our condolences over the lack of material. Come, come, men, buck up!" But for the most part, the sportswriters agreed with Blaik. Army would have talent, certainly, but they looked awfully thin on the depth charts and would have to depend too much on untested plebes. Blaik would have a nice squad, the football writers agreed, but nothing like Notre Dame's or Navy's. Now *they* would have teams.[10]

In truth, between the returning lettermen and the talented plebes, Army enjoyed an overflowing cornucopia of talent. If Blaik had wanted to put his best eleven players on the field, it would have been impossible for him to choose. Instead he decided to build two teams. Although in 1941 a new NCAA rule allowed free substitutions except in the last 2 minutes of the first half, coaches during the war years did not fully exploit the change by moving to the two-platoon football of today—that is, offensive and defensive teams comprising different personnel. Players of the era "went both ways"; they played offense and defense.

Blaik's 1944 two-platoon system comprised two teams that each went both ways. The idea was for the A team to play the entire first quarter and the B team to play the second. Then, depending on the score or the importance of the game, in the second half Blaik could repeat the sequence, substitute true reserve players, or use some combination of both teams. Blaik and his players normally referred to the teams by the names of their quarterbacks. The A was Kenna's team and included mostly upperclassmen. The B was Captain Tom Lombardo's team and included most of the finest plebes. The starting lineups of the two teams, with a few variations, were:[11]

Kenna's Team	Position	Lombardo's Team
Dick Pitzer	LE	George "Barney" Poole
Archie Arnold		Tom Hayes
Bill LaMar	LT	DeWitt "Tex" Coulter
Jack Green	LG	Shelton Biles
Bob St. Onge	C	Herschel "Ug" Fuson
Joe Stanowicz	RG	Art Gerometta
Al Nemetz	RT	Harold Tavzel
Bill Webb		
Ed Rafalko	RE	Henry "Hank" Foldberg
Doug Kenna	QB	Tom Lombardo
		Young Arnold Tucker
Dale Hall	LH	Glenn Davis
Max Minor	RH	Dean Sensanbaugher
		Dick Walterhouse
Bobby Dobbs	FB	Felix "Doc" Blanchard

Blaik wanted each team to develop into a perfectly coordinated unit. For the first time in his coaching career, he had two sets of players capable of executing his precise plans perfectly. In their only real scrimmage, they battled to a 21–21 tie.

September practices were exercises in precision. "Run it again," were Blaik's most frequent three words. He was less concerned with the number of plays the teams could run than how many they could execute to his exact standards. Every player had not only an initial assignment but secondary ones. An offensive tackle, for instance, might explode off the ball into the defensive end, hold for a one count, and take one step, pivot, and block the linebacker moving toward the play. If the opposing team acted as expected, it would work brilliantly. In the short, intense sessions, Blaik demanded complete attention. "Practices were not supposed to be fun," recalled Doug Kenna.[12]

Occasionally, however, there were light moments, usually supplied by the Falstaffian Herman Hickman. In one September practice he became upset with a lineman who was too high in his stance. Bob Woods, who was now Cadet First Captain and serving as an assistant coach, recalled that Herman approached the player and yelled, "Get down. You're too high. Get your ass down. Like this." And then Hickman got down in a perfect three-point stance: ass low, back straight, and legs coiled. It was as if he were back at Tennessee and 75 pounds lighter. "Herman was big," Woods said. "Even wearing baggy canvas football pants, a sweatshirt, and an old duck jacket with big pockets, you could see how powerful he was. Had legs like tree trunks. He got down and—POW—he fired right out into a defensive tackle. Perfect block. Then all of a sudden a head popped out of one of the right pockets in his duck jacket. It was Tiny, his Chihuahua, with the damnedest look on his face. Like—What just happened?"[13]

Meanwhile, down by the Severn River, the Annapolis squad got ready for a season that everyone agreed held great expectations. Their hopes centered squarely on a new wartime NCAA rule that permitted four years of varsity eligibility. After a period of some debate, Navy decided to use fourth-year players. When Rear Admiral John Beardall, superintendent of the Naval Academy, announced the decision in September, Navy's football captain, Big Ben Chase, shouted gleefully, "Now we've got the stuff."[14]

Beardall's decision gave another year of eligibility to Don

Whitmire, Navy's All-American tackle. Whitmire had played at the University of Alabama in 1941 and 1942. In his second season with the Crimson Tide, he received first-team All-American votes and led Alabama to an Orange Bowl victory. In 1943 Alabama dropped football, and Navy coach Rip Miller recruited Whitmire to the Naval Academy, where in 1943 he was picked as a consensus All-American. In 1944 he would win the Rockne Trophy as the nation's top lineman. In an age when a team's fate hinged on the play of the tackles, the quick, smart, mean Whitmire was Navy's anchor.

Along with Whitmire, the decision gave another year of play to blocking back Dave Barksdale, who had been the captain-elect at North Carolina before entering the Academy; Ben Martin, the 250-pound standout at center; Jack Martin, the 1943 starting wingback; and Hal Hamberg, the triple-threat leader of the 1943 team. In 1943 Navy had won the Lambert Trophy as the best team in the East. The additional players did not alter Coach Oscar Hagberg's plans for the 1944 season. "I planned on winning every game, and this will help," he told reporters.[15]

Blaik agreed that on paper Navy looked nearly unbeatable. "The middy team will be a superduper, lollypalooza," he remarked to a *Time* reporter. Then he added, "That doesn't mean we won't beat Navy."[16]

Navy's linemen were so big, their backs so quick, that Blaik's addendum seemed like rare braggadocio. Lawrence Robinson of the *New York World-Telegram* announced: NAVY LINE GOOD ENOUGH TO MOVE INTO PRO LEAGUE. Further confirmation of their strength came in a September scrimmage against Bainbridge Naval Training Station, a team of football ringers who had gone undefeated in 1943 and outscored their opponents by a combined total of 313–7. Bainbridge was a team of college stars and professionals, former All-Americans and future All-Pros, a tough bunch of sailors playing football before they shipped off to war. They were led by the young sensation Charlie "Choo-Choo"

Justice of North Carolina at tailback. But after a brief period of adjustment against the bigger, older Bainbridge men, the Midshipmen, commented a reporter, "gathered their wits and their strength and fought the enlisted men evenly." The scrimmage left no doubt in the sportswriters' minds that Navy was the team to beat in 1944. As Robinson commented, "The U.S. Navy today is the most powerful in its history. So is the Navy football team!"[17]

"Army is very likely to have one of the best football teams in the country this season, but—Lieut. Col. Earl Blaik shudders every time he thinks of it—Navy will have a better one," noted Arthur Daley of the *New York Times*. Blaik admitted that he had a fine, day-laborer team, but he became "rapturous" when discussing Annapolis, rattling off Navy statistics "with such enthusiastic ease that in no time at all he had convinced everyone in the vicinity that the middies will be twice as powerful as the pre-war version of the Chicago Bears."[18]

Tim Cohane of the *World-Telegram* undoubtedly had Blaik in mind when he summed up the college football scene in verse:

> *Press agents are stirring,*
> *Their mimoes [sic] whirring,*
> *Superlatives airing*
> *North, South, East and West;*
>
> *Of backs quick and nifty,*
> *Of backs strong and shifty,*
> *Of linemen two-fifty*
> *And loaded with zest;*
>
> *Yet, in the same mailing,*
> *You'll read, without failing,*
> *The head coach is wailing*
> *And beating his breast.*[19]

In college football in the 1940s, most of September was taken up with preseason drills and games of words. Football writers feasted on coaches' fantasies and nightmares, their dearest hopes and deepest fears, because if they didn't they would starve. But on Saturday, September 20, 1944, most of the major college teams began their seasons, and sportswriters could begin to dine on realities.

Army opened in Michie Stadium against the University of North Carolina. In 1943 the Tarheels had been brimming with V-12 talent, but by 1944 most of the Marines were fighting in the Pacific and European theaters. At many V-12 schools, the game once again belonged to the civilians. "[M]ost of the service stars of last year are gone from the campuses now," wrote Al Laney of the *New York Tribune,* "and many schools are presenting teams of seventeen-year-olds and men who have received medical discharges." UNC was one of those teams. Army wasn't.[20]

Doc Blanchard had played freshman ball at North Carolina in 1941 and Barney Poole had started on the varsity team in 1943, and both reported that the best players they knew were "long gone—off to some place that they were not playing much football." Poole recalled, "When I left North Carolina, they were pulling all those V-12s." That left UNC with inexperienced youths and older men with punctured eardrums, flat feet, or some other sort of disability.[21]

A few weeks before the North Carolina game, Blaik told his team: "I expect you to be the greatest team in the history of West Point." Better than the undefeated 1916 team led by the All-American Elmer Oliphant. Better than the 9-1 1927 squad led by three-time All-American Red Cagle. Better than any of Coach Ralph Sasse's elevens of the early 1930s. North Carolina was their first test, a relatively easy one, admittedly, but he did not expect his players to demonstrate any signs of weakness.[22]

Kickoff was scheduled for two-thirty, and the game was broadcast over WEAF, WABC, and WNYC. The 2,500-member

Corps of Cadets made up more than a quarter of the spectators in Michie Stadium. Most of the rest were nearby residents. Only a few came from as far away as New York City.[23]

In the first 10 minutes nothing much happened. Blanchard kicked off to North Carolina, and in two plays the Tarheels lost yards and punted on third down. Army failed to make a first down on three tries and Kenna punted. UNC failed to move the ball and punted, Army punted after a drive stalled, and UNC again could not get a first down and punted. But this time Kenna returned the punt to the North Carolina 35 and led Army toward the goal line from there. Nothing spectacular—a nice catch, a few short runs, until at the 10:10 mark Dale Hall made a 6-yard touchdown plunge. It was Army's first score of the 1944 season, a product of good defense and workmanlike offense. Nothing special.

Toward the end of the first quarter Blaik sent in the Lombardo team, and the game's tempo shifted into a different speed. Early in the second quarter Glenn Davis threw a short ball to Barney Poole—and, like the flash of a camera bulb, a star was born. "I'll never forget to the day I die," Poole remembered. "I considered myself a pretty good receiver-type tight end–type. [Glenn] threw me a little pass and I flipped it out to Doc Blanchard. . . . They'd converged on me and [he] got the ball and headed up. I don't know how many little light blue North Carolina shirts had a shot at him, but he left them strewed from there to the goal, and went all the way. . . . [It was] Davis to Poole to Blanchard against our ex–alma mater."[24]

The play covered 63 yards and sent a jolt of electricity through Michie Stadium. Before the play sportswriters knew about Kenna and Davis, and they thought that Dean Sensanbaugher would add depth to the Army attack. Blanchard, on the other hand, was almost unknown, just some guy who had played freshman ball at UNC and spent a year in the service. Everything changed when he latched on to Poole's lateral. As Jesse Abramson of the *New York Herald Tribune* commented, "Blanchard really didn't play much, but while he was there with a so-called second team he was more than slightly terrific." Al Laney agreed. The guy was a game-changer. Blanchard, he wrote, "places Army almost on a par with Navy."[25]

Blanchard's run also started a rout. Lombardo's team scored twice more in the second quarter. Davis reached the end zone after a "gaudy catch" of a pass from Lombardo, and Kenna initiated another pass-lateral play that covered 61 yards. The score was 26–0 at the half, and it seemed worse as the North Carolina players slumped to their locker room. In an effort to keep the score down, the last two quarters were shortened from 15 to 12 minutes. It made little difference. Davis scored on two more long runs and Kenna threw another touchdown pass to complete Army's 46–0 victory. If the other teams on Army's schedule were searching for a ray of hope, Abramson noted, "The third team didn't score, proving there is a limit to Army's depth."[26]

While Army easily handled UNC up on the Hudson, down on the Severn, in a misty rain, Navy stumbled against the powerful North Carolina Preflight Cloudbusters. Led by Otto Graham, an All-American back from Northwestern who had finished third in the 1943 Heisman Trophy balloting, the service team defeated the Midshipmen, 21–14. The game was tied, 14–14, with less than 3 minutes remaining when Graham received a punt on the Fliers' 30 and began to twist, weave, and sidestep his way down the field. Hemmed in at midfield, he coolly tossed a lateral to Frank Aschenbrenner, who streaked 55 yards for the winning touchdown.

In two plays involving laterals, one to Blanchard and the other to Aschenbrenner, the course of the 1944 season shifted, however slightly. In his pregame picks, football writer Lawrence Robinson had noted, "The Midshipmen are the power and the glory this year." By Saturday evening the picture had changed. Navy had a loss on their record. Army had Doc and Glenn.[27]

If North Carolina was intended to be a test, it wasn't. And Army's next games, against Brown, Pittsburgh, and the Coast Guard Academy, could not even be considered quizzes. Tim Cohane immediately diagnosed the situation. The team was great. Not only was it more familiar with the T offense, but it now had what every T attack needed, a powerful running and blocking fullback. In 1943 Davis had played fullback because the team did not have a bruising presence. The addition of Blanchard freed him to return to his more natural left halfback position. The change was dramatic, giving Army power between the tackles and speed around the ends. And Poole and Coulter added size and power on the line, something that had often been Army's downfall. Army, in short, had everything—speed and power, youth and experience, quality starters and abundant substitutes.[28]

The problem, and the real test for the team, would be not only how they performed on Saturdays but how they studied and were graded between the games. From their first classes, it was clear that Coulter, Poole, Blanchard, and Sensanbaugher were not cutting it in the classroom. "At some point in time, it became obvious that Tex and I were not very academically inclined, and hadn't spent a lot of time with books," Blanchard recalled. They studied, trying their best to stay up with their classmates, but it was difficult. "There was hardly any wiggle-room at West Point," Kenna noted. "Everyone in your class took the same courses and none of them were really easy. When I arrived there I was strong in English, history, and those courses, but weak in mathematics because I had little background. It took me a while to adjust and my class standing slipped, but eventually I got the hang of it and learned to like chemistry and science courses." That was the point: you either got the hang of it or you didn't. There was not a third option—no switching majors, no searching for gut courses, no finding the easy professors, and no dropping a troublesome subject. If Glenn Davis could be busted out, anyone could.[29]

With tests every day in every class, trouble was spotted early. The coaching staff arranged for tutors and allowed players to skip practice to study. Poole and Coulter managed to keep barely afloat in the academic waters, but by the time the leaves began to change colors in October, Sensanbaugher, a transfer from Ohio State, began to sink. Backfield coach Major Andy Gustafson said he suffered from "Plebeitis"—a hard time adjusting to Army life. He missed practice after practice, and Blaik finally announced that the Lombardo team would have a new backfield. He replaced the former Ohio State star with Dick Walterhouse, a former Michigan standout. With Davis and Blanchard as the running mates, however, it didn't appear to matter which other former Big Ten runner Blaik used.[30]

On October 7 Army ungenerously hosted Brown. The Bruins boasted that for the 1944 season they had a fresh class of fighting V-12 Marine students, but if the game had been a boxing match the referee would have stopped it after the first quarter. Army scored nine touchdowns in the 59–7 slaughter, and the one score that Brown managed was a gift from the officials. (A Bruin back fumbled the ball into the end zone and it squirted out of bounds, but after some consultation—and perhaps some compassion—the officials called it a touchdown.) Virtually everything Army tried worked. Davis scored three touchdowns, Dale Hall two, and Kenna had the longest run of the afternoon. Equally impressive, on defense Army's linemen seemed to spend more time on the Brown side of the ball than did the Bruin backs.

More interesting than the game was its coverage in the press. Sportswriters increasingly compared the fortunes of the Army football team to the success of the U.S. Army in Europe. The metaphors quickly became clichés. The Cadet backs had "the versatility of jeeps and the irresistibility of tanks," wrote one scribe. "While the United States Army was cracking the Siegfried

Line its future generals were breaching a less formidable Brown forward wall," added another. Army's drives were "advances into enemy territory," its scores "assaults against the foe's end zone." The squad was no longer a football team, it was a "juggernaut," an "avenging army," a "swift infantry." Even articles about individual players extended the theme. In an overview of Blanchard's path to West Point, a journalist noted, "It seems particularly fitting . . . that the finest army in the world should have the best fullback. . . ." As never before, Army was becoming America's team.[31]

On October 14 the master met the pupil when Clark Shaughnessy brought his Pittsburgh Panthers and the T offense to Michie Stadium. No one in the country understood the beautiful complexities of the T better than Shaughnessy. Blaik's T lacked the subtle nuance of Shaughnessy's former unstoppable Stanford team, but Blaik had the advantage of Davis, Kenna, Blanchard, Minor, and a stable of other backs. On a clear, warm fall day and a dry, fast field, there was nothing to stop them from running until twilight.

For Blaik, Pittsburgh also stirred bitter memories. In the 1930s, when he was an assistant coach at Army and Jock Sutherland was head coach at Pitt, the Panthers had twice beaten the Cadets. One of the games had been a lopsided shutout. Sportswriter Oscar Fraley contended that "the men from the Point had not forgotten" the losses, or Pittsburgh's aggressive, perhaps even dirty, play. Certainly Blaik never forgot any defeats—and he believed in reckonings.[32]

Exceeding their previous week's total, the Cadets tallied ten touchdowns and won by the adding-machine score of 69–7. In the second quarter alone Army crossed the Pitt goal line four times. Al Laney, the thoughtful *New York Herald Tribune* writer, put it best: "The details of such a game are unimportant and under the circumstances it is impossible to gauge accurately Army's strength beyond saying that it is obviously great." Laney believed that Davis was the fastest back in the country, Kenna the finest ball handler, and Blanchard simply incomparable. The fullback scored on a pass and a pass interception, shredded Pitt's defense on several runs, and kicked consistently and long.[33]

Doc even said a mea culpa after the game, jogging over to Shaughnessy and telling him, "Coach, I don't feel very happy about this." It was a nice gesture. Doc's father had played fullback for Shaughnessy in 1915 at Tulane and always spoke highly of his old coach. Shaughnessy replied that he would have been disappointed if Blanchard had given anything less than his best, adding that he believed Doc was the best fullback he had ever seen. Later, reporters questioned him about the statement, suggesting that he had "spread it on a bit thick." Shaughnessy, whose sense of humor was about as well developed as Red Blaik's, replied, "No, sir. I'm not kidding. The boy is the best I've ever seen." Comparing him to Norm Standlee, the Stanford All-American and outstanding professional fullback, the Pitt coach added, "He's better than Standlee. He's just as big and he's faster. Yes, he's faster than Standlee and more powerful. He could play halfback just as well as fullback. He can also pass, and you saw the way he can kick. He's absolutely at the top of the heap as far as I'm concerned."[34]

The following week, the national football poll rated Army second behind Notre Dame. New York sportswriters focused almost exclusively on the Army–Notre Dame match as if it were the next week's game. A few mentioned that Army had to face a quality Duke team before taking the field against the Irish. Duke's losses had come in close games against Penn (7–18), North Carolina Preflight (6–13), and Navy (0–7), so they were a team worth mentioning. None of the columnists bothered to note that the Cadets also had games against Coast Guard and Villanova before Notre Dame.

Only a few sportswriters questioned Army's victories. Dan Daniel suggested that Blaik's team had defensive problems, especially in the secondary. Pitt had completed 24 passes for 230 yards, disturbing numbers in such a one-sided game. Tim Cohane wondered if the success of Army's backs was the product of their greatness or their opponents' incompetence. Resorting to doggerel, he wrote:

> *Doc Blanchard, Max Minor, Glenn Davis, Dale Hall.*
> *Four Army T Terrors at running the ball.*
> *But so far they've run against nothing at all.*[35]

The early line on the Army–Coast Guard game picked Army to win but to face their "best test yet." The early line was right on the first point, frighteningly wrong on the second. In a cold, dark, drizzling rain at West Point, Army scored eleven touchdowns, added a safety for good measure, and won, 76–0, the most points they had scored in a game in fifteen years. The Coast Guard never advanced into Army territory and appeared mystified by the Cadets' spinning, whirling offense. Everyone on the Army team played, and a host of them scored. Kenna and Lombardo both tossed a touchdown pass, Blanchard and Davis ran for two scores each, and Barney Poole was all over the field, blocking punts, intercepting passes, scoring a safety, and catching a touchdown pass.[36]

Blaik tried to hold down the score. In the last quarter, "in a spirit of mercy," he suggested cutting the period to 10 minutes. The Coast Guardsmen, however, "registered a tremendous objection and insisted on tasting defeat to the bitter end." Had the game been shortened, the Coast Guard players could have taken some consolation with a mere 69–0 defeat.[37]

Blaik had been here before. In his first three years as Army's head coach, his team had won its first four games. Soon after it had begun to stumble, limping through the rest of the season, losing more than they won. A cartoon in the *New York World-Telegram* made the point by picturing an Army player shooting rabbits labeled North Carolina 46–0, Brown 59–7, Pitt 69–7, and Coast Guard 76–0. The final scene depicted a Duke Blue Devil with his finger in the gun, asking, "Ya sure that isn't just a hot-air rifle?" "We'll know more when they draw a bead on their first big game Saturday—the Blue Devils from Durham." It was a valid point.[38]

Duke was one of the best teams in the South, even though it had lost three close games. It would finish 1944 with a winning record and a victory over Alabama in the Sugar Bowl. Along with Notre Dame, USC, and Michigan, Duke was able to keep most of its 1943 Navy V-12 players. Tom Davis, an All-Southern and honorable mention All-American, was a superb runner, and its linemen were experienced. Making the game even more important, Army would play its first game of the season away from Michie Stadium. Scheduled for the Polo Grounds, the contest would be the first New York City game for the plebes. For almost a month Army had been a newspaper and radio team, an almost mythical scoring machine that played in a faraway spot up above a river and a plain. Now more than 50,000 people would get a chance to watch them perform, and the game would be televised to a very limited market.[39]

It will be a "crucial" game against "as fine a team as there is in the South," Blaik told reporters. "Of course we're scared. Our scouts tell us Duke is tough and rugged. We should have real rough opposition, but to date we have just run away from our rivals." What he really expected he kept to himself. His players anticipated another high-scoring affair. "We were just rolling through our opposition," recalled Kenna, "wearing them out with our two teams and scoring about any time we set our minds to it." It seemed impossible that any team except perhaps Notre Dame or Navy could stop them.[40]

Overlooking the Harlem River at West 155th Street, the Polo Grounds was one of the sacred sports facilities in America. In 1923 Jack Dempsey had knocked out the Argentinean Luis

Firpo in the Polo Grounds. In 1941 Joe Louis had flattened Pittsburgh's Sweet Billy Conn to retain his heavyweight crown in the Polo Grounds. Babe Ruth had blasted towering home runs there, Joe DiMaggio had made gliding, balletic catches there, and several Army-Navy games had been played there. It was in the Polo Grounds in 1924 that Notre Dame had defeated Army, inspiring Grantland Rice to write the most famous opening line in sports history: "Outlined against a blue, gray October sky, the Four Horsemen rode again. In dramatic lore, they are known as Famine, Pestilence, Destruction, and Death. These are only aliases. Their real names are Stuhldreher, Miller, Crowley, and Layden." Perhaps even as much as Yankee Stadium, the turf of the Polo Grounds was a place of magic and legends.

Some 45,000 people crowded into the stands. "There was an obvious air of expectancy in the crowd about the unveiling of that precious fullback, Felix A. Blanchard," noted a football writer. An unlawful spectator who sneaked a field badge remarked, "As a ball carrier, they tell me Felix is really the cats."[41]

At 1:10 the full Corps of Cadets marched into the stadium in neat, perfect lines. The next day the *New York World-Telegram* ran a large photograph of the Corps in the center of the field. The sight of their gray uniforms and military precision was an "ever-thrilling" sight. Duke coach Eddie Cameron took one look and said, "I knew Army had plenty of manpower, but this is *the deepest I've ever seen.*" Cameron's quip did not detract from the mood of patriotism.[42]

Only the week before, General Douglas MacArthur had waded ashore on Leyte in the Philippines, the surf destroying the neat creases in his trousers. "People of the Philippines," he said in a broadcast, "I have returned." At virtually the same time, the last German troops in Aachen surrendered to the Allies, but only after savage street fighting and after the city had been reduced to burning rubble. Across the battlefronts, from Leyte Gulf and the Marianas to the Hurtgen Forest and the Vosges Mountains,

American forces were on the move. In the Polo Grounds on the afternoon of October 28, the football team from West Point was the totem of those forces.

If the spectators in the stands needed a reminder, they only had to open their game program and read. "Young Americans everywhere are inspired by the heroes which the game of football has produced," wrote Joe Cahill in an essay, "Beyond the Call of Duty." "In this war, more than any other, literally thousands of America's outstanding gridmen have written distinguished service into the record books of history. Naturally, the names of West Pointers predominate throughout for that is the mission of the United States Military Academy." The last time Army played in the Polo Grounds, Cahill noted, was 1927, when they had defeated Navy to finish 9-1. "Light Horse" Harry Wilson had scored both touchdowns. Now Colonel Wilson "has matched his scoring ability via devastating raids on Jap shipping in the Pacific." Little Art Meehan was the quarterback on the team. Now Colonel Meehan is in the Pacific, where recently he "guided the mighty armada [of planes] over the target at Wake Island and 'bombed the hell out of them!'" The list continued. It included Generals La Verne "Bloody" Saunders and Charles "Chuck" Born. Years before, Cahill reminded his readers, Knute Rockne commented that one thing consoled him after a "bitter defeat" by Army: "If this nation ever goes to war it's going to be comforting to have those same Army men on our side instead of fighting against us."[43]

Duke's players, clad entirely in blue and wearing no stockings, were not cowed. "They were big, strong, unafraid looking fellows," observed Tim Cohane. "They looked as if they'd eaten a hearty breakfast, but didn't act as if they were walking the last mile." They had come north to win a football game, not celebrate West Point or pay homage to the Long Gray Line. Up in the press box Chick Meehan reminisced about his days as NYU coach and the intersectional 1931 game against Tennessee, when Herman Hickman had come to the Polo Grounds. "We built several mousetraps for Hickman," he said, "but he chewed up the cheese and spit out the trap."⁴⁴

It was a "pretty tough ballgame," Doc Blanchard recalled years later. Perhaps, as several reporters claimed, the Cadets were "too keyed up" at the start and pressed too hard. In Army's first possession Max Minor fumbled, and for the rest of the first quarter the Cadets worked to reverse bad field position. Several times Duke mounted drives but could not get into the Army end zone. For their part, the Kenna team could not break through the Duke defensive line and hurt themselves with assorted penalties, interceptions, and fumbles. The quarter ended scoreless.⁴⁵

Lombardo's plebe team showed more poise. As soon as Blaik sent them onto the field, commented a sportswriter, "Army's team took on the real Army look." The reason was Blanchard. Duke had scouted Army and saw what Shaughnessy saw—Blanchard was the best fullback in America. With that in mind, Duke keyed their defense on stopping him. On his first play from scrimmage he was stopped for no gain. On the second, he went over left tackle for 7 yards. On the third, Lombardo faked the ball to Blanchard going left and handed it off to Davis, streaking right. It took the Duke defense a second to adjust, but it was a second too long for Glenn Davis. Two Duke players lunged at him, grabbing only an armful of air. "Like a deer," wrote Allison Danzig, "the blinding-fast Davis tore down the side line, outstripping the opposition on a 53-yard gallop across the goal line." Army led, 6–0.

Davis's speed startled even his own teammates. Sometimes they simply gawked at his greatness. Barney Poole later set national receiving records catching passes from Charlie Conerly at Ole Miss, but none of that glory compared to "making a block out ahead of Glenn Davis and then rolling up and watching that son of a gun." It was a thing of beauty. Other teammates agreed with Poole. Kenna said, "When Glenn found himself one-on-one against any tackler, he was apt to make that other fellow look silly. He didn't do it intentionally. But he did it."[46]

Duke maintained their poise. Later in the quarter they blocked an Army punt, recovering it on the Cadet 13. Army threw Duke runners for several losses, but on third down Tom Davis threw a pass that was broken up by Tom Lombardo. As the ball fell to the ground, a referee reached into his pocket, pulled out his red flag, and tossed it into the air, calling pass interference. It was a questionable call, but it saved the Blue Devils' drive and Davis scored on the next play. The conversion gave Duke a 7–6 lead. For the first time that season Army was behind. And for the rest of the half it stayed that way.

"Well, he wasn't very happy," Kenna said of Blaik. "In the locker room he said that in the second half we were going to run the ball. That was it. Just run right at them." Blaik didn't yell or plea or shake down the thunder. He wasn't that sort of coach. "There is nothing of the Rockne, the Warner or the Dobie about him," popular sportswriter Joe Williams commented. "It is difficult to picture him delivering a fire-worksy pre-game pep talk." And he didn't in the locker room in the Polo Grounds. He was emphatic, Rafe Rafalko recalled. Just run the ball, starting "between the ends, no sweeps or fancy-Dan stuff."[47]

And one more thing—run the ball with Doc Blanchard in the game. "That was Blanchard's style of game," Rafalko said, and "it was something to watch him work because he was a player who seemed to love contact. He was never happier than when he was taking it to someone." In the second half, the Army passers did not attempt one throw, but after establishing the inside game, Blaik used his running game to widen the field of play. In the 1930s and 1940s teams rarely used the full width of the field, preferring to play a tackle-to-tackle game. The T offense opened the game up dramatically. By using a man in motion, pitches off fakes to Blanchard, and the sprinter speed of Davis and Minor,

Blaik forced Duke to cover more of the field just when its two-way defenders were beginning to tire.[48]

In one 15-minute stretch with Blanchard playing with both the Kenna and Lombardo teams, Army scored three touchdowns. Aided by a "vital block" by Kenna, Dale Hall went 26 yards for the first of the TDs. Then Minor scored on an end run that capped a 74-yard drive. On the last play of the third quarter, Barney Poole blocked a punt that was recovered by Tex Coulter. Blanchard busted off the right end 22 yards to the Duke 1 and scored a touchdown on the next play. In 15 minutes the score had gone from 7–6 Duke to 27–7 Army, and the game was effectively over.

After the game Danzig pronounced that Army's "glamour" had faded under the impact of Duke's defense. Al Laney agreed that if Duke had had an offense, the game might have had a different outcome. Both felt that no one would know how good Army was until it played Notre Dame in two weeks. The Irish had the number one–ranked team in the country and would prove the ultimate test of the greatness of the West Point squad.

But Army had passed Blaik's exam. The first half against Duke was "exactly the way I would have ordered it," he told reporters. "I wanted to see how these men of ours would react to that sort of situation. We had been feasting on soft stuff and sought a test before moving into the November schedule." It might have been coach-speak, but it wasn't. The comeback had demonstrated something to the exacting coach. As he wrote to General MacArthur: "It showed the soul and will of a champion."[49]

General Henry "Hap" Arnold, head of Army Air Forces, felt the same way. Not long after the game he wrote to Blaik: "I was tremendously pleased to see that you had backs and line all coordinated in their operations, but the one thing that stands out in the team above all others I have seen for several years is the fact that there is a fight in the individual players, an aggressiveness coupled with the schooling of the individual, that has been missing heretofore." Praise from up the line always pleased Blaik, and he proudly passed it along to MacArthur. His team, the generals believed, showed what the Army was all about.[50]

There was one more game before Notre Dame, another easy workout before the three teams that had traditionally added even more gloom to the dark, dreary West Point winters. On November 4 the Cadets hosted Villanova, a team with little talent and no chance. The outcome was such a foregone conclusion that Bobby Dobbs and Doc Blanchard, the fullbacks of the Kenna and Lombardo teams, did not even play. The outcome was so certain that Blaik and most of his staff skipped the game and hopped a train to Baltimore to watch the Navy–Notre Dame contest.

For the cadets at the game, the contest was a little like cheering at an execution. Kenna's team scored three touchdowns in the first quarter, Lombardo's tallied six in the second quarter. In the second half, the quarters were mercifully cut to 8 minutes and the substitutes did their best not to score, although on several occasions they failed in their mission. Army began attempting—and failing—to kick field goals on first and second downs to keep from scoring. They limited their rushes to the space between the two guards. They seemed to be doing their best not to do their best. It was not fun to watch. Thankfully, when it ended, 83–0, very few people were watching.[51]

In fact, by the end of the game many of the people still in Michie Stadium were huddled near a large chart showing the progress of the Navy–Notre Dame game and were cheering wildly. Something unexpected was happening. Red Blaik had picked the right game to attend that Saturday.

10

★ ★ ★

Payback

Brazil can cheer about its coffee as Ceylon raves about
its tea. Let Florida and California speak with passion
of their orange groves as Kentucky points with a finger
of pride to the thoroughbred.

But out in Notre Dame, South Bend, Indiana,
football grows on trees and bushes. It blossoms upon
the vine and leaves the air redolent with the fragrance
that comes from the skin of the mole.

— GRANTLAND RICE

Suppose the Fighting Irish played on some Tibetan hill,
In some dark jungle fastness or along some ancient rill,
In some deserted village or some deep antarctic point —
The magic name of Notre Dame would still sell out the joint.

—TIM COHANE

O N NOVEMBER 4, 1944, a personal advertisement,
which had first run in the *Buffalo Evening News,* found
its way to the top right of the front page of the *New
York Post:*

NOTRE DAME–ARMY GAME.
I HAVE AN EXTRA ROOM AT HOTEL PENN-

SYLVANIA, BUT NO TICKETS. IF YOU HAVE TWO
EXTRA TICKETS, BUT NO ROOM, I'LL SWAP, OR
IF YOU PREFER, I WILL SWAP POPULAR BRANDS
OF CIGARETTES FOR TICKETS.[1]

The game had been sold out for months. But hotel rooms
and smokes were hard to come by as well. As a result of lower
production, nearly every tobacco store had signs in the window
announcing NO CIGARETTES. When cigarettes did go on sale,
lines formed before the doors opened. According to thousands
of smokers, it was nothing short of a national crisis.[2]

In the last months of 1944 Americans were ready for the war to
end. In the summer, during the heady two and a half months
between the D-Day landings and the liberation of Paris, a mood
of optimism swept the country. Officials in the War Production
Board talked confidently about reconverting to peacetime activities and even permitted the production of such necessary house-
hold items as irons, stoves, and refrigerators. The Office of Price
Administration (OPA) relaxed its rationing efforts. Some previ-
ously unavailable canned goods and meats suddenly appeared
on grocery store shelves.

But the buoyant mood faded with the chilly fall winds. Nazi
Germany was dying more slowly than expected. The failure
of Operation Market Garden to leapfrog the Allies across the
Rhine River, the terrible fighting in the Hurtgen Forest, and the
fuel problems all along the line on the Western Front made the
point: the war was not almost over. Talk of food and fuel crises at home spurred the OPA to restore its full rationing program, causing a howl from Americans who were tired of going
without beef, eating lungs and tripe, driving 35 miles an hour,
searching in vain for a bottle of Scotch, never having sugar for
their coffee, and never having real coffee for their last spoonfuls
of sugar. They knew that the boys overseas were making heroic

sacrifices, but they wanted peace. They wanted their America back.

The big football game—the crush of large crowds in a cavernous stadium, the feel of autumn in the air, and everyone dressed for an outdoor occasion—was a visible expression of the America they wanted back. That fall, football attendance began to rise. It increased 38.5 percent over 1943, and more than a hundred colleges reinstituted the sport. And nothing signaled big-time football as much as a November game between Notre Dame and Army in New York City. Allison Danzig could read the mood. "As harbingers of good years ahead," he commented, "the Army–Notre Dame game had sold out earlier than ever before. All 76,000 seats in the Yankee Stadium were gone by August." Colonel Biff Jones, director of athletics at the Academy, added that ten times as many had been applied for. Perhaps they could have sold a million ducats.[3]

For more than a decade Notre Dame had beaten Army like a rented mule. Since November 1932, when Franklin Delano Roosevelt was elected to his first term, the Irish had defeated the Cadets ten times and tied them twice. Army had not won a single game. The last touchdown the Cadets had scored was in 1938, when Charles "Huey" Long had lobbed a left-handed pass to Riggs Sullivan for a score. It was a record of ineptitude unmatched in recent Army history. Now, finally, Blaik had a team that stacked up in every position to the powerful Irish squad.

For that reason he had abandoned his own team on November 4 and gone to Baltimore to scout the Notre Dame–Navy contest. It was an uncomfortable trip. As Blaik was beginning to cut into a boiled egg for breakfast, an old acquaintance came into the diner and sat at a table across from him. "Earl, I remember another coach who left his team to scout. It was Knute Rockne, and that day Notre Dame lost to Carnegie Tech." A sick feeling ended any hope of a pleasant breakfast. Blaik had been in Chicago on that day in 1926 to watch the same Army-Navy game Rockne attended. Before 110,000 spectators at Soldier Field the academies had tied, 21–21. That same day Carnegie Tech coach Judge Walter Steffen had told his team, "Rockne thinks you're so poor he's gone to Chicago to see some real football players in the Army-Navy game." The players burst from the locker room ready for carnage and went on to win, 10–0. When he arrived in Baltimore, Blaik arranged to take a portable radio to the stadium so he could watch one game and listen to another, the Army-Villanova contest.[4]

Notre Dame–Navy underscored the return of the big game. The military brass was there in full force — Commander-in-Chief of the United States Fleet Admiral Ernest J. King, Undersecretary of the Navy Ralph Bard, Assistant Secretary of War John McCoy, and head of the Office of Strategic Services Brigadier General William J. "Wild Bill" Donovan, among others. But sitting in the press box, soaking in the pregame activity, Al Laney of the *New York Herald Tribune* was taken back to a time before Pearl Harbor and cigarette shortages: "This was the real authentic big-game atmosphere. Here were two fine and colorful teams, a huge crowd, a contest about which there were divergent opinions, and here was tradition in abundance. It does not happen often in these war times." Almost on cue, just before kickoff, as an omen of the football gods, "the mist lifted and the sun broke through strong and bright." Everything seemed just right for an epic contest.[5]

While Laney was watching the sun break through the clouds, in the Navy locker room the Midshipmen were receiving their marching orders. Fleet Admiral King had come down to say a few words. No one ever accused him of being warm. He was all Navy, all the time, a man of few words, uncompromising, totally devoid of tact, never warm. Someone once asked him if he was the one who said, "When they get in trouble they send for the sonsabitches." He said no, but added he would have said it if he had thought of it. Now, just minutes before kickoff, he looked into the faces of the Middies and said, "Let's go, boys." Navy's coach Oscar Hagberg thought it sufficient. "You have your orders, men," he added. It was a very short and very effective pregame talk.[6]

Navy ran onto the field as if they were Marines assaulting a beachhead. For the first time in the season, Navy fulfilled their potential. Playing single-wing football, they mostly stayed between the tackles and physically overpowered the Irish. On several occasions they ran reverses for large gains. "Navy demonstrated that the single-wing could be as thrilling as the T if the proper men are available to make it work," wrote Shirley Povich in the *Washington Post*. Don Whitmire and Ben Chase, two of Navy's best linemen, dominated the offensive and defensive lines, and runners Bob Jenkins and Clyde "Smackover" Scott ran over and around the Notre Dame defenders. Early on, it was clear that the Irish had no answer for the Midshipmen's brute force. Allison Danzig summed it up in military language: Navy "sailed through full steam ahead, pouring broadsides into the outgunned and outmanned Fighting Irish."[7]

"At least we came out of the game alive," grimaced Notre Dame coach Ed McKeever, the man who had replaced Frank Leahy when he was called into the Navy. When a reporter asked him about having to play Navy and Army back-to-back, he winced. "This is the week we could have used a breather, a soft touch," he said. "But what the heck. That's the way the schedule reads, and there is nothing you can do about the schedules once they are made." Making a first-year coach mistake, he added, "[B]esides, I think this is a fitting time for Army and Navy to have great teams."[8]

No sooner were the words out of his mouth than he wanted to take them back. "I don't mean to say," he amended, "that I'm conceding anything. I think we'll give Army something more than just a pleasant workout." Yet in an unintended way, the

Navy game increased the pressure on Army. Now Blaik's team would jump ahead of the Irish in the national polls and be favored. Notre Dame could play loose and mean. A victory over Army would all but erase the Navy defeat and catapult them back on top.

This was not the time to start to read press clippings and get "fat, dumb, and happy." On Tuesday Blaik held a 15-minute scrimmage on Cullum Field. He matched the Kenna backfield with the Lombardo line against the Lombardo backfield and the Kenna line. He told both teams to use the special Notre Dame defense he and his staff had worked out. The result was an offensive shootout. Neither team could stop the other. Both scored three touchdowns in what Blaik believed was "the best football I ever saw." He later wrote to General MacArthur that the coaching staff "came to the conclusion that either we had one of the great offensive teams of all times or that we had designed a poor set of defenses for the 'T' formation."[9]

The scrimmage also underscored the improvement of Army's linemen and in particular that Tex Coulter and Barney Poole were coming into their own. In the last several games, the New York press had noticed that opponents seemingly could not block them. Blaik believed that tackle was the key position on the team, and he was pleased by Coulter's success. He "conservatively says [Coulter] will be the greatest tackle Army has ever had," reported Jesse Abramson. But the coach was startled by the pure violence of the tackle's play. There was something in Coulter's eyes, a hard, mean expression, that set him apart from his teammates. Barney was tough, too, but he knew when to turn it on and off. He scrimmaged hard, but it was not a matter of life or death.[10]

Tex played the same way in practice scrimmages as he did in the games—with a hot rage. As Blaik later told one of his players, "Now, look. If when I blow my whistle Tex Coulter is anywhere in your vicinity, lay down. Because if you stand up, he's going to hit you." "Tex was a little fuzzy about exactly when a play was over," agreed another player. "Maybe he thought that once you heard the whistle it was all right to finish what you had started—or what you were thinking of starting." "DeWitt never played dummy scrimmage," another player added. "If anybody blocked him or anything he'd just start swinging elbows. . . . It was just an instantaneous reaction with DeWitt." With Coulter on the field, everyone paid attention. "You had to have your head on a swivel—do what you were supposed to on the play and watch the hell out for Tex. If you didn't you were on your ass."[11]

Even Blaik wasn't sure how to handle Tex. Occasionally in practice, when Tex would hurt another player with some questionable—or just out-and-out dirty—shot, Blaik would intervene with a sharp, "Now I don't want to see any more of that." But mostly he just kept quiet. Football was a game of aggression, and he did not want to curb his tackle's instinct. And he had a positive effect on the team. Coulter, Blaik wrote to General MacArthur, had done "the most to spread the aggressive spirit among our linemen." Among the coaches, the question of what to do about Tex sometimes arose. Blaik decided to allow Tex to be Tex. He had "the ability to be a heavyweight champion," Blaik thought. So why not permit him to warm up for the ring on a football field?[12]

Meanwhile sportswriters prepared for one of the premier games of the season. The sheer amount of words devoted to the contest was staggering, especially for the week in which Americans elected Franklin Roosevelt to his fourth term in office. In his election-day column, Tim Cohane reminded readers that the world did not revolve entirely around the fortunes of Army, Navy, and Notre Dame:

> *For weeks avid fanatics, who keep on the beam,*
> *Have raved about Army and Navy.*

The one has a backfield that plays like a dream,
  The other sends foes down to Davey.

Today neither service school fits in the scheme,
  Instead fans are thirsting for knowledge.
Of who is to captain the varsity team
  At good old Electoral College![13]

The outcome of the Roosevelt-Dewey election had to share the front page of the *South Bend Tribune* with news from the gridiron. Columnist Joe Williams asserted that South Bend was "probably the only city in America where the results of an election are of secondary interest to what's going to happen in the football game between Notre Dame and Army in Yankee Stadium Saturday." He thought the city "live[d] in a dream world," obsessed with the fate of its team. The biggest news of November 7 was that Frank Szymanski, the center from the 1943 team who had been called into service after the season, had been discharged from naval aviation for medical reasons. He promptly came back to Notre Dame and enrolled for the semester, making him eligible for the Army game. The addition of Szymanski considerably strengthened the Fighting Irish's line.[14]

All week, Coach McKeever's four-year-old twin daughters greeted him and visitors with a stout "Beat Army!" Students at Notre Dame shuffled by one another on campus, shouting "Beat Army!" Shop owners greeted patrons with "Beat Army!" Notre Dame had never lost to Navy and Army in the same year. The team, Joe Williams concluded, never wanted "to win a ball game as they do this one."[15]

The game transfixed the cadets as well. Sheets with BEAT NOTRE DAME! rippled in the November winds outside cadet windows. Plebes saluted upperclassmen: "Beat Notre Dame!" Football players walking across the post were held in awe. They were the Long Gray Line itself. Harold "Hal" Moore, a member of the Class of 1945 who gained enduring fame in the Vietnam War battle of Ia Drang and rose to the rank of lieutenant general, recalled the importance of the football players to the other cadets: "They were one of us, but something more, too. Wonderful men. We were so proud of them."[16]

The climax of the week before the game was a full corps rally after Friday's mess. Blaik addressed the cadets, praising the efforts of his players and extolling the abilities of Notre Dame's stars, especially quarterback Frank "Boley" Dancewicz and halfback Bob Kelly. They could make Army's first team, he said. But the Corps of Cadets didn't buy any of it. They whooped and cheered, sure that no one who was not already on their team could even make the team, let alone start. An illustration in the *New York World-Telegram,* "Last Man," captured the mood. It shows two marching cadets, shoulders back and smartly uniformed. One gives the command "EYES RIGHT!" as they pass a statue of Cadet H. Riggs Sullivan, the last man to score against Notre Dame.[17]

Blaik's address, while characteristically cautious, was nonetheless accurate. Even with the loss to Navy, Notre Dame had an outstanding team. It still had some of the best V-12 Marine players in the nation — and V-12 athletes continued to dominate the game. In 1943 the Irish won the national championship with V-12 Marines, and V-12 players starred on other leading teams. Eight of the top nine Heisman Trophy candidates were V-12 or V-5 players, as were eight of the eleven Associated Press All-Americans. Every ranked team in the final poll was aided by the Navy's V programs. Although in 1944 the programs had shrunk, they continued to supply the Irish with superior players.[18]

At noon on Friday the West Point team left the post. As usual for New York games, they planned to spend the night at the Knollwood Country Club at Elmsford, just north of White Plains. It was a beautiful, tranquil, late-nineteenth-century club with a magnificent golf course. Bobby Jones once held the course record. Whitelaw Reid, William C. Durant, William G. Rockefeller, and H. M. Harriman were once members. For many of the players, it was a glimpse into a world of wealth and luxury they hardly knew existed.

After checking in, they got back on the bus and went to Yankee Stadium for a light practice. The workout was unimportant. Blaik had closed all his practices during the week, but he now allowed reporters to watch his boys stretch their muscles in the House That Ruth Built. What Blaik mainly wanted was for his plebes to see the historic place. On opening day in 1923 Babe Ruth had hit the first home run in a 4–1 victory over the Red Sox. Asked his opinion after the game, the Babe had answered, "Some ball yard." It had been or was the home of Lou Gehrig, Lefty Gomez, Frank Crosetti, Tony Lazzeri, and, of course, Joe DiMaggio, names revered by the Army players. Joe Louis had knocked out Max Schmeling in Yankee Stadium. He also had done the same thing to Tony Galento and Arturo Godoy there. Knute Rockne had given his "win one for the Gipper" speech at halftime in a 1928 game against Army in Yankee Stadium, and Army's years of futility against the Irish had sadly taken place on the field as well. Blaik wanted his players to jog around on the turf and soak in the place before it was filled with 75,000 cheering spectators. They went through their rituals in a gray downpour, hardly aware of the rain at all.[19]

Returning to Knollwood, the team ate dinner and then took a walk along the fairways, throwing footballs back and forth and loping after long, lazy passes. The players mentally reviewed their assignments—some quietly kidding one another, others deep in their own thoughts.

Back in the clubhouse they gathered around a fire. One player recalled the standard routine: "[O]ld Herman Hickman then would start telling us stories about his professional wrestling career." With everyone laughing, he would move into verse. He'd begin:

> You may talk o' gin an' beer
> When you're quartered safe out 'ere,
> An' you're sent to penny-fights an' Aldershot it;
> But if it comes to slaughter
> You will do your work on water,
> An' you'll lick the bloomin' boots of 'im that's got it.
> Now in Injia's sunny clime,
> Where I used to spend my time
> A-servin' of 'Er Majesty the Queen,
> Of all them black-faced crew
> The finest man I knew
> Was our regimental bhisti, Gunga Din.

And he would continue to:

> Din! Din! Din!
> You Lazarushian-leather Gunga Din!
> Tho' I've belted you an' flayed you,
> By the livin' Gawd that made you,
> You're a better man than I am, Gunga Din!

"He'd recite 'Gunga Din' and other poems from start to finish. Telling jokes and all, he really kept everyone loose."[20]

While they ate, listened, and laughed, the exclusive annual Army–Notre Dame rally in the Grand Ballroom of the Waldorf-Astoria attracted luminaries from both schools and their guests, raising hundreds of thousands of dollars for the Notre Dame Service Fund. Other less prestigious gatherings erupted in bars and saloons around the town. There were plenty of excellent gridiron rivalries, Arch Ward of the *Chicago Tribune* observed. "But there's none that thrills the metropolitans like Army–Notre Dame. . . .

Come prosperity or depression, war or peace, Gus and Gussie fans save enough money to guarantee their presence at the big game."[21]

The rains stopped, the clouds blew away, and "glorious football weather" embraced the city. The sun made the boat trip down the Hudson from West Point seem like a vacation for the Corps of Cadets, who marched into Yankee Stadium impeccably attired and went through their parade maneuvers more flawlessly than a veteran *New York Times* writer had ever seen. Sitting on the sideline was Colonel Russell "Red" Reeder, an inspiring link between past and present at West Point. The son of a Spanish-American War veteran, Reeder had entered the Academy shortly after the Great War and picked up six demerits in his first two hours on the post. "I majored in football and baseball," he later claimed. On the football field he excelled as a kicker. In the classroom he struggled. He was turned back several times, laboring six years to graduate and receive his commission in the infantry. On June 11, 1944, five days after D-Day, during the hedgerow fighting on the Cherbourg Peninsula, he was hit by shrapnel from a German .88mm shell, which almost severed his leg. He was evacuated to England and then transferred to Walter Reed Army Hospital in Washington, but surgeons could not save the leg. Scarcely four months later, Reeder flew from Walter Reed to New York in the private plane of Chief of Staff General George C. Marshall. Once again, he was on the Army sideline, resting in a wheelchair, a white blanket covering his missing leg.[22]

The presence of Reeder was a reminder that it was Armistice Day, twenty-six years since the guns had gone silent at the end of the First World War. "There will be no bloody cease-fire order around here today," a private fighting in northern Holland said. There was none for General Patton's Third Army, slogging through the mud around Metz; none for the First Army, battling for survival inside Germany; none for General MacArthur's men on Leyte; none for the American troops in northern Italy.[23]

Thousands of people had gathered earlier that morning in Madison Square to pay tribute to the dead of both wars. Mayor Fiorello La Guardia had cautioned that "we must profit by the mistakes of the past in building the second peace," adding his confidence that President Roosevelt would lead the world to an enlightened future. At 11 a.m. the crowd went silent for several minutes, just as they did everywhere in the United States on the eleventh hour of the eleventh day of the eleventh month.

Shortly after the ceremony in Madison Square, a war bond rally was held in Times Square. Two tickets for the Army–Notre Dame game went on the auction block, and Seaman Second Class Robert Hedges opened with a $25 bid. A football fan, he desperately wanted to see the game but had limited resources. Quickly the price climbed, Hedges dropping out when it reached $200. The bidding finally ended at $5,000. As the crowd cheered, the winning bidder, Mrs. Betty Bentley of Boston, gave the tickets to Hedges.

Just shy of 75,000 spectators joined Reeder and Bridges at Yankee Stadium. If Reeder represented the American fighting spirit, the Madison Square ceremony Americans' desire for a lasting peace, and Bentley's Times Square gesture Americans' generosity, then the game signified a slice of what the country was fighting for. It wasn't an abstraction or a slogan or a political promise but a simple event, one of many taking place that day in every corner of the country. No other country played American football. Like baseball, it was something that united the troops in the field and the citizens on the home front. It had survived during the war largely because of the deep emotions it evoked. America loved its games, and needed them.

The Armistice Day events, the pageantry of the Corps of Cadets, the crispness of that fall day, the traditions of Army and Notre Dame, the fragility of a nation at war, the sense that in an uncertain world this event seemed oddly important—everything fused at the two o'clock kickoff. Glenn Davis was not the most reflective player on the team, but he was very much aware that the game was broadcast around the world on Armed Forces radio. He believed everyone on the team "felt a little responsibility to . . . entertain the Armed Forces, the guys who were overseas that . . . were glued to their radios. Yeah, I had a picture of that in my mind."[24]

Notre Dame won the toss and elected to receive the kick, which Blanchard booted high and deep. The Irish were able to return it only to their own 13-yard line. It was the start Blaik had hoped for. Even if Army had won the flip of the coin, he would have had Doc pin Notre Dame back deep on their side of the field. So often in the past, the games had been low-scoring slugfests hinging on field position. Irish quarterback Frank Dancewicz began conservatively by testing Army's line. Three times he gave the ball to his runners, but they were unable to gain a first down, forcing Bob Kelly to punt.[25]

The punt stayed on Notre Dame's end of the field, and immediately Doug Kenna led a methodical drive toward the Irish goal line. Three first downs advanced the ball inside the 10, and two running plays pushed it to the 1. But on the next play an Irish lineman dropped Minor for a 5-yard loss. On fourth and goal from the 6, Kenna was supposed to take the snap, spin, and hand off to Minor on an off-tackle play. But he spun the wrong way, bobbled the ball, and missed the exchange. With the action moving left, he managed to run a near naked bootleg to the right corner of the end zone. "Everyone was going one way, and I just sort of acted like I knew what was going on and ran the other way for the score," he recalled.[26]

Most of the newspaper reporters thought that the touchdown was a called play that Kenna executed brilliantly. He "ran with magnificent stride," read the *New York World-Telegram*. He faked a pass and "tricked" the Irish before sweeping around the end, judged the *Washington Post*. But when Kenna ran to the sideline before the next kickoff, Blaik shook his head and asked, "What were you thinking about? You were lucky." Lucky or not, it was Army's first score against Notre Dame in five years. Every battle plan, no matter how meticulously prepared, becomes obsolete the instant the shooting starts.

The play was a sign of good things to come—for Kenna and Army. Soon after, Kenna intercepted a Dancewicz pass, and on the next play Minor ripped through a hole and streaked, untouched, 26 yards for another touchdown. The contest had barely begun, and Notre Dame was behind by two scores and desperate to get back into it. They had two options: (1) stay with the game plan and work methodically; (2) scrap the plan and go for broke. The Irish now lacked confidence in the conservative option. Besides, Coulter and the other Army linemen were controlling the scrimmage line. So Notre Dame decided to "roll the bones" and put the ball in the air.

In a game in which they had no viable options, the one they selected quickly led to disaster. On Notre Dame's next series Doc Blanchard intercepted a pass, and on the following play Kenna threw a touchdown pass to Ed Rafalko. At the end of the first quarter Army led, 20–0, at which stage Glenn Davis came into the game and promptly intercepted another Dancewicz pass and returned it to the Irish 6. On the following play he scored. And so it continued. A long, brilliant punt return by Kenna set up another Davis touchdown. The score was 33–0 at the half.

Early in the second half, on another punt return, Kenna drew the Notre Dame defenders to him and pitched the ball to Minor on a reverse, ending in a 60-yard touchdown run. Soon after, Kenna threw a pass to Dick Pitzer for a touchdown, then Davis ran in his third score of the afternoon. Late in the fourth quarter the score was 52–0 and Blaik was no longer trying to score. But Army scored even when they didn't try. Hal Tavzel, described in several reports as "an obscure plebe tackle from Cleveland," made the eighth Army interception of the game when he was so deep in Irish territory that all he had to do was virtually fall into the end zone for Army's ninth touchdown. After scoring, he delivered the ball to the referee and then ran back to his teammates, flapping his hands over his head like a kid at a birthday party. It was as if he had just scored the game-winning touchdown on a last-second, 100-yard kickoff return. The extra point made the score 59–0—one point worse than the drubbing the Irish took at the hands of Wisconsin in 1904. Never before or since would they be so badly drilled.

Shirley Povich wrote in the *Washington Post,* "There was no 'cease fire' order from the Army command on this Armistice Day, and the Cadets from West Point poured it on the Fighting Irish." In truth, it could have been worse. "Had not the great Samaritan (and Army coach) Lieutenant Colonel Earl H. Blaik hobbled his forces, the margin might have been anything, even a hundred points," concluded Stanley Woodward in the *New York Herald Tribune.* It was more than Army had scored in their fifteen previous games against Notre Dame. In just the first half they had tallied more against the Irish than Navy had in its entire game. Although the Corps of Cadets chanted "More yet" for most of the second half, Army's desire for revenge was sated.

After the game the Army team enjoyed a long-overdue celebration, singing "On, Brave Old Army Team." The ease of the victory surprised everyone. As Herman Hickman remarked to Blaik when they were sending in third- and fourth-teamers for clean-up duty, "My goodness! I never thought we'd ever be sending in subs like this in the Notre Dame game." Stunned, rowdy surprise fueled the locker room festivities. Finally Captain Tom Lombardo called for quiet. Solemnly, holding the game ball, he spoke a few words about the victory as a team win and their duty to one another. Then he handed the ball to Red Reeder, the footless former drop-kicker.[27]

. . .

It took a few days for the sportswriters to digest what they had seen. The debate was no longer "how great" but "what made them the greatest." Many reporters singled out Kenna. After two years of high hopes and injuries, he made for a compelling story line. Kenna "passed, kicked and ran with consummate artistry," wrote one columnist. "If Army has an indispensable man, Kenna appears to be it," added another. Other writers concentrated on the brutal blocking of Coulter and Blanchard. Tex knocked one Irish player cold in the game, and Blanchard leveled John "Tree" Adams, Notre Dame's enormous tackle. Legendary coach Pop Warner later told Blaik that Blanchard's crushing block was the hardest he had ever seen.[28]

Blaik, however, quickly moved past the Notre Dame game and made late-night trips to his office to work on offensive and defensive schemes to use against Pennsylvania. He feared Penn, he told reporters. "We were pretty high for the [Notre Dame] game. And that may mean letdown." In 1941 his team had held the Irish to a 0–0 tie and then lost to Harvard and Penn in consecutive weeks. In 1943 his team had tied Penn and lost badly to Notre Dame the following week. To break the pattern, he put his team through strenuous drills, impressing on them that the final two games of the season would be the most competitive of all.[29]

Throughout the war years Penn had a very good team. It was their lopsided victory against Army in 1940 that had convinced Superintendent Robert Eichelberger that West Point needed the coaching services of Red Blaik. And in three tries against the Quakers, Blaik had managed only a single tie. Though he was normally tight-lipped about his feelings, several people close to him knew that Penn was one school that he wanted to take to the woodshed.

Penn's coach, the thoughtful, bespectacled George Munger, was considered the thinking man's coach, particularly able to confuse offenses with his imaginative specialty defenses. He also had a well-deserved reputation for freely speaking his mind and twitting fellow coaches. It was not that he thought he was smarter than the other members of the coaching fraternity; he knew it. Maybe it was his exclusive education—Hill School, Episcopal Academy, and Penn. Perhaps it was his wire-rimmed glasses and slight, all-knowing half-smile. Or it might have been his quirky sense of humor. Whatever it was, he was never able to charm Blaik, and his penchant for beating Army did not help.

Goble Bryant, one of Blaik's players, was convinced that the colonel was "scared to death" of Munger's single-wing, unbalanced-line attack. Munger was Blaik's "nemesis," Bryant thought, and he suspected that there was a history between the two that went back to the coach's Dartmouth days. He just wanted to "beat the stew" out of his rival.[30]

Convincing the team that Penn actually had a chance was Blaik's primary problem. After the Notre Dame game, all the sportswriters wanted to discuss or write about was Army's December 2 contest against Navy. After some early struggles, Navy was playing its best football and had climbed to number three in the nation, behind Army and Ohio State. More than ever before, it was a game with a variety of angles—political, military, and athletic. But Blaik castigated any reporter who even mentioned Navy. "What about Navy?" he shot back at one journalist who broached the topic. "I will not discuss the Navy game. We play Pennsylvania on Saturday, and right now that's the game we're all thinking about."[31]

By "we" Blaik was evidently referring to himself and his coaching staff. Everyone else at the Academy was thinking, talking, and dreaming about Navy. Cadets did not greet each other with "Beat Pennsylvania!" There were no articles in the *New York Times* discussing the importance of the Army-Pennsylvania game. And the cadets were required to read one paper, usually the *Times*, every day.[32]

Doing so helped keep them abreast of the war news. In many ways West Point was a paradoxical institution. In no other school were students so cloistered. Every one of them went to classes, ate their meals, studied, and slept on the post. Passes to get off the post were as rare as extra rack time and given only as a last resort. Bob Woods vividly recalled an incident during his time at West Point when he was serving as duty orderly with the responsibility of checking out cadets in his Company B-1. John S. D. Eisenhower, Class of 1944, came down from his room and asked Woods to sign him out. "It was such an odd request, because it was a weekday and nobody, I mean nobody, signed out on a weekday. You just couldn't leave your room at that time. I thought it was some sort of plebe test—one I better not fail. But John was not very tough on plebes, so it made no sense." To be on the safe side, Woods called the officer of the day, who said that it was fine to sign out Cadet Eisenhower. "I have a reason," Eisenhower told Woods, "which I will explain to you when I can." A few weeks later he went to Woods's room and explained that his dad, General Dwight Eisenhower, had made a secret return trip to the United States and had come to visit him. Only a few people on the post knew about it, and he was not allowed to say anything at the time.[33]

Yet even though they lived in a virtual lockdown, West Point cadets might have been the best informed student body in the country. They knew in great detail what was happening in America and the world. It might have been true, as the old saying went, that at the Academy they got a free $10,000 education "shoved up the ass one nickel at a time," but they did get an outstanding education. Woods and Kenna and others remembered that in their military tactics/history course they studied the campaigns of Napoleon and the Civil War. "We were taught about offensive campaigns," said Woods. "I don't recall much discussion about World War I and the stalemate on the Western Front. The teachers liked to talk about Napoleon, Grant, and Lee. But they always compared what we were learning to the actions of the day.

We followed the American campaigns around the world. Many times the leaders were West Point graduates."[34]

They also followed the careers of recent graduates. Announcements in the mess often included the fates of West Pointers. Some had received one commendation or another. Others had died in action. For Woods, Kenna, and the other first classmen, everyone they knew from the classes of 1942, 1943, and 1944 was in "the big show."

In turn, GIs and Army officers gloried in the successes of the West Point football team. Around the world, the shortwave broadcasts of the games were like presents from home. Captain Tom Misereau, a lineman on the 1941 and 1942 teams en route from New Guinea to Leyte, gathered with nine other Academy graduates in the middle of the night to listen to the Army–Notre Dame game. Lieutenant Colonel August Farwick, Class of 1925 and an All-American guard, was in the Italian Apennine Mountains when he heard that Army had clobbered Notre Dame. "Just a lot of damned German propaganda," Gus quipped.[35]

The game might not have mattered to the *New York Times,* but it mattered to Tom Misereau, Gus Farwick, Robin Olds, Riggs Sullivan, and all the others who followed the exploits of the team. "[W]e represented the Army, we represented the service," a player later said. "[I]t gave [soldiers] a feeling that if your team won, that you could win." And that was something to play for.

Before they took the field, Blaik made sure that his team realized what was at stake: respect. "This team beat Army worse than any other team ever beat Army," he said. "Penn humiliated us." That was back in 1940. It was time, he said, to settle old scores.[36]

More than 66,000 spectators gathered at Franklin Field in Philadelphia. They had read about the speed of Glenn Davis, the power of Doc Blanchard, and the deceptiveness of Doug Kenna.

They were in for a few surprises. "Army fizzled, fumbled, contributed a profusion of missed blocks and football malfeasances of other categories," observed the *New York Post*'s Stanley Woodward. Often the Cadets treated the ball like an unappreciated Christmas tie, just looking for a place to dump it. They fumbled four times, threw several interceptions, bobbled and dropped passes, committed unpardonable penalties, and at times seemed baffled by Penn's defensive formations.[37]

As usual, Kenna's team started the game, but a series of turnovers and miscues ended drive after drive. The only sign of life was a long touchdown run by Max Minor. He found a gap over right tackle, swept past Penn's 252-pound George Savitsky, veered to the sideline, and then with sprinter speed outraced the defenders 67 yards to the end zone. Still Blaik was frustrated, and shortly after 10 minutes of action he sent in nine substitutes, including an entirely new line. The shakeup seemed to momentarily awaken Army. Davis intercepted a Quaker pass and returned the ball to Penn's side of the field. But on the next play a Penn lineman knocked down a Lombardo lateral, and a teammate scooped it and returned it 51 yards for a touchdown. With the quarter almost over the score was 7–7. The Army team that had inspired all the fabulous press clippings had yet to take the field.

Fortunately for the soldiers listening to the shortwave broadcasts, the combination of Blanchard and Davis—with some help from their friends—took over. Before the quarter ended, Davis broke several tackles on a long kickoff return. Then, on the second play from scrimmage, Dale Hall broke past the highly touted Savitsky, dodged two defensive backs, and sprinted 45 yards to the end zone. The quarter ended with Army leading, 13–7.

The Philadelphia spectators had cheered wildly when Penn scored, but their exuberant we've-got-a-chance cheers ended with that first—and last—Pennsylvania touchdown. Starting in the second quarter, Army asserted its power. "From there on it was not touch and go but only go," wrote William D. Richardson of the *New York Times.* In the second quarter both Blanchard and Davis scored short touchdowns. In the third quarter Kenna pitched the ball to Davis on a deceptive punt return, and the Californian went 45 yards for the score; Davis registered another on an 8-yard run; Lombardo passed to Blanchard for another tally; and third-team quarterback Young Arnold Tucker threw a touchdown pass to Barney Poole. After Dean Sensanbaugher returned a fumble 90 yards for a touchdown in the fourth quarter, Blaik began to substitute liberally and hold down the score. It was already 62–7, the worst beating Penn had taken since the 76–10 pounding by Princeton "back in '85, the days of the middle part, the moustache, the turtle-neck and flying wedge."[38]

During the game, placekicker Dick Walterhouse tied Tulsa's Clyde La Force's season record for points after touchdown. After Davis's final tally, Walterhouse booted his forty-fourth conversion of the season. He might have broken the record after any one of the next three Army scores, but angry fans prevented him. The crowd behind the goalpost had turned larcenous. When Walterhouse kicked a ball into the stands, they refused to return it, unmoved by the cajoling by officials, players, and coaches. Finally Army abstained from kicks and resorted to running or passing for points after touchdowns. By the end of the game the rude behavior had forced the two teams to play with an old, blackened, lumpy practice ball. In a time of leather shortages and rubber rationing, the actions of the few malcontents and their abettors were unconscionable.

It was the overwhelming victory Blaik desired, a soupçon of revenge for Penn's 48–0 throttling of Army in 1940. General Robert Eichelberger was in the Philippines that day. Perhaps he thought about his role in enticing Blaik back to the Academy. But both Blaik at West Point and Eichelberger in Leyte knew the campaign was not yet over.

11

★ ★ ★

Cause for Thanksgiving

> [I]n three or four years the United States has in sober
> fact become the greatest military, naval, and air power
> in the world—that, I say to you in this time of war, is
> itself a subject for profound thanksgiving.
>
> —WINSTON CHURCHILL

> *Army and Navy, more is the pity,*
> *Will play in Annapolis, not a big city.*
> *Although countless gridiron followers rue it,*
> *Forrestal says so, that's all there is to it.*
>
> —TIM COHANE

RAIN AND SLEET pounded West Point and New York
for two days before Thanksgiving Day, November 23.
Several inches of snow still blanketed the Academy's
gray buildings and covered the grass on the Plain. The winds tore
into the painted sheets inscribed with BEAT NAVY and SINK THE
NAVY that had begun to appear on the Post. In New York City
the snow had melted, but winds bent and snapped trees in Central Park and knocked out telephone lines. Weather conditions
forced the cancellation of most flights in and out of La Guardia
Field, flooded several low-lying areas, and snarled traffic.[1]
Before the holiday Mayor La Guardia had responded to

frightful rumors: his city's housewives would be able to buy turkeys—but only after Thanksgiving. For now, he confessed, "[t]he turkey situation was bad." He encouraged everyone to eat chicken on America's most recently declared national holiday: "I think we have reached the point where Americans celebrate Thanksgiving, even if they have to delay their turkey eating for one week. . . . There are many ways in which we can give thanks for all of the blessings we have."[2]

Turkey wasn't the only missing ingredient that year. The War Food Administration had issued warnings that New York faced a severe sugar crisis. La Guardia noted that it had given seven reasons for the shortage of sugar: "One reason is that sugar is scarce, so we are not interested in the other six reasons." Bakery shelves were bare, and the government had not sent in any emergency supplies. The forecast looked grim for pie lovers.

It was America's third Thanksgiving at war, and there was a note of bitter melancholy in the air. Maybe next year there would be turkeys and pies for Thanksgiving and gifts and laughter on Christmas. Perhaps next year entire families would be united for the holidays—alive, safe, and secure about the future. The mood was perfectly captured by a successful MGM film released toward the end of the month. *Meet Me in St. Louis* traffics in nostalgia for a time when girls thought about snagging boys, boys about catching balls, and parents about what was best for the whole family. It was set in 1903 and 1904, when the biggest event on the calendar was the opening of the Louisiana Purchase Exposition—the St. Louis World's Fair.

Beneath the film's surface, however, a sense of loss broods. Families move, friends disappear, communications become confused. Judy Garland sings "Have Yourself a Merry Little Christmas" to her terrified younger sister, who wonders how Santa will know how to find her. Like the enormously successful "White Christmas"—the biggest hit of the war—"Have Yourself a Merry Little Christmas" is scored in a minor key. The song promises a restored America of light hearts: "Yuletide gay," "happy days of yore," and an untroubled gathering of friends. But the promise is just a wish or, in the context of the film, an almost pointless prayer. The dream is that "next year all our troubles[1]/[1]will be out of sight." But until then "we'll all have to muddle through somehow," referring to the British wartime refrain of "muddling through."

"Have Yourself a Merry Little Christmas" speaks to the desire for restoration. "White Christmas" dreams of restoring a mythical New England of snow-covered treetops, horse-drawn sleighs, and youthful innocence. Many wartime songs tapped into the same vein of restoration. "I'll Be Seeing You," "Don't Get Around Much Anymore," "I Don't Want to Walk Without You," "The White Cliffs of Dover," "You'd Be So Nice to Come Home To," "Don't Sit Under the Apple Tree with Anyone Else but Me"—the list is long. By Thanksgiving 1944, Americans had been hearing the message in songs and movies for almost three full years. They were hungry for more than turkey and pie. They were starved for the America the war interrupted.

A college football championship—at least, a game that would effectively decide who would be ranked number one for the season—would have been a front-page spectacle in that normal America. And by that inclement Thanksgiving the Army-Navy game looked to be such a contest. Newspapers were full of details about it, Americans across the country discussed it, soldiers and sailors thousands of miles from home looked forward to the broadcast. There had never ever been an Army-Navy game quite to match it. In the November 27 football poll Army was ranked number one in the country and Navy number two. Both teams were on extended winning streaks that included decisive victories over Notre Dame. The game would almost certainly anoint the 1944 national champion.

In the last weeks of November, however, the question that aroused the most debate was whether the game would be a "normal" spectacle. President Roosevelt had once again decreed that the Army-Navy game would be played at Annapolis before a handful of spectators living within ten miles of the Naval Academy. It would remain "a cloistered affair," wrote Joe Williams in the *New York World-Telegram*. The new secretary of the Navy, James Forrestal, had said so. The Corps of Cadets would not be allowed to go to the game, nor would Army and Navy officers stationed even as close as the Capitol. In essence, the 1944 national championship game would be contested in a cozy football facility before a small group of people who overwhelmingly favored Navy. The most important Army-Navy matchup in history would have the look and feel of a high school football game.[3]

Part of the problem was not the recently installed Forrestal but the veteran secretary of the Army, Henry L. Stimson, who continued to oppose sporting events that diverted attention from the war. This was particularly true for professional sports like boxing, which Stimson, a product of Andover, Yale (Skull and Bones), and Harvard Law School, looked down on with a sniff of disdain. In 1942, when the sporting public had clamored for a rematch of the heavyweight title between Joe Louis and Billy Conn, Stimson had squashed the idea. Like Chief of Staff General George Marshall, he was sensitive about the fact that many college football players — some of whom had All-American ability — had been declared medically unfit for military service but played like supermen on Saturday afternoons.[4]

Marshall and Stimson were flinty, high-minded men who misjudged the public relations value of college football. In 1943 and especially in 1944, the big college game had returned to America. In 1943 Navy had played Notre Dame in Cleveland before 80,000 delighted fans, much like the 1944 Army–Notre Dame game at Yankee Stadium. Both Army and Navy had played big games against Penn in Philadelphia. And in 1944 Navy had already played "home games" in Baltimore, not Annapolis, against Duke, Notre Dame, Cornell, and Purdue. From a purely logical standpoint, Stimson's position made little sense. "Is this just another instance of where the reasoning and the logic cannot be justified on the facts," asked Congressman John E. Sheriden of Pennsylvania, "or another demonstration of the 'Army' way of doing things . . . ?"[5]

Only a few weeks before the Army-Navy game, two other teams of Army and Navy athletes stationed in Europe played each other in London for the European championship. The contest was held on November 12 before 60,000 "football-starved Yanks." Though not a particularly close contest—Army won, 20–0—the servicemen hooted and hollered throughout. The Navy goat tried to butt the Army mule at halftime. After one play a sergeant screamed, "Wotta tackle!" into the ear of the man sitting beside him; looking over, he saw he was next to the famed pilot Lieutenant General Jimmy Doolittle. It wasn't just the public that craved a big game, it was the servicemen themselves.[6]

Desperate fans looked to President Roosevelt to cut through the red tape and reverse himself. It was well known that FDR was a football fan, partial to Navy. Rumors had circulated widely that he would attend the Army–Notre Dame game in Yankee Stadium. (He was one of the few no-shows who could have obtained a ticket.) It seemed like an easy matter for FDR to handle. "When the election is out of the way," suggested Arthur Daley in the *New York Times,* "perhaps President Roosevelt will have the time to think about it and order the change. It has reached such a point now that he alone can destroy that Washington bottleneck that is hemming in the year's greatest game."[7]

What Americans did not know, and what was only discussed in whispers at the highest levels, was that President Roosevelt was dying. Even before the election, politicians and friends had been shocked that he had developed a chronic hacking cough, shed pounds, and visibly aged. He seemed to be shrinking. Once a buoyant, handsome man, now his eyes, frequently watery, had dark rings, his skin was a sickly gray, and his cheeks were melting wax. His jaw often dropped, leaving his mouth hanging open like a lizard waiting to catch a fly. His shirt collars were a size or two too large and his suits hung loosely on him, though he had always been a natty dresser, fastidious and proper.[8]

The old political warhorse mustered enough energy to run his final race. He addressed the Teamsters Union at the Statler Hotel in Washington, D.C., but he had to deliver the talk sitting down. He braved a cold rain in New York, riding hatless in an open Packard through Brooklyn, Queens, the Bronx, and Manhattan. He said all the right things, made all the correct moves, and won the race against Dewey. Then he traveled to his Warm Springs retreat to rest.

Meanwhile politicians in and out of the Capitol were organizing and executing a campaign of their own. As early as August, Congressman Samuel A. Weiss of New York had attempted to make Stimson see the folly of his position. England, he wrote, "has continued her Socker [sic] Football Games, while only a few hours away from the luft waffe [sic]. Many of these events were attended by over 100,000 spectators; and after five years of war the leaders of Great Britain believe these athletic events have fully justified themselves." Weiss believed it was time to use major sports events to raise money for the Army Emergency Relief Fund and promote the sale of war bonds.[9]

By mid-November both journalists and politicians increased their attacks on Stimson and Forrestal. The old bureaucratic excuse about clogging the railways and using up tires and gasoline was ridiculous, politicians suggested, for the game could be moved to a large eastern city that could easily provide enough interested spectators to pack any stadium. Mayor Theodore McKeldin of Baltimore, Mayor Bernard Samuel of Philadelphia, and Governor Herbert O'Conor of Maryland wired Stimson with essentially the same message—give the game to us, it will be good for America.[10]

Nobody, especially money-hungry mayors and governors, was

going to sway the stiff-backed secretary of war. But their message found supporters on Capitol Hill who agreed that the game was too important to receive anything short of special treatment. Senator Edwin C. Johnson of Colorado, the ranking member of the Senate Military Affairs Committee, said that he was "one-thousand percent for transferring" the game to a bigger city. He predicted that it would be the greatest game in the history of the rivalry. Representative Joseph W. Martin of Massachusetts thought it was "foolish" to limit spectators because of "alleged transportation" issues. Besides, there were more important things at stake. The government needed money to fight the war and the recent war bond drives had begun to lag. Now, in the opening phases of the Sixth War Bond Drive, the Army-Navy game presented literally a golden opportunity.[11]

These arguments caught the ears of people in the Treasury Department. A source identified as a "gentleman close to Henry Morgenthau, Jr., Secretary of the Treasury," told Joe Williams of the *New York World-Telegram* that the department's only interest in the game was "in using it as background for selling Bonds." Baltimore, Philadelphia, New York—the place didn't matter. "It is inconceivable to me," Williams wrote, "that if Mr. Morgenthau made an energetic effort to have the game switched it wouldn't be switched. Mr. Morgenthau has banked heavily on sports promotions in peddling his bonds and getting his message across the sports pages. Now Uncle Sam finds himself with a natural of naturals on his hands, the biggest sports show of the year, one of the biggest of all time, and unless someone acts and acts darn quickly it will go completely to waste, especially from the angle which should concern Mr. Morgenthau most."[12]

Morgenthau certainly believed the matter was worth a second look. Although as late as November 16 most of the power brokers in the administration still opposed changing the site of the game, the Treasury secretary spoke publicly about it. When a reporter asked him how much he was talking about, Morgenthau suggested between $5,000,000 and $10,000,000 worth of war bonds. Then Ted R. Gamble, director of the War Finance Division of the Treasury, quietly interrupted him. "I don't like to butt in, Mr. Secretary," he said, "but it would be more like $50,000,000." "That's even more money," Morgenthau responded.[13]

For a few days, the political football was tossed from one end of Washington to the other. Morgenthau came out full for the switch in location. Stimson remained staunchly opposed. Forrestal balanced on top of the fence, ready to jump in either direction. FDR said that he would have to think about the matter, though in principle he was "not opposed" to changing direction. If the site of the game were not changed, wrote *New York Post* columnist Leonard Cohen, "something is rotten in Denmark, U.S.A."[14]

Finally, less than two weeks before the showdown, FDR ordered the site of the Army-Navy game changed from Annapolis to Baltimore, where it would be a featured event in the Sixth War Bond Drive. "Like a last-minute field goal, the decision to shift the game came just in time," commented a reporter. Treasury officials again claimed the game would raise about $50,000,000 for the war effort.[15]

Ten thousand tickets had already been sold for the Annapolis stadium. Now the game would be at Municipal Stadium, with a seating capacity of nearly 70,000. The Treasury and the Maryland War Finance Committee were charged with selling the extra tickets. Potential spectators were required to purchase a Series E war bond, widely regarded as the "little man's bond" because of its low face value. The bond values were scaled to the desirability of the seats, beginning at $25 and ranging up to $1,000, although a handful of box seats required the purchase of a $1,000,000 bond. Many sportswriters encouraged all Americans interested in the game to help support the military by buying a Series E bond whether or not they wanted to attend. One scribe even suggested that the game be filmed and shown in theaters across the country to sell even more bonds. "The big thing," wrote Arthur Daley, "is that all of us must buy extra bonds."[16]

Selling the tickets was a nightmare. The game was an instant sellout. Within a day of the decision, the Maryland War Finance Committee workers were crushed by the number of ticket requests. Chairman Frank W. Wrightson said his office had received "literally tons of mail," adding that he would not open any more envelopes. Even more irksome was the number of special requests from politicians, seeking tickets for themselves, their friends, and their constituents, regardless of travel restrictions or price. After some wrangling, the committee decided that each senator and congressman could buy four tickets. But that did not quiet the requests. From all reports, there had never been an event that generated such a demand. Newspaper photographs showed committee secretaries being attacked by King Kong–sized bundles of ticket requests, and newspaper articles reported on the power of people in high places to disrupt the process. A cartoon in the *New York World-Telegram* best captured the mood of that Thanksgiving. It pictured two men, one holding a wrapped turkey, the other clutching an Army vs. Navy ticket. Looking enviously at the ticket-holder, the other one says, "Who do you know?!!!" Licking his lips, the other replies, "That's what I wuz gonna ask you!"[17]

In an age when virtually every standout football player carried a moniker, when there seemed always to be a Bronko, Bubba, Buster, Reb, or Tex on the field, Clyde "Smackover" Scott may have had the best of all.

Scott was raised in Smackover, Arkansas, and in 1944 he was at the beginning of a college career that would span two years at the Naval Academy and three years at the University of Arkansas. In all five years he would receive mention on various All-

American teams, and in his last year he would receive consensus first-team All-American status. Although only 175 pounds, he played the game with abandon, running and tackling at top speed. He feared no injury, and perhaps as a result he was often injured. Smackover Scott was fast, even faster in the 100-yard dash than Glenn Davis. His fastest hundred was 9.4 seconds, close to world caliber. In the 1948 London Olympic Games he would finish second in the 110-meter high hurdles, in 14.1, second fastest in the history of the Olympics. And that was after several football injuries had cut into his speed.

Nor was Smackover the only talented Navy back. In 1944 he wasn't even the best in the backfield. The finest runner, a classic single-wing tailback, was Bobby Tom Jenkins, a transfer from the University of Alabama who in 1944 was a first-team consensus All-American. "Tough" was the most common single word used to describe Jenkins, "dependable" the second. In Navy's 13–0 victory over Army in 1943, he scored the crucial first touchdown. Joe Stanowicz, the Cadets' All-American tackle, brutally collided with Jenkins on the 3-yard line, but the Navy runner continued into the end zone with the tackle clinging to his back. Even Tim Cohane, biased toward Blaik and Army, admitted, "For all its galaxy of backs, Army hasn't anyone, including Doc Blanchard, who can run as hard as Jenkins." The previous week, Cornell's star player had attempted to level "Ruby Robert." He "ended up in the hospital with a concussion."[18]

Off the field Jenkins was gentle and considerate. In high school he had been a straight-A student, president of his class, an All-State football player, and a paperboy, "more to be admired," said his hometown journalist, "for his character than for his prowess as an athlete." His hobby was catching butterflies.[19]

"Little" Hal Hamberg was Navy's third outstanding back. "Little" wasn't his nickname, but it might as well have been. It seemed that throughout his career sportswriters could not imagine mentioning the former University of Arkansas standout without at least once using the adjective. Captain John Whelchel, his Navy coach, described the 150-pound Hamberg as a "PT boat amid a squadron of dreadnoughts," but on the field he played like a destroyer.[20]

A brilliant runner, passer, and kicker, Hamberg had been the star of Navy's 1942 defeat of Army, and he had broken open the 1943 game with his all-around play. Although he was injured for part of the 1944 season, he had a way of playing his best when he was counted out. Coach Oscar Hagberg expected him to be in prime condition for Army. More than any other quality, the coach knew that Hamberg added an element of imagination—even a touch of the sandlot—to the Navy offense. "Army, from Col. Blaik down, fears Hamberg more than any other Navy back," wrote a reporter.[21]

Smackover Scott, Bobby Tom Jenkins, Little Hal Hamberg—they gave Blaik something to think about during his team's two weeks of preparation for the Navy game, but even they were not his primary concern. Most of the sportswriters were willing to give Army's two backfields a slight edge over Navy's, but almost all of them thought that the Middies had the superior line. Lawrence Robinson of the *New York World-Telegram* summarized the conventional thinking: "The United States is divided today—between those who believe Army's backs will run to glory and those who think Navy's line will stop the Cadets at the source of their plays." All of Navy's linemen were outstanding, and two, Don Whitmire and Ben Chase, were 1944 consensus All-Americans.[22]

Navy's players were fighters, some literally so. Chase had been the regimental heavyweight boxing champion at Annapolis, which had the finest boxing program in the country. Coached by Spike Webb, the program included such other football players as end Leon Bramlett, blocking back Dave Barksdale, guard

Stansfield Turner, and Jenkins. These boxers characterized the ferocious nature of the team. "Navy can play rough, if that's the way the opposition wants it," concluded a reporter. "It will be recalled that the Army-Navy game at Michie Stadium last year was graced by seven incipient fist fights with two different combatants involved in each. [Leading boxing promoter] Mike Jacobs himself hasn't had a better card since Joe Louis enlisted."[23]

Undoubtedly the best fighter, the toughest of a tough lot, was Whitmire, who was in a class of his own at tackle. Whitmire was from Decatur, Alabama, where his father was the chief of police and the entire family prized duty to state and country. He had an older brother serving in Italy and a younger one in the Army Air Forces. He had gone to the University of Alabama, where he had roomed with Bobby Tom Jenkins and earned All-American honors for the Crimson Tide. Both at Alabama and Navy, Whitmire played football with unbridled aggression. Like Tex Coulter, he used his elbows, knees, and fists to get the job done, earning a reputation as a player who was not too concerned about the nuances of the rule book.[24]

His teammates and coaches called him "the Rock." One of his coaches said that Whitmire played like Jack Dempsey fought, adding, "I don't mean he's rough or tough. I mean he's in love with the game, and that also explains why he's a tackle; because that's where the most bruising play develops; that's where most of the action is, and the Rock likes to be in the thick of things." Like Dempsey, he had a reputation for knocking opponents out. Earlier in the season he had hit George Savitsky, Penn's standout tackle, so hard that the Quaker had to be carried from the field on a stretcher.[25]

The players at West Point considered Whitmire rough and dirty. Bob Woods believed that the Navy tackle figured prominently in the thinking of many of his Army teammates: "I was in the 1942 game when Robin [Olds] was slugged and had a couple of his teeth knocked out. I wasn't ten feet from him and never heard a scream like that on a football field. It was piercing. There was a feeling on the 1944 team that Whitmire had hit him. I don't know if that was true, but I do know that some of the players thought it was. There was a desire to get even for what had happened to Robin. Col. Blaik didn't have to worry about the team being ready to play in 1944."[26]

Whitmire hadn't been anywhere near Robin Olds that day—he had played tackle for Alabama in 1942. And Olds knew that he had evened the score with the player who shattered his teeth. But Whitmire had been a terror in the 1943 game at West Point, throwing elbows, hitting after the whistle, and initiating fights. Robin Olds's 1942 injury and the vicious combat of the 1943 game created a dark and angry mood among the players in 1944. It was a feeling so strong that more than sixty years later Woods recalled that the Cadets had a score to settle. And the Army team had a few players who understood how to settle scores.

As the game approached, it rained without letup at West Point. Blaik reluctantly moved his team indoors. He was in a foul humor, and virtually any subject set him off. Joe Williams believed coaches were the strangest people on earth: "They live in a dream world. A bad dream world. They are never happy unless they are unhappy." Blaik bristled at every topic the reporter broached. Army was the 2–1 favorite to win, he suggested. "How do those characters arrive at such odds?" Blaik answered. "On what do they base their calculations? With the exception of Stanowicz, at guard, this is the same line Navy tore to pieces a year ago, and it's in the line games are won and lost." Furthermore, his offense excelled on a fast track, but the damn rain, rain, rain was promising a mud bowl.[27]

To make matters worse, Blaik learned that Navy was tampering with the field at Baltimore's Municipal Stadium. Evidently someone in charge at Annapolis decided that the old, worn patch needed a good sprucing up for the big game. Since it was technically a Navy home game, Naval Academy officials chose to resod the field between the 30-yard lines. Blaik tried to prevent the groundskeeping but failed. The continual downpour meant that the resodded field, even if covered, might be wet, slippery, and ever so slow.[28]

The best news from West Point was that, with the change in the game site, the entire Corps of Cadets would be shipped down to watch what sportswriters had begun to call the most important game in the seventy-five-year history of football. At the news, waves of ecstasy swept over the corps. "The Army team's the pride and dream of every heart in gray," went the opening lines of "On, Brave Old Army Team." Visiting West Point and seeing the enthusiasm, Tim Cohane wrote a parody of Kipling's "Tommy." It began:

> *If you would go to West Point, lad, and someday earn your stars,*
> *You'd better be a man or learn some other trade than Mars,*
> *For up there on the Hudson, lad, where Benny set 'em up,*
> *The only one a plebe outranks is the superintendent's pup.*
>
> *O, it's "Mr. Dumbjohn this and that. Hey, Mister, blow your nose!"*
> *But it's "Thank you, Mister Blanchard," when the football whistle blows.*
> *When the football whistle blows, my lad, when the football whistle blows*
> *O, it's "Thank you, Mister Blanchard," when the football whistle blows.*
>
> . . . .
>
> *O, it's "Suck your gut in, Mister," and it's leather you'll define,*

But it's "Thank you, Mister Blanchard," when you're back-
ing up the line.
When you're backing up the line, my lad, when you're back-
ing up the line,
O, it's "Thank you, Mister Blanchard," when you're backing
up the line.[29]

Blaik's comments notwithstanding, Army was favored to win the game. Their team was fit—every paper in New York and America said so. Rollie Bevan said that even Johnny Sauer, who broke his arm in the Notre Dame game, would be ready for action. And Navy was hurting—or might be hurting, depending on which sportswriter was covering the story. At a time when American men were injured and killed by the hundreds nearly every day in Europe and the Pacific, no subplot of the Army-Navy game was more closely scrutinized than the exact condition of one of Bobby Tom Jenkins's toes. Navy was less than forthcoming about which toe might be a little below par, but enterprising reporters confidently asserted that it was one of the ones on his left foot and it was definitely infected. For several days the fate of Jenkins's toe dominated stories about the game. Finally the Navy team physician said Bobby Tom would play.[30]

The one event that might have sent off shock waves of doubt among the corps didn't. In the annual Turkey Day clash between the Engineers and the Goats, the top students won, 7–0. According to tradition, "As the Goats go so goes the Army." But who cared about the old saw, anyway? A cadet writer for *The Pointer,* the Academy's paper, confidently argued: "[O]ur departmental statistics show so many upsets to this tradition during the last few years (the Goats have been winning but so has Navy) that it has been commonly accepted that perhaps this timely win by the Engineers is a good luck omen for our 'Big Rabble.'"[31]

Perhaps the only cadet not caught up in the giddy excitement was Bob Woods, whose role in the contest was even larger than it had been when he played for Annapolis or West Point. In his last year, now First Captain, he was responsible to Cadet Headquarters for the general condition, morale, and attitude of the corps, as well as Fourth Call Customs and control of the mess. When it was announced that the corps would go to Baltimore, it fell to Woods to develop a plan to transport, feed, and move the cadets from place to place. The tactical officers were concerned about every detail—how long it would take to seat each cadet for meals, how long it would take for the corps to board the ship, how long it would take to march from the Baltimore dock to Municipal Stadium. It was not D-Day, but it was an important assignment and would happen exactly as planned.

It would be difficult to exaggerate how intensely reporters covered the buildup to the 1944 Army-Navy game. The daylight bombing of Tokyo by American B-29s from Saipan, the Soviet push into Hungary, and Allied convoys reaching Antwerp were given lower billing. The condition of Jenkins's toe, the state of the field, the mood of the academies, the predictions of coaches, the alignment of the stars—anything and everything, and sometimes nothing, that had to do with the game was fodder for the papers. Without any sense of hyperbole, a week before the contest Lawrence Robinson wrote, "Undoubtedly this is one of the climactic games of football history." A week later it wasn't just one of several. The 1944 Army-Navy game was widely described as the most important game of football ever played in America.[32]

The sportswriters may have been right. In 1944 Army and Navy did occupy a central place in the minds of Americans. They represented millions of young men in uniform in the United States and around the world, defending their country against Nazi and Japanese aggression. Those soldiers and sailors knew better than most that there was no such thing as a "Good War" but that their conflict was a "Just War." It was time to win and come home. The Army-Navy game symbolized the continuation of peacetime rivalries in a time of national crisis. In a very real sense, it stood for exactly what Americans most desired, a return to the normality of American life.

Millions of Americans around the world listened to the game. There had never been a wider coverage of an athletic event—or probably any other event. It was unquestionably the greatest shortwave hookup in radio history. The Armed Forces Radio Service broadcast the game live to troops in northern Europe, Egypt, Italy, and the Mediterranean, as well as those in Alaska, the Aleutians, and the Southwest Pacific. In Iceland, Greenland, Central Africa, and islands in the South Atlantic, where conditions did not permit a live broadcast, troops heard a play-by-play rebroadcast. In the Burma-India Theater the game was broadcast through a relay by the British Broadcasting Company.[33]

Army and Navy were the top two teams in the nation for the first time in their history. Although Navy had lost two early-season games, they had played the more difficult schedule and had defeated highly ranked Penn, Notre Dame, Cornell, and Purdue in the previous month. Army's schedule was weaker, but they had decisively won every game and performed better against common opponents. It was an intriguing matchup—Army's backs vs. Navy's line, Army's T vs. Navy's single wing, Army's string of failures vs. Navy's years of success. Although most reporters predicted Army to win, the coaching fraternity was split. Eight of the eleven Notre Dame players who had seen the most action against the two teams picked Navy. The majority of the Penn Quakers who had played against both squads agreed. The majority of Duke Blue Devils, however, favored Army. If ever there was a "pick 'em" game, this was it.[34]

Rarely had so many all-stars played in a regular-season game. Only days before the contest, the United Press announced its All-American team. The first team included end Barney Poole, tackle Don Whitmire, guards Ben Chase and Joe Stanowicz, and backs Bob Jenkins, Glenn Davis, and Felix Blanchard. Seven of the eleven All-Americans played for either Army or Navy! Although Les Horvath of Ohio State won the Heisman in 1944, he won only 412 votes. Together, Davis and Blanchard tallied 524. Whitmire, Jenkins, and Kenna also finished in the top ten in the Heisman race. Never in the history of the modern game had two institutions so dominated the nation's football talent.[35]

And never in the history of the sport would there be a more important game.

12

★ ★ ★

A Game for America

If I were a Navy man and saw Blanchard coming, I'd
resign from Annapolis immediately.
— JOHN MCEWAN

It was America's No. 1 sports event of World War II.
— JOHN F. CHANDLER

It was the greatest football game I've ever seen.
— BOB WOODS

ON FRIDAY BEFORE D-Day, shortly after breakfast
mess, First Captain Bob Woods led the Corps of Cadets down the steep hill to south dock on the Hudson,
where they boarded the USS *Uruguay* for the trip to Baltimore.
It was a cold, breezy day, but hardly anyone noticed at first. All
the way down the river to New York City, the cadets talked about
Blanchard, Davis, Kenna, and beating Navy. None of them had
been at the Academy for the last Army victory.

As the *Uruguay* headed into the Atlantic, it was joined by an
escort of warships, submarines, and a few dirigibles. The threat
of a German U-boat attack necessitated precautions. Then the
mood changed. "It was very cold and the waters were really

choppy," Woods recalled. "About half of the Corps became violently sick." But they were buoyed by anticipation, and whether hugging a john or bending over the side of the transport, none wanted to miss the trip.[1]

As the cadets bedded down in tight quarters, Baltimore was a "veritable madhouse." The *New York Post*'s Leonard Cohen wrote, "The place is jumpin', not with jive talk, but with the phraseology peculiar to football. The Army T, the Navy line, Davis' speed, Blanchard's power, Kenna's passing, Whitmire's tackle play, Scott's plunging, Jenkins' toe infection, Duren's blocking, Hamberg's forwards—put them all together and you get the gridiron jargon that assails your ears in hotel lobbies, bars, grill and street corner gab-fests." It was as if a seven-game World Series had been jammed into a couple of days, with a heavyweight championship fight and a Fourth of July celebration added for good measure.[2]

Mixing in with the football crowd was an assortment of gamblers, prostitutes, pickpockets, ticket scalpers, and out-and-out crooks. With a few exceptions, the ticket-holders were supposed to be from the Baltimore area, but a mob of out-of-towners seemed to be hanging around the fringes of all the activity, looking to score a black market profit for anything anyone could desire. "My, oh, my, it was a raw gathering," recalled one woman. "I saw some things I had never seen or heard of before."[3]

The police raided one gambling establishment, which was a little like a guard catching one convict after a general prison break. They arrested forty-eight men, and when they were asked what they were doing there, almost to a man they replied, "We're trying to find tickets to the Army-Navy game." There were none to be found. The sellout contest added $58,637,000 to the coffers of the Sixth War Bond Drive.[4]

After Army's last practice at West Point, the sun had broken through the clouds and a "glorious rainbow spanned the Hudson, one end appearing to emerge right out of the Academy."

The coaching staff accepted it as an omen. Blaik had just been promoted from lieutenant colonel to full colonel and now had a pair of silver eagles pinned to his khaki blouse. When a reporter asked about the key to the game, he ran out of words. "It's been Navy's line that beat us these last two years. I hope it doesn't happen this year. If it does . . ." He trailed off. Herman Hickman picked it up: "If it does ah'm goin' to keep right on walkin' South."[5]

First Captain Woods's force arrived at the Baltimore harbor on a sunny Saturday morning. "After the rugged voyage it was good to get my feet on terra firma," he recalled. "It took a while for the ground to stop swaying under me." Formed into their companies, the corps began the 5-mile uphill march from the docks to Municipal Stadium. It was clear and cold; 32 degrees was the predicted high for the day. As the cadets marched through the streets, the residents cheered and called out greetings. About halfway to the stadium the group stopped for a planned john break. Sheets had been strung up in an empty lot surrounded by high apartment buildings. As the cadets relieved themselves, curious onlookers stretched their necks out of windows to watch the soldiers complete their tasks. "There was a wonderful amount of good-natured cheering and ribbing," said Woods.[6]

They continued to march. A man with "half a load on" fell in beside Woods, but even in his inebriated state he marched strong and steady, talking with the First Captain all the way to the gates of the stadium. There the corps stopped, waiting for the call to march onto the field. Suddenly Woods heard someone behind him call his name. "Bob, you look terrific!" Woods looked around and saw Swede Larson, his old football coach from Annapolis, who had gotten permission from the Marines to attend the game and cheer for his former team. Larson had never lost to Army as a player or coach.[7]

Finally, at 1:15, the call came to lead the corps onto the field. Eight companies of cadets marched in perfect rhythm, forming in midfield and facing the empty section reserved for the midshipmen. They cheered the middies' vacant seats, wheeled around and cheered their own stands, then broke ranks and flowed like a gray stream to their seats.[8]

The cadets were not yet seated when the Midshipmen marched into the stadium, their band playing "Anchors Aweigh." The Maryland crowd broke into wild applause. The Navy Regiment returned the Cadets' salute, then raced to their seats while "the stadium resounded with the cheers of the proud, home-town audience."

Last came a moment of drama—and camp. It was clear that President Roosevelt would not attend the game, but unexpectedly the public address system announced the arrival of "a very special distinguished guest." All eyes watched a large black limousine, accompanied by three motorcycle policemen, drive into the stadium. Guards armed with tommy guns rode on the running boards. The motorcade circled the field and stopped at the official boxes in front of the Navy cheering section. Out stepped two heralds, trumpets blaring. Two counterfeit cadets followed, rolling out a red carpet. Then the trumpeters began a swing beat, and out pranced the Navy mascot Bill the Ninth, his coat long and lustrous, his goat horns perfectly curved and painted a brilliant navy blue. As Bill's two escorts led him to the center of the field, the Midshipmen in the stands raised a banner: WE ARE READY NOW.

Normally a cool technician before the game—a dispenser of information about tendencies, options, and last-minute information—Red Blaik gathered the team around him for a few final words. Reaching into his pocket, he pulled out a telegram from General Eichelberger, then in the Philippines. As Glenn Davis remembered, the telegram asked the players "to win for all the soldiers scattered throughout the world." Adding nothing else, Blaik sent the team out to play.[9]

· · ·

Nearly 70,000 spectators had been waiting for just this pageantry. Some had arrived as early as eight-thirty, though the gates did not open until ten o'clock. At noon 75 percent of the spectators were in their seats. There they sat in snow flurries, with a harsh wind coming off Chesapeake Bay. Their faces were raw and pinched. Men covered their ears with gloved hands. Women stamped lightly covered feet on the stadium's concrete floor to encourage the circulation of blood. Sitting in the press box, Al Laney watched the condensed breath emerge like smoke from tens of thousands of mouths and wondered if he would ever be warm again. Yet he could not think of another place in the world he would rather be.[10]

As he wrote, "[T]here never has been a sports event, perhaps never an event of any kind, that received the attention of so many Americans in so many places around the world." He knew that in France and the Low Countries, on a severely cold night, American soldiers were huddled around receiving sets in the frozen mud, listening to the game on Armed Forces Radio. And that soldiers and sailors in the Pacific and on the beaches of Leyte, sweating on a hot, humid Sunday night, were doing the same. It was a game played by boys training to be soldiers and sailors, listened to by hardened soldiers and sailors dreaming of being boys once again.

Across the field from each other, midshipmen and cadets hurled friendly insults. Then the cadets began to sing some verses to a favorite song:

> Come fill your glasses, fellows, and stand up in a row,
> To singing sentimentally, we're going for to go,
> In the Army there's sobriety, promotion's very slow,
> So we'll sing our reminiscences of Benny Havens, oh!

> To our kind old Alma Mater, our rockbound highland home,
> We'll cast back many a fond regret as o'er life's sea we roam.

Until on our last battlefield the light of heaven shall glow.
We'll never fail to drink to her and Benny Havens, oh!

Let us toast our foster-father, the Republic, as you know,
Who in the paths of science taught us forward for to go;
And the maidens of our native land, whose cheeks like roses
*   glow,*
They're oft remembered in our cups, at Benny Havens, oh!

May the Army be augmented, promotion be less slow;
May our country in the hour of need be ready for the foe;
May we find a soldier's resting-place beneath a soldier's blow;
With space enough beside our graves for Benny Havens, oh!

Inspired by a nineteenth-century tavern-keeper, it was West Point's old drinking song, sung by cadets for almost a century. It managed to celebrate getting drunk, finding a woman, and the company of friends, along with service to country and fighting and dying for something grander than themselves. As they sang, the stadium grew quiet. The midshipmen listened respectfully. The theme of the song—"May his ghost never grow pale nor his memory ever fade"—spoke to them all. "I've never been so moved by a song in my life," recalled a woman who had attended the game.

More songs followed from both sides of the stadium, and then everyone was on their feet and roaring as the two teams ran onto the field. In the presidential box Anna Boettiger, President Roosevelt's daughter and the unofficial White House hostess, and her guests politely cheered for both teams. The shouts of encouragement were more partisan in the Army and Navy boxes. Secretary of War Stimson and Secretary of the Navy Forrestal led the distinguished military leaders in full regalia. There was more high brass in the stadium than in virtually any council of war, and their names were familiar to most Americans. On the Navy side were Admiral William D. Leahy, chief of staff to the president; Admiral Ernest J. King, commander in chief of the Navy; and Admiral Jonas H. Ingram, commander of the Pacific Fleet. The Army side included General George C. Marshall, Army chief of staff, and General Henry H. Arnold, chief of the Army Air Forces. Surrounding each one was a convoy of lower-ranking admirals or generals.[11]

Just before kickoff, the stadium fell to a hush. A final group of spectators were ushered across the field to a section of honor. They were all badly wounded soldiers, the armless, the legless, and the terribly scarred. As they came closer, the spectators on the south end of the field stood silently, removing their hats. More than the heavily muscled players huddled near their benches, the wounded men reminded the spectators that this was no ordinary time or game.

The thick, well-illustrated program was filled with advertisements, all reminders of a nation at war. Chevrolet touted its armored car: "Ever since the North African Campaign these unique cars have been in action in Europe, yet only recently have we been permitted to tell you about them." Fisher boasted of its Strato-Flack gun: "[W]hen bombers took to the stratosphere, Army Ordnance engineers realized the need for a 120-millimeter gun, deadly to both air and ground targets at long ranges, and capable of a high rate of fire. So they worked it out with Fisher Body." General Motors praised its amphibious truck, the "Duck," which had been in the "vanguard of invasions from Normandy to New Guinea." Page after page they continued—the Grumman Hellcat, the Graham-Paige Amphibious Tractor, and the Buick 76-mm Gun Motor Carriages.[12]

Included were biographical sketches of the players that underscored that they were from every corner of the country—midwestern farms and southern small towns, eastern cities and western ranches. They were descendants of immigrants from Ireland,

England, Sweden, Germany, France, Hungary, Poland, Italy, and Czechoslovakia. "They represent many racial strains," commented Lieutenant Bill Sullivan in an article, using an old-fashioned sense of that term, "and yet from a physical and mental point of view there is no better group of American youths than those who wear the colors of their respective Academies." Photographs of each player as a child or a young boy accompanied the biographies.

At two o'clock Doc Blanchard kicked off to Scott. The opposing players charged one another across a damp, slick field. Army had won the toss and elected to kick, planning to pin Navy deep in their territory, but Scott slashed up the center of the field, cut right, broke a couple of tackles, and made it past the 30-yard line before he was forced out of bounds. It was a fine run. For a moment, Jenkins' infected toe was forgotten.[13]

Less than a minute later, Jenkins had a problem at the northern extreme of his body. On the third play from scrimmage he carried the ball on a power play to the right. It seemed like half his line and backfield pulled to run interference, and for a moment the Alabama back had an opening. But from his middle linebacker position, Joe Stanowicz read the play, moved down the line to his left, brushed aside a blocker, and clotheslined Jenkins. It was a brutally hard, perfectly legal tackle. Even before Jenkins hit the ground, Bobby Dobbs slammed into him, too. He lay on the turf for 10 long seconds before several teammates helped him off the field. In football parlance, he had had his "bell rung." Though ambulatory, he had no idea what had happened or where he was. Reporters later wrote that he had been kicked on the play. Maybe he had. Or maybe Stanowicz's high hit had knocked him unconscious. Whatever the case, he was effectively done for the day. Although he returned briefly in the second half, he played as if he was in a fog.

It was a sign of the type of play both teams favored. Brutal. Power on power. And, at least in the early going, the advantage lay with Army.

Navy punted, and the ball—a rounder, bouncier ball than is used today—bounded deep and out of bounds inside the Army 15-yard line. Kenna took his position under the center and surveyed a Navy defense stacked to stop the run—six down linemen and two linebackers close to the scrimmage line. He ran a quarterback sneak, testing the center of Navy's defense. Then he ran a few off-tackle plays for Max Minor, who picked up 8 yards and fumbled, but recovered, for a first down. On the next play, however, Minor fumbled again. Navy recovered.

Throughout the season so far, Army had scored 481 points, an average of more than 60 points per game. But the story of the first quarter was all about defense. The field limited Army's offensive speed, yet the Cadets' defensive alignment also stopped Navy's powerful single-wing attack. The key to Navy's ground game was its "inside mousetrap" plays, essentially trap blocking schemes that featured Whitmire as the pulling blocker. All season Whitmire had been successful in springing Jenkins on long runs. But Jenkins was out, and Army's linemen played slightly off the line, hesitating a moment before attacking, a tactic that disrupted the timing of the trap blocks. Instead of breaking through the line of scrimmage and taking off, Navy backs were consistently smothered for little or no gain.

Kenna's team did no better against Navy's line. Whitmire played like a rock, making tackles himself or clogging holes and allowing others to finish the job.

To the uninitiated, nothing was happening, but to knowledgeable fans, the game was shaping up as a beautiful struggle. The hitting was intense. Allison Danzig said it was marked by "the unusual stark ferocity of the give and take." The first quarter was exceedingly violent, and the hard hitting continued throughout the game. It was a "savagely fought game, full of 16-caret crashes and fierce action," noted Stanley Woodward in the *New York Herald Tribune*, "but it did not get out of hand as did the game last year at West Point." He credited the referees for preventing the contest from descending into a brawl. When the quarter ended, the contest was scoreless.

Blanchard, Davis, Poole, Coulter, Fuson, and the rest of Blaik's plebes reported in at the beginning of the second quarter. Navy responded with a series of brutal tackles. Navy defenders stopped Minor for a 1-yard gain, nailed Davis for a 7-yard loss, and threw Minor for a 5-yard loss, forcing a Blanchard punt from Army's end zone. Scott fielded Blanchard's 45-yard punt and returned it to Army's 35. Finally, they had achieved ideal field position.

Four plays later, Ug Fuson intercepted a Hamberg pass and Navy's elation was instantly over. But in the second quarter the character of the game subtly began to shift. Each time Army got the ball they moved a little farther. Davis, Blanchard, and Minor ran for several first downs, and if each time the drives stalled, they got farther into Navy's territory. On one drive Army reached the Navy 16 before turning the ball over on downs. Davis's and Minor's speed and Blanchard's raw — Danzig called it "terrifying"—power created problems Navy had not faced all year. On the sideline, sportswriter Lawrence Robinson noted that Navy's coaches "stirred with alarm."

On the line of scrimmage, Tex Coulter was beginning to have his way with Whitmire. Perhaps, as the coaches said later, Whitmire had hurt his knee in the first quarter. The huge tackle was not limping, but he was learning what Tex's teammates already knew—DeWitt played according to a whistle in his own head. When Army punted, Tex took off after Whitmire. When Whitmire pulled off the line and moved laterally, Tex took off on a search-and-destroy mission. Whitmire began to tire. Then, shortly after the halfway mark of the second quarter, DeWitt hit him with a Masonic Home School special: a shoulder punch, right under the chinstrap. Whitmire went down—and out of the game. "It was a legitimate clean type of block seldom seen in football," Blaik later wrote to General MacArthur. DeWitt had seen lots of them as a barefoot boy in Fort Worth.[14]

The slow, steady momentum in Army's favor suddenly leaped up a notch. Navy's defense noticeably worsened without Whitmire. After a Navy quick-kick, Army began to drive. Davis twisted and turned on end runs and Blanchard banged into the line, gaining yards with his leg drive. On a 20-yard gain that took the ball deep into Navy territory, Davis looked as if he might go for a touchdown before Hamberg forced him out of bounds. Relaxing as he crossed the sideline, another Navy player hit him late, throwing him to the ground. Today, it would have drawn an instant flag and a 15-yard roughing penalty. Then, it hardly drew a second thought. Davis jumped up, smiling, without a word of complaint. More than just stoic, his response was psychologically powerful.

With the Navy defense focused on Davis and Blanchard, Dale Hall was the back who did the most damage, gaining chunks of yardage on misdirection and trap plays. With first down on the Navy 24-yard line, Lombardo faked a handoff to Davis, causing the Navy defenders to veer toward the dangerous runner. Lombardo then slipped it into the arms of Hall, who broke off a trap block and outraced everyone to the end zone. He crossed the goal line standing up at about the 11-minute mark of the quarter. After Dick Walterhouse's conversion, Army led, 7–0. It was their first lead against Navy in six years.

In the halftime locker rooms there were no Rockne speeches. Blaik simply covered details, most of which his players already knew. He trusted execution more than inspiration. If everyone did his job, made the plays he was supposed to make, Army would win. Nor did Navy's first-year coach Oscar Hagberg find anything memorable to say. Unlike Swede Larson coaching his last game in 1941, he could think of no incendiary "now let's go out there and win for some person or cause" address.

About halfway through the game there was an air raid alert on Leyte, as General Eichelberger and his staff listened to the contest. The broadcast had begun at about 2:30 a.m. local time. If the general was willing to get up in the middle of the night to listen to the game, he certainly wasn't about to shut it off because the Japanese were bombing his position. His aides quickly blackened out his shack, then settled down for the third quarter.[15]

The temperature had dropped even more by the beginning of the second half. Doug Kenna's father had come up from Jackson, Mississippi, for the first game he had seen his son play for West Point. "By now it was bitterly cold," Kenna remembered. "It couldn't have been more than ten or fifteen degrees, and that was too cold for my dad. Eventually he just had to leave."[16]

As cold as it was, the Corps of Cadets were soon cheering themselves warm. Blanchard began the second half the way he had started the first, kicking the ball deep to Scott. But the Navy team that received the ball was not the one that had started the game. Jenkins and Whitmire were both out. Guard Stansfield Turner was playing hurt and soon would leave. After three plays and a penalty, Navy had lost 13 yards and was forced to punt. On that play, Army guard Joe Stanowicz and tackle Archibald Arnold ran a stunt. Arnold drove into the Navy player across from Stanowicz, pushing him to the side and giving Stanowicz an open lane to the punter. It worked perfectly. Stanowicz blocked the punt and the ball bounded back into the end zone, where the punter dove on it for a safety. Army now led, 9–0.[17]

Navy still had All-Americans in the game who were capable of making plays. "Scott and Hamberg were exceptional players," Kenna recalled, "who could score from anywhere on the field. Back in the '40s a 9–0 was a two-touchdown lead, but we knew

Navy could score two touchdowns and beat us if we let up an iota."

Navy kicked the ball to Army after the safety, and on the first play from scrimmage a Midshipman broke through the Cadet line and forced a fumble. "For the rest of this quarter," Danzig wrote, Navy "came back so fiercely to outplay the cadets that the hopes of the midshipmen in the stands were revived." As the Navy band struck up "Anchors Aweigh," Scott and Hamberg began to move the ball.

After mistakes stopped two drives, Navy began a third toward the end of the quarter. As he had before, "little Hal Hamberg"—"148 pounds of brains and Arkansas heart," wrote Grantland Rice—took over the game. From his deep position in the single wing, he ran the ball on sweeps and traps up the middle or faked runs and passed. Several vicious Army tackles slammed him to the frozen turf, but each time he got up and trotted back to the huddle.[18]

There was no single spectacular play in the fifteen-play drive, just a series of 5-, 6-, and 7-yard gains and a string of first downs until the ball was on the Army 1. "The Arkansas Kid ran and passed the ball against the great Army defense for 73 yards," commented Rice. "He faked and ducked and fought," struggling for every extra inch. Just short of the goal line he called the number of the other Arkansas back. With just over a minute remaining in the quarter, Smackover Scott carried the ball into the end zone. The extra point narrowed the score to 9–7. Fifteen minutes remained.

The stadium exploded with cheering. Navy's band struck up "Anchors Aweigh," and the Maryland crowd roared its approval. Admiral Leahy and Admiral King stood and shouted along with the midshipmen. Colonel Swede Larson, who had earlier predicted a Navy victory, smiled confidently. Now, wrote Craig E. Taylor in the *Baltimore Sun*, "it looked like either side could win."[19]

Then Blaik made his move.

All season long, he had alternated his two teams—Kenna's in the first and third quarters, Lombardo's in the second and fourth. Only rarely did he mix the backfields. Now it was time. He put his best in—Kenna, Minor, Blanchard, and Davis. On the Navy sideline, Oscar Hagberg had the same idea. He wanted his best backs in the contest, and that meant Bobby Jenkins. In the last quarter of the most important game in the history of football, five backs who had been named to at least one of the 1944 All-American teams—Davis, Blanchard, Kenna, Jenkins, and Scott—were in the game at the same time. The sight of those five jerseys created waves of cheers from both sides of the stadium.

Jenkins, however, was playing with a concussion. His head throbbed, he had trouble remembering plays, and he should not have been on the field with the likes of Tex Coulter, Barney Poole, and Doc Blanchard out to hit him. Still, as Glenn Davis recalled, Jenkins's return was "like a shot in the arm to the Navy rooters and players. Those Middie linemen started hitting us like raging madmen."[20]

No sooner did Navy get the ball back than they began another drive. Scott shook off a tackler and moved into Army territory, and two more runs advanced the ball to the 39. Then Jenkins took the center snap, faked a run into the line, took a quick step back, hopped to avoid a tackler, and threw a pass toward a receiver in the center of the field. The pass was behind its target. As the receiver made a balletic spin to catch it, his arm reaching out like a first baseman's stretching for an errant throw, Davis shot forward and intercepted the ball, taking it to near midfield.

Earlier in the season George Trevor of the *New York Sun* coined nicknames for Blanchard and Davis—"Mr. Inside" and "Mr. Outside." Doc, he suggested, pounded holes between the tackles, and Glenn glided around the ends. After Mr. Outside's timely interception, Mr. Inside went to work. He ran off tackle for 26 yards and up the middle for shorter gains. He moved toward defenders with a high, powerful knee action, challenging them to hit him. Before the age of face masks, tackling Blanchard was daunting. One man who tackled him said it was an unforgettable experience "if you live through it. . . . He came into the line with his head down and his knees churning up a couple of thighs that were as big as giant tank traps. You were really lucky to ever get a good piece of him by yourself because he simply sent tacklers sprawling who tried to take him one-on-one. . . . If he got into the open, then he was a more fearsome weapon against linebackers and defensive backs who were smaller than him." One of his own teammates claimed "it hurt to hit Doc. He was such a solid person and he loved to deliver a full package of pain."[21]

In the 52-yard drive Navy got the full package. In a nine-play scoring drive Doc carried the ball seven times, accounting for all but 4 of the yards. On the 10-yard line, he broke up the middle, his body leaning forward and to the left at a preposterous angle. Three Navy tacklers dove at him fruitlessly. Blanchard just bulled his way into the end zone. If no one had touched him he would have fallen on his face. He depended on people hitting him to remain upright. Army led, 16–7, with only 9 minutes left, and the game was all but over.

All that remained for Army was a perfect punctuation point. After forcing Navy to punt, Lombardo called the "California Special," a new play that featured Davis. Blanchard lined up outside the right end, Minor went in motion to the left, and Lombardo pitched the ball to Davis. Minor's block on a linebacker gave Davis a sliver of an opening to the outside. It was all the space he needed. Two tacklers had perfect angles on him, but Davis faked out Hamberg with a stutter step and a change of speed, and then outran Scott for a 50-yard touchdown. Blaik wrote to General MacArthur that it was "one of the most beautiful runs in Army and Navy history." It was Davis's twentieth of the season, and he now led the nation in scoring.[22]

The final score: Army 23, Navy 7. After more than a half century of football, Army was finally, indisputably the number-one
team in the nation.

It was fitting that Blanchard and Davis scored the last two
touchdowns of Army's undefeated 1944 season. "Yes, sir," Herman Hickman declared after the game. "I'm coming around to
Shor's with my cigars on Monday for the Football Writers' Association meeting and I'm going to be as egotistical as hell. I'll
even compose a poem for the occasion."[23]

After Davis's run, the cadets came down from the stands and
gathered behind Army's sideline, cheering. But on the field there
were no wild celebrations at the final whistle. To a man, the players from both teams came together and shook hands, draping
arms around each other's shoulders and wishing one another
well in the future. They were all part of the same team in the end.

Modesty reigned in the Army locker room. As always, Davis
talked about his great teammates. The magnificent 50-yard
touchdown, he said, was nothing. With the blocking he received,
any old back could have scored. All he had to do was not trip
over any of the yard lines. He had only one request. "Sir," he
asked backfield coach Andy Gustafson, "my cousin is here in
Baltimore. May I see him?" "You can do anything you want," the
coach answered. "There goes one of the greatest ball carriers I
have ever seen," he added to a reporter when Glenn was out of
hearing range.[24]

Blanchard, hardly feeling the effects of all the impacts, was
a trifle melancholy. Earlier in the season when a Notre Dame
scout had watched Doc against Villanova, he had reported to
Coach Ed McKeever, "Cancel the game!" But today Doc had
played better than he had against Villanova or Notre Dame or
any other opponent of the season. He had played the game of his
life. But he was thinking of his father, who had died just before
he entered the Academy. His cousin Ed Tatum, who had come

north for the game, told him that he wished Big Doc had been there to see his performance. "He was there, Ed," Doc reassured him. "I could feel him patting me on the back after each play and saying, 'Hit like your daddy did, son.'"[25]

It was a game for America, Blaik said when it was all over. A game for Americans in the Ardennes and outside Strasbourg in France, near Florence in Italy, on Leyte in the Philippines — wherever Army forces were, they were celebrating. General Eichelberger was so happy that he went out looking for Colonel Charles "Monk" Meyer, a standout Army back from the mid-1930s. He found him in the north end of the Ormoc Valley on Leyte, where he was leading an assault. When he heard the score, Meyer was as happy as if he had scored the last touchdown himself. He was so happy he could have eaten his hat.[26]

Soon after the game Blaik received a telegram:

> 3 DECEMBER 1944
> URGENT URGENT URGENT URGENT
> TO LT COL EARL BLAIK
> US MILITARY ACADEMY
> WEST POINT NY
>   THE GREATEST OF ALL ARMY TEAMS STOP
> WE HAVE STOPPED THE WAR TO CELEBRATE
> YOUR MAGNIFICENT SUCCESS
> MACARTHUR[27]

Epilogue

The country can now return to the normalcy of fight-
ing the most terrible war ever inflicted upon mankind.
The Army-Navy game has passed into history.
— Allison Danzig

IT WAS OVERCAST and snowing in the Ardennes, and GIs
patrolling there said it was so cold that it froze your grand-
father's ass. Snow blanketed the hills and the pines, and a
thick fog stuck to the low ground. The arctic cold mixed with
the frozen chill of fear of an enemy lurking just out of reach. On
December 16 German forces, led by elite SS Panzer divisions,
poured out of their wooded lair in the Eifel and attacked across
a 60-kilometer front, initially delivering death and destruction
to American forces in front of them. No event caused greater
fear and anger among American GIs than the Malmédy massa-
cre that took place on the seventeenth. A German SS officer and
soldiers under his command had opened fire directly into some
150 POWs, killing more than 80 of them and leaving the dead
and wounded to freeze in the snow.

Within only hours, with a speed that could not be matched
anywhere outside a military force, news of Malmédy spread
through the ranks, taking on extra layers of exaggeration and
details. A hundred had been killed—no, two hundred, five hun-

dred, more. The Germans had stripped off the GIs' boots and jackets before they shot them. Soldiers who had not been killed by the machine-gun and small-arms fire had froze to death, their bodies covered by snow. Malmédy spoke to all American soldiers anywhere near the front—the war had reached a new stage. POWs had no place in the new order of things.

The problem for Americans on the front was identifying the enemy. As part of the Ardennes offensive, Hitler had ordered Obersturmbannführer Otto Skorzeny to organize a special brigade of English-speaking German troops to infiltrate enemy lines and create havoc. Disguised in authentic U.S. uniforms, they would seize vital objectives, cut telephone lines, change road signs, and kill the military police in charge of directing troop movements. Once again, a small amount of news went a long way, increasing in size like a snowball rolling down one of the Ardennes' snow-covered hills.

How do you quickly and reliably identify a genuine American soldier from a German counterfeit in an American uniform speaking perfect English? Quick. Your life and the lives of your friends could depend on your judgment. Information, soldiers determined, was the key. Ask for information that only a true American, one raised and educated in the good old U.S. of A., would know. One MP, seeking to ascertain a general's bona fides, asked General Omar Bradley the name of Betty Grable's husband. When he confessed his ignorance of that bit of cultural knowledge, the MP took pity and asked the capital of Illinois. "Springfield," Bradley answered. "No, Chicago," the MP shot back.

But there was some information that every American soldier knew, from the lowest private to five-star Ike himself. West Point graduate Red Reeder gave one example. In 1945 he wrote to a friend at the Academy:

"[A] smart M.P. went up to an officer, suspected of being a phony, and said:

"'Who won the Notre Dame game?'

"The 'officer' did not know what the M.P. was talking about, so he was promptly locked up for further questioning, and shooting. The method of checking phonies spread around and it did the trick."[1]

At the time, there were at least a few men at the Academy who felt that the authorities could have skipped the questioning stage.

After the 1944 Season

Earl "Red" Blaik became West Point's most successful football coach. From 1941 until 1958 his teams compiled an astounding 121-33-10 record, going undefeated in 1944, 1945, 1946, 1948, 1949, and 1958. He coached three Heisman Trophy winners (Doc Blanchard, Glenn Davis, and Pete Dawkins) and helped to produce such famous coaches as Paul Dietzel, Bobby Dobbs, Sid Gillman, Bill Yeoman, Murray Warmath, and Vince Lombardi. He died on May 5, 1989. At the bottom of his tombstone is the line: "On, Brave Old Army Team."

Felix "Doc" Blanchard in 1945 became the first junior to win the Heisman Trophy. The same year he also received the Sullivan Trophy as the leading amateur athlete in the country. In his three seasons between 1944 and 1946, Army's record was 27-0-1. Denied the chance to play professional football after graduation, he coached for a few years at Army before entering the Air Force. During the Vietnam War he flew 84 missions over North Vietnam. He retired as a colonel in 1971. He died on April 19, 2009.

DeWitt "Tex" Coulter never graduated from West Point. After achieving consensus All-American status during the 1945 season, Tex lost his battle with mathematics and busted out of the Academy. In 1946 he joined professional football with the New

York Giants, making the All-Pro team in 1948 and 1949. After football he became a commercial artist and worked as the athletic director at a home for mentally handicapped men. He died on October 2, 2007.

Glenn Davis costarred with Blanchard on the Army teams of 1944, 1945, and 1946. All told, he scored 59 touchdowns, had a career rushing average of 8.26 yards per carry, and was awarded the 1946 Heisman Trophy. He also excelled in baseball and track. While on leave from the Army in 1947, he and Doc Blanchard played themselves in the movie *Spirit of West Point*. While filming a football scene, Davis badly hurt his knee. Although he later played in the NFL for the Los Angeles Rams, his blazing speed and illusiveness were gone. Davis dated Elizabeth Taylor and was married for two years to the actress Terry Moore, but he remained the same soft-spoken, friendly, humble person who played at West Point. Davis died in La Quinta, California, on March 9, 2005.

Herschel "Ug" Fuson lost his brother, Clyde "Ig" Fuson, two days after the 1944 Army-Navy game. Ig, a standout player at the University of Tennessee, was killed in Germany. Ug played with Glenn Davis and Doc Blanchard on the 1945 and 1946 undefeated West Point teams. Graduating in 1947, he was assigned to Armored Cavalry. He served in Japan during the occupation, and coached and played for the First Cavalry Division football team. He went to Korea at the outbreak of the war. On September 17, 1950, he was wounded by mortar fire and returned to the U.S., where surgeons decided against removing shrapnel lodged near his heart. On June 14, 1951, he died of a heart attack in Middlesboro, Kentucky.

Herman Hickman coached the line at West Point until 1948, when he accepted a head coaching position at Yale University.

In four seasons under Hickman, Yale went 16-17-2. His last season was his worst. But Herman had a stellar subsequent career as a speaker, humorist, television personality, and sportswriter. He was a regular on the TV quiz show *Celebrity Time* and hosted *The Herman Hickman Show* on NBC. In the 1950s he was a popular writer for *Sports Illustrated*. He died on April 25, 1958.

Doug Kenna graduated from West Point in the top portion of the Class of 1945. While at the Academy he excelled in football, basketball, and tennis. During his last year, the teams he played for had a combined record of 34 wins and 1 loss. He coached and played for General George Patton's Army football and basketball teams in Europe, coached at West Point under Red Blaik, played professional basketball, and won national amateur titles in tennis. He went on to a highly successful business career with the Avco Corporation, Fuqua Industries, R. B. Anderson and Company, and Carrier Corporation. Both before and after retirement he was actively involved in volunteer and philanthropic work and was a tireless supporter of West Point. In 1994 he received the West Point Association of Graduates' Distinguished Graduate Award. He lives in Florida when he is not traveling the world or at Michie Stadium watching West Point play football.

Tom Lombardo, captain of the 1944 team, graduated in 1945 and selected infantry service. He was assigned to the occupation forces in Japan, then was chosen by Red Blaik as an assistant coach at West Point. During the Korean War he commanded a company that was part of the breakout of the Pusan Perimeter after the Inchon invasion. On the afternoon of September 24, 1950, while crossing a wide valley, his regiment came under fire from a nearby hill. First Lieutenant Lombardo led a group of volunteers against the enemy stronghold, but he was killed in the action. In 1962 the football field at the Yongsan Reservation, South Korea, was designated Lombardo Field.

Robin Olds, flying P-38s and P-51s, became a double ace during World War II. After the war he was the wingman for the first acrobatic team in the Air Force, recorded record distance-speed flights, and married the movie star Ella Raines. During the Vietnam War, Olds once again became a fighter pilot ace. In the late 1960s, he was commandant of cadets at the U.S. Air Force Academy. He retired from the Air Force in 1973 at the rank of brigadier general. He died on June 14, 2007.

Barney Poole played football for three years at Army and earned All-American honors, but he busted out before graduation. He returned to the University of Mississippi and starred for two more years, earning All-American honors both years. Altogether, Barney played seven years of college football, after which he enjoyed a successful playing and coaching career. Afterward, he lived happily in his home state of Mississippi. His one major regret was his failure to graduate from West Point. He died on April 12, 2005.

Ed Rafalko lettered in football, basketball, and baseball at West Point and graduated in 1945 with a pilot rating and a second lieutenant commission. During his military career he served in Europe, Asia, and the United States, rising to the rank of major general. He also served as director of athletics at the U.S. Air Force Academy. He retired from the Air Force in 1973 and remains interested in Army football.

Joe Stanowicz, standout lineman in 1943 and 1944, as well as two-time Eastern Intercollegiate Wrestling champion, graduated in 1945 and joined the 20th Infantry in Korea, where he met Nell, an Army nurse. The two married in Seoul. He retired from the Army in 1966 and died on September 21, 1999. Nell said that she never heard him complain about anything.

Robert Woods met Geraldine Harrington at a West Point dance, and they were married on June 6, 1945, the day after he graduated as First Captain of his class. Sixty-six years later, they are still married, living in Darien, Connecticut. A lifelong musician, Woods plays trumpet in a popular jazz band.

Acknowledgments

Once again we are at war; in fact, at this writing it has been true for more than a decade. American men and women are again fighting for our values and ideals, suffering and dying on contested ground far from home. But back at home, the games go on. Jets streak over football stadiums, flags are saluted before games, maimed victims of Iraq and Afghanistan sit in places of honor and watch others do what they no longer can.

Perhaps it is as it should be. The games, after all, are part of the American fabric, as fundamental and iconic as home and apple pie. But as I teach hundreds of Purdue University students about World War II, I am often struck by the differences between then and now. Today relatively few young people stand in harm's way; then some 16 million did. During World War II, virtually every family had a father, son, brother, cousin, or uncle in uniform. Few neighborhood blocks did not see a home with a gold star flag hanging in the window. Yet even during the worst of the war, news of professional baseball and college football games filled the sports sections of newspapers.

For years I have wanted to tell some part of that story. As time passed, I began to focus on the West Point football team during the war, when Colonel Earl "Red" Blaik struggled to build a championship team. Never was the Academy more on the thoughts of Americans than in the 1940s, and never was it represented by finer teams. What was the relationship, if any, between war and football? How was the sport kept alive during a war that demanded so much from so many American boys? What was the relationship between the soldiers on the battlefields and the cadets on the gridirons? I have tried to answer these and other questions, and, even more important, I have sought to describe what it was like for the players, spectators, politicians, soldiers, and sailors.

The World War II cadets I studied were terrific athletes, but in all other ways they were typical of the sort of men who have attended West Point for more than two hundred years. Several in the group later died in or as a result of combat. Several rose to the rank of general. Several became successful business leaders. A few busted out or quit before they graduated. They made it through Beast Barracks, formed lasting friendships, and loved West Point, if they did not always enjoy it.

I was guided in my search for answers by an inspiring group of men who were cadets and soldiers during the 1940s. I'm not sure who I talked to first; it might have been Doug Kenna. From the first time I contacted him, Doug could not have been more helpful. The quarterback of the 1944 team, he remained a confident, indefatigable leader. He told me who I should talk to, gave me phone numbers and addresses, introduced me to the leaders of the Academy, escorted me to a football game at Michie Stadium, and told me countless stories about West Point, Red Blaik, and his teammates. All I can do in return is to thank him.

I talked with scores of cadets who had attended West Point from the 1940s to the 1960s, and they were all uniformly helpful and supportive. Bob Woods, Ed Rafalko, and Joe Steffy answered hundreds of questions during many interviews. Robin Olds recounted his years at West Point and in the sky during the war. His friend Henry Romanek shared his wartime experiences. James Salter and Hal Moore recounted their time at the Academy and in the service. Morris Herbert shared his encyclopedic knowledge of West Point football. George Troxell and Peter Vann talked about their relationship with Red Blaik. George Benson told me about West Point during the war. Bob Sorley took time from his own research to give me a tour of an area of the Academy he knew well. In countless ways, so many people have helped me during the past decade. Some of them have died since we talked, but I hope they all knew and know how important they were to the book.

A special debt of thanks goes to Henry E. Mattox, who interviewed many players for his own book, *Army Football in 1945: Anatomy of a Championship Season*. He permitted me to use his interviews with players who had since died. They allowed me to get closer to such men as Barney Poole, DeWitt Coulter, Doc Blanchard, and Glenn Davis, as well as many others.

A number of people at the West Point Special Collections and Archives helped me with research requests, including Elaine McConnell in the archives, Suzanne Christoff and Brian Gunning with photo searches, and Tammy Flint with requests for contact information. At Notre Dame's Joyce Sports Research Collection, George Rugg was once again an enormous help.

Of course, another group of readers helped me write the book. Johnny Smith took time from writing his own book to help me with the research and carefully read each draft chapter. Sorry about the long drives, Johnny. Andrew Smith read a later draft. David Welky read everything, closely and critically. All writers should have such readers.

For the publication of the book I owe another cast of characters. I can't imagine better literary agents than Christy Fletcher and Don Lamm of Fletcher & Company. Both were supportive from the first and carefully placed it with the right publisher. Christy, thanks for your advice. Don, thanks for your reading, and I'm sorry if it took you away from the early snowfalls.

Bruce Nichols at Houghton Mifflin Harcourt is my ideal editor. We've done a few books together, and I'm beginning to learn his method. He's so nice and funny, his authors don't mind his pen knifing through their pages. Thanks, Bruce, for your continual support, and most of all for your friendship. This is our book. Thanks also to Luise Erdmann for expert copyediting.

My daughters, Kelly and Alison, were away at school while I was writing most of this book, though I'll take any chance I get to tell them how much I love them. It's a lot. My wife, Marjie, was around when I disappeared to write, woke at night to scribble down a thought, and generally was not there even when I was there. She never complained. She never does. Amazing.

Notes and Abbreviations

I relied on a wide range of primary and secondary historical sources for *A Team for America*. Rather than include a large bibliography, I have credited my sources in the notes. Much of the story, however, came from interviews and contemporary magazines and newspapers. I conducted many of the interviews, but also of supreme importance was a series of interviews compiled by Henry E. Mattox for his book *Army Football in 1945: Anatomy of a Championship Season* (1990), which he allowed me to use.

The following abbreviations appear throughout the notes:

AEC—*Annapolis Evening Capital*
BS—*Baltimore Sun*
CDN—*Chicago Daily News*
CT—*Chicago Tribune*
HMC—Henry Mattox Collection, U.S. Military Academy Archives
LAT—*Los Angeles Times*

NYHT—*New York Herald Tribune*
NYP—*New York Post*
NYT—*New York Times*
NYWT—*New York World-Telegram*
PI—*Philadelphia Inquirer*
WP—*Washington Post*
WTH—*Washington Times-Herald*

Prologue

1 *NYT,* November 28, 1943.
2 *NYWT,* October 27, 1944.
3 Doug Kenna interview.
4 Doug Kenna interview; Stanley Woodward, "Football's Greatest Father-and-Son Act," *Saturday Evening Post,* October 7, 1950, 34.

5   Robert Woods interview; Glenn W. Davis interview (HMC); Doug Kenna interview.

6   Robert Chabot interview (HMC); John Sauer interview (HMC).

7   Army-Navy 1943 game films.

8   Wilbur D. Jones, Jr., *"Football! Navy! War!": How Military "Lend-Lease" Players Saved the College Game and Helped Win World War II* (2009), 133.

9   Doug Kenna interview.

10 *NYWT,* November 14, 1944.

11 *NYT,* November 28, 1943.

12 Stanley P. Hirshson, *General Patton: A Soldier's Life* (2002), 388–96.

1. A Week in November

1   *NYT,* November 17, 1940.

2   Earl H. Blaik with Tim Cohane, *You Have to Pay the Price* (1960), 160.

3   Ibid., 161.

4   *WP,* November 17, 1940; *NYT,* November 18, 1940, Blaik, *You Have to Pay the Price,* 162.

5   *NYT,* November 23, 1940.

6   Ibid., November 17, 1940.

7   Ibid., November 18, 1940.

8   *CDT,* November 17, 1940; *WP,* November 17, 1940.

9   *CDT,* November 18, 1940; *NYT,* November 18, 1940.

10 Blaik, *You Have to Pay the Price,* 163; *NYT,* November 19, 1940.

11 Ibid., November 19, 1940.

12 Tim Cohane Papers, Box 2, Folder 14, USMA Archives.

13 Robin Olds interview.

14 Robert L. Eichelberger (and Milton MacKaye), *Our Jungle Road to Tokyo* (1950), xviii.

15 Henry E. Mattox, *Army Football in 1945: Anatomy of a Championship Season* (1990), 9.

16 Eichelberger, *Our Jungle Road to Tokyo,* xix; Blaik, *You Have to Pay the Price,* 169.

17 Eichelberger, *Our Jungle Road to Tokyo,* xix.

18 Ibid.; Blaik, *You Have to Pay the Price,* 170–71.

19 R. L. Eichelberger to Earl Blaik, November 25, 1940, Vertical File, Football, USMA Archives.

20 Ibid.

21 Earl Blaik to R. L. Eichelberger, November 26, 1940, Blaik Papers, USMA Archives; Blaik, *You Have to Pay the Price,* 169–70.

22 For Blaik's trip to West Point, see Eichelberger, *Our Jungle Road to Tokyo,* xx; Blaik, *You Have to Pay the Price,* 172–73.

23 Mattox, *Army Football in 1945,* 14.

24 *NYT,* February 12, 1942.

25 Ibid.

26 Earl Blaik to R. L. Eichelberger, December 16, 1940, Blaik Papers, USMA Archives; also see drafts of letter.

27   R. L. Eichelberger to Earl Blaik, December 19, 1940, Vertical File, Football, USMA
     Archives.
28   Ibid.
29   R. L. Eichelberger to E. M. Watson, December 23, 1940, Vertical File, Football,
     USMA Archives.
30   Ibid.; Doug Kenna interview. .
31   R. L. Eichelberger to E. M. Watson, December 23, 1940, Vertical File, Football,
     USMA Archives.
32   *NYT,* December 26, 1940.

2. Where the Most Football Games Are Lost

1   Lars Anderson, *The All Americans* (2005), 90.
2   *NYT,* December 7, 1941; Richard Lingeman, *Don't You Know There's a War On? The
     American Home Front 1941–1945* (2003), 11–24.
3   *LAT,* December 7, 1941.
4   Unless otherwise noted, the story of Blaik's years as a cadet are from Blaik, *You Have
     to Pay the Price,* 20–49.
5   For West Point during World War I, see Theodore J. Crackel, *West Point: A Bicenten-
     nial History* (2002), 185–88.
6   D. Clayton James, *The Years of MacArthur,* Vol. I, 1880–1941 (1970), 261.
7   Ibid.
8   Earl Blaik, "A Cadet Under MacArthur," *Assembly* (Spring, 1964), 8.
9   Ibid.
10   Ibid., 9.
11   James, *The Years of MacArthur,* Vol. I, 280.
12   Tim Cohane, *Gridiron Grenadiers: The Story of West Point Football* (1948), 116; Blaik,
     "A Cadet Under MacArthur," 9.
13   Blaik, *You Have to Pay the Price,* 47.
14   Ibid., 41–48.
15   For Blaik's service career, see ibid., 50–63.
16   Cramerer, "The Toughest Coaching Job," 92.
17   Cohane, *Gridiron Grenadiers,* 220–21; Robin Olds interview.
18   For Blaik's schedule and routine, see Blaik, *You Have to Pay the Price,* 176–77, and
     David Maraniss, *When Pride Still Mattered: A Life of Vince Lombardi* (1999), 97–115.
     Most helpful was the Doug Kenna interview.
19   Maraniss, *When Pride Still Mattered,* 101.
20   *WP,* February 6, 1941.
21   *WP,* September 23, 1941; interview with Robin Olds. For Murphy's experiences, see
     Anderson, *The All Americans,* 67–68.
22   Anderson, *The All Americans,* 68.
23   Maraniss, *When Pride Still Mattered,* 102.
24   *NYT,* October 22, 1941.
25   Ibid., October 28, 1941; ibid., October 31, 1941.
26   Ibid.

27 Ibid., November 2, 1941.

28 Henry E. Mattox, *Army Football in 1945,* 17.

29 *NYT,* November 6, 1941; Ibid., November 13, 1941; *WP,* November 12, 1941; Robin Olds interview.

30 Anderson, *The All Americans,* 99.

31 Ibid., 102; Robin Olds interview.

32 *NYT,* November 30, 1941; *WP,* November 30, 1941.

33 Anderson, *The All Americans,* 116–22.

34 For the game, see ibid.; *NYT,* November 30, 1941; and *WP,* November 30, 1941.

35 Anderson, *The All Americans,* 129.

36 Ibid., 130.

37 Robin Olds, *Fighter Pilot: The Memoirs of Legendary Ace Robin Olds* (2010), 11; Robin Olds interview.

38 *NYT,* November 29, 1941; Anderson, *The All Americans,* 134–35.

3. A Few Good Boys

1 For the details of Winkelman's and Lieser's stories, see "Football Under Fire at Pearl Harbor," ed. Walter R. Okeson, *The Official 1942 National Collegiate Athletic Association Football Guide* (1942), 25–31. It contains the accounts of Winkelman and Lieser.

2 Jim Campbell, "Who Could Forget," *College Football Historical Society Newsletter* (November 1998), 7.

3 Ibid.

4 Doug Kenna interview. Unless noted, all of Kenna's statements come from these interviews.

5 Program for the Army-Navy game (1944), 106.

6 This section is constructed from interviews with Doug Kenna, Robin Olds, Joe Steffy, Edmund Rafalko, Harold Moore, James Salter, and several other West Point graduates. See especially James Salter, *Burning the Days: Recollection* (1997), 43–74. Two other books were also helpful: James Blackwell, *On Brave Old Army Team: The Cheating Scandal That Rocked the Nation: West Point, 1951* (1996), 7–25, and Rick Atkinson, *The Long Gray Line* (1989), 9–50.

7 The Cadet Prayer is from *Bugle Notes* (1942), 61–62; also see Don M. Snider and Lloyd J. Matthews, eds., *Forging the Warrior's Character: Moral Precepts from the Cadet Prayer* (2008).

8 Robert Woods interview.

9 James Salter interview; Doug Kenna interview; *Bugle Notes* (1942), 90–92.

10 Joe Steffy interview (HMC).

11 Blaik, *You Have to Pay the Price,* 181.

12 Earl Blaik to Douglas MacArthur, December 15, 1942, Blaik Papers, USMA Archives.

13 Ibid.

14 Michael Oriard, *Reading Football: How the Popular Press Created an American Spectacle* (1993), 1–2.

15 Theodore Roosevelt, "The American Boy," *St. Nicholas* (May 1900).

16 Brooke Leman, "The Soul of Football," *Athletic Journal,* 22 (November 1941), 7. Quoted in Donald W. Rominger, Jr., "The Impact of the United States Government's Sports and Physical Training Policy on Organized Athletics During World War II," (Ph.D. diss., University of Oklahoma, 1967), 27–28. (Hereafter, Rominger, diss.)

17 Mattox, *Army Football in 1945,* 30.

18 Rominger, diss., 4; Wilbur D. Jones, Jr., *"Football! Navy! War!,"* 16, 76–82; Mattox, *Army Football in 1945,* 36.

19 Rominger, diss., 63.

20 *NYT,* April 15, 1942.

21 Ibid., Franklin Roosevelt to Kennesaw Mountain Landis, January 15, 1942.

22 Rominger, diss., 43; *NYT,* August 20, 1942.

23 National Collegiate Athletic Association, *The Official 1943 Football Guide* (1943), 31–36.

24 National Collegiate Athletic Association, *The Official 1942 Football Guide* (1942), 23–25.

25 Donald W. Rominger, Jr., "From Playing Field to Battleground: The United States Navy V-5 Preflight Program in World War II," *Journal of Sport History,* 12, No. 3 (Winter, 1985), 260–61; National Collegiate Athletic Association, *The Official 1943 Football Guide* (1942), 21–22.

26 Jones, *"Football! Navy! War!,"* 58.

27 Rominger, "From Playing Field to Battleground," 255.

28 National Collegiate Athletic Association, *The Official 1943 Football Guide,* 30.

4. Lost Teeth and Lost Chances

1 *NYT,* February 12, 1942; Blaik, *You Have to Pay the Price,* 179.

2 Robin Olds interview.

3 Doug Kenna interview. Unless noted, quotes from Kenna are from this interview.

4 *The Pointer,* November 5, 1943.

5 Blaik, *You Have to Pay the Price,* 131–32.

6 *WP,* October 4, 1942; *NYT,* October 4, 1942.

7 Robin Olds interview. Unless noted, quotes from Olds are from this interview. Olds, *Fighter Pilot,* 12.

8 *NYT,* October 30, 1942.

9 *WP,* October 22, 1942; ibid., October 30, 1942.

10 *NYT,* October 30, 1942.

11 Robert Woods interview; *NYT,* October 19, 1942; ibid., November 1, 1942.

12 Robert Woods interview; *NYT,* November 5, 1942; "The Long Gray Line," *Time* (June 11, 1945), 65–68.

13 Doug Kenna interview.

14 *NYT,* November 6, 1942.

15 Ibid., November 8, 1942.

16 *WP,* November 18, 1942; *NYT,* November 19, 1942; ibid., November 21, 1941; ibid., November 22, 1942.

17 Brehon Somervell to George C. Marshall, "Memorandum for the Chief of Staff," August 18, 1942, Vertical File, Football, Army-Navy, USMA Archives.

18 F. B. Wilby to George C. Marshall, August 21, 1942; Wilby to Irving J. Phillipson, June 4, June 18, 1942; Wilby to Joseph T. McNarney, August 22, 1942; Wilby to Ernest Graves, August 22, 1942; Graves to Wilby, August 26, 1942;. Wilby to Philip B. Fleming, August 22, 1942; Fleming to Wilby, August 26, 1942. All letters in Vertical File, Football, Army-Navy, USMA Archives.

19 Joseph T. McNarney to F. B. Wilby, October 7, 1942, Vertical File, Football, Army-Navy, UNSMA Archives.

20 Meade Wilrick, "Memorandum for the Superintendant," September 25, 1942, Vertical File, Football, Army-Navy, USMA Archives; *WP*, November 15, 1942; *Sporting News*, November 26, 1942.

21 Earl Blaik to Douglas MacArthur, December 15, 1942, Blaik Papers, USMA Archives.

22 Robert Woods interview.

23 Earl Blaik to Douglas MacArthur, December 15, 1942, Blaik Papers, USMA Archives.

24 *WP*, November 28, 1942; *NYT*, November 28, 1942; Rominger, diss., 147.

25 *NYT*, November 29, 1942; Robin Olds interview; Doug Kenna interview.

26 For the Olds episode, see Olds, *Fighter Pilot*, 14; Blaik, *You Have to Pay the Price*, 183–84; Lars Anderson, *The All Americans*, 184–86; Robin Olds interview; Henry Romanek interview.

27 Blaik, *You Have to Pay the Price*, 183–84; Olds, *Fighter Pilot*, 14.

28 *NYT*, September 4, 1943; Blaik, *You Have to Pay the Price*, 182.

5. "God Gave Me That"

1 Forrest C. Pogue, *George C. Marshall: Education of a General* (1963), 54–55.

2 George C. Marshall to F. B. Wilby, n.d., Vertical File, Football, USMA Archives.

3 William Webb interview (HMC); *LAT*, November 25, 1941; ibid., February 5, 1941; ibid., December 20, 1942.

4 *LAT*, October 21, 1943; Glenn Davis interview (HMC).

5 *LAT*, December 13, 1942; ibid., October 21, 1943.

6 Glenn Davis interview (HMC); Earl Blaik interview (HMC).

7 Earl Blaik interview (HMC); Ron Fimrite, "Mr. Inside & Mr. Outside," *Sports Illustrated* (November 21, 1988), 79–80.

8 Rominger, diss., 145–46.

9 Ibid., 152–53; *NYT*, February 13, 1943.

10 Ibid.

11 Ibid., February 21, 1943.

12 Rominger, diss., 157–70; Jones, *"Football! Navy! War!,"* 59–62.

13 Doug Kenna interview.

14 Blaik, *You Have to Pay the Price*, 184.

15 Robin Hardin, "Herman Hickman: Talented On and Off the Field," *College Football Historical Society Newsletter* (August 2001), 11–15. See article for details of Hickman's career.

16 Grantland Rice, *The Tumult and the Shouting: My Life in Sport* (1954), 114.

17 Herman Hickman to Tim Cohane, March 15, 1946, Tim Cohane Papers, USMA Archives.

18 Rice, *The Tumult and the Shouting,* 202.

19 Blaik, *You Have to Pay the Price,* 185.

20 Maraniss, *When Pride Still Mattered,* 98.

21 Blaik, *You Have to Pay the Price,* 185.

22 Maraniss, *When Pride Still Mattered,* 105; Doug Kenna interview.

23 Robin Lester, *Stagg's University: The Rise, Decline & Fall of Big-Time Football at Chicago* (1995), 164–68.

24 Ron Fimrite, "A Melding of Men All Suited to a T," *Sports Illustrated* (September 5, 1977), online.

25 Ibid.

6. Making the Grade

1 Jack Clary, *Field of Honor: Duty, Honor, Country, and Winning the Heisman* (2002), 56–58.

2 *NYT,* September 4, 1943.

3 Henry F. Pringle, "What Good Is West Point," *Collier's* (August 24, 1940), 17, 48; Wayne Whittaker, "West Point at War," *Popular Mechanics* (September 1943), 82; *NYT,* September 4, 1943.

4 *NYT,* September 18, 1943.

5 Ibid.; *WP,* September 18, 1943; *The Pointer,* September 10, 1943.

6 Ibid., September 24, 1943.

7 *NYT,* September 26, 1943.

8 *WP,* October 3, 1943; *NYT,* October 3, 1943.

9 *The Pointer,* October 8, 1943.

10 Doug Kenna interview; *WP,* October 10, 1943; *NYT,* October 10, 1943.

11 Ibid., October 16, 1943.

12 Ibid., October 17, 1943.

13 *The Pointer,* October 3, 1943.

14 Ibid.

15 *NYT,* October 24, 1943.

16 Blaik, *You Have to Pay the Price,* 187.

17 Glenn Davis interview (HMC).

18 Joe Steffy interview (HMC).

19 Doug Kenna interview.

20 *WP,* October 28, 1943; *NYT,* October 30, 1943.

21 *The Pointer,* October 22, 1943; *NYT,* October 30, 1943; *WP,* October 30, 1943.

22 *NYT,* October 31, 1943.

23 Rominger, diss., 163.

24 *NYT,* October 22, 1943; ibid., October 30, 1943.

25 Ibid., October 31, 1943; ibid., November 1, 1943.

26 Athletic Board Proceedings, November 5, 1943, Athletic Board Proceedings, USMA Archives.

27   MEMORANDUM FOR: Colonel L. McM. Jones, Graduate Manager of Athletics, from C. L. Fenton, November 5, 1943, Athletic Board Proceedings, USMA Archives; Robert Woods interview.
28   *WP,* November 2, 1943; *NYT,* November 5, 1945.
29   Ibid., November 6, 1943.

7. Historic Hours

1   "Address by Lieutenant General Brehon B. Somervell," *Assembly* (July 1944), 6–8; *NYT,* June 7, 1944.
2   *Greenville News,* June 14, 2006.
3   Henry Romanek interview; Anderson, *The All Americans,* 3–17, 210–15, superbly reconstructs Romanek's D-Day experience. Along with my interview with Romanek, I relied on Anderson.
4   Olds's actions and thoughts come from Robin Olds interview; Olds, *Fighter Pilot,* 40–55; and Anderson, *The All Americans,* 207–15.
5   "The Invasion," *Time* (June 12, 1944), online; "Battle of France," *Time* (June 19, 1944), 22–28.
6   "Beaches of Normandy," *Life* (June 19, 1944), 25–29.
7   Mattox, *Army Football in 1945,* 31.
8   Dwight D. Eisenhower, *At Ease: Stories I Tell to Friends* (1967), 16.
9   Whittaker, "West Point at War," 82–87, 154, 156.

8. "I've Just Seen Superman"

1   Thomas "Shorty" McWilliams interview (HMC); Pete Martin, "Portrait of a Fullback," *Saturday Evening Post* (December 1, 1945), 116.
2   Barney Poole interview (HMC); DeWitt "Tex" Coulter interview (HMC).
3   Ibid.
4   Barney Poole interview (HMC); Doug Kenna interview. Unless noted, Poole's quotes are from the Poole interview.
5   *Clarion-Ledger Jackson Daily News,* July 8, 1984. For more on the Poole family, see the Barney Poole file, College Football Hall of Fame.
6   Ibid.
7   Stan W. Carlson, "A Long College Career," *College Football Historical Society Newsletter,* (August 1995), 1–2.
8   Atkinson, *The Long Gray Line,* 39.
9   Col. Morris Herbert interview (HMC).
10   Doug Kenna interview.
11   Barney Poole interview (HMC).
12   Goble Bryant interview (HMC).
13   DeWitt "Tex" Coulter interview (HMC). Unless noted, Coulter's quotes are from the Mattox interview.
14   Jim Dent, *Twelve Mighty Orphans: The Inspiring True Story of the Mighty Mites Who Ruled Texas Football* (2007), 26–30.
15   Ibid., 29.

16 Ibid., 89.
17 Ibid., 240, 272.
18 "Most Feared Tacklers," ESPN.
19 Felix "Doc" Blanchard interview (HMC).
20 Goble Bryant interview (HMC); Joe Steffy interview (HMC).
21 Ibid.; Goble Bryant interview (HMC).
22 William Webb interview (HMC); Albert Joy interview (HMC).
23 Joe Steffy interview (HMC).
24 Fimrite, "Mr. Inside & Mr. Outside," 84; Fimrite, "A Melding of Men All Suited to a T."
25 Fimrite, "Mr. Inside & Mr. Outside," 84.
26 Martin, "Portrait of a Fullback," 18, 116.
27 Ibid.
28 Ibid.; *Army-Navy Program* (1944), 151.
29 Martin, "Portrait of a Fullback," 18; Doc Blanchard interview (HMC).
30 Doc Blanchard interview (HMC).
31 Blaik, *You Have to Pay the Price*, 192; Martin, "Portrait of a Fullback," 115–16; Doug Kenna interview.
32 Thomas "Shorty" McWilliams interview (HMC).
33 John Sauer interview (HMC).
34 "Army's Super-Dupers," *Time* (November 12, 1945), 58.
35 Fimrite, "Mr. Inside & Mr. Outside," 87.

9. Warm-Up

1   Blaik, *You Have to Pay the Price*, 192.
2   Doug Kenna interview.
3   Earl Blaik to F. B. Wilby, May 25, 1944, Army-Navy, USMA Archives.
4   Ibid., September 11, 1944, Army-Navy, USMA Archives.
5   F. B. Wilby to Earl Blaik, September 12, 1944, Army-Navy, USMA Archives.
6   *Army-Navy Program* (1944), 91; Joe Steffy interview (HMC).
7   Thomas "Shorty" McWilliams interview (HMC); Doug Kenna interview; Joe Steffy interview (HMC); Joe Steffy interview.
8   Edmund Rafalko interview.
9   Doug Kenna interview. Blaik later cleaned up Rafalko's comment in his autobiography.
10 *NYWT,* September 8, 1944; *WP,* August 15, 1944; ibid., September 1, 1944; *NYP,* September 8, 1944.
11 Blaik, *You Have to Pay the Price*, 195.
12 Doug Kenna interview.
13 Robert Woods interview.
14 *NYWT,* September 7, 1944.
15 Ibid.
16 "Teens and TNT," *Time* (September 25, 1944), 68.
17 *NYWT,* September 9, 1944; ibid., September 11, 1944.
18 *NYT,* September 12, 1944.

19   *NYWT,* September 29, 1944.

20   *NYHT,* September 30, 1944.

21   Barney Poole interview (HMC).

22   Blaïk, *You Have to Pay the Price,* 196; Doug Kenna interview.

23   *The Pointer,* September 22, 1944.

24   Barney Poole interview (HMC).

25   *NYHT,* October 1, 1944; ibid., October 2, 1944.

26   Ibid., October 1, 1944.

27   *NYWT,* September 28, 1944.

28   Ibid., October 2, 1944.

29   Doc Blanchard interview (HMC); Doug Kenna interview.

30   *NYWT,* October 12, 1944; *NYT,* October 12, 1944; Ibid., October 17, 1944.

31   *NYHT,* October 8, 1944; *NYWT,* October 9, 1944; *NYT,* October 8, 1944; *NYWT,* October 10, 1944; *WP,* October 17, 1944.

32   Ibid., October 15, 1944.

33   *NYHT,* October 15, 1944.

34   Ibid., October 16, 1944.

35   *NYWT,* October 16, 1944; ibid., October 17, 1944.

36   Ibid., October 19, 1944; *NYHT,* October 22, 1944.

37   Ibid., October 22, 1944.

38   *NYWT,* October 23, 1944.

39   *The Pointer,* October 20, 1944; *NYWT,* October 27, 1944.

40   *NYT,* October 25, 1944; *NTWT,* October 25, 1944.

41   Ibid., October 28, 1944.

42   Ibid.; *NYT,* October 29, 1944.

43   Joe Cahill, "Beyond the Call of Duty," *Army-Duke Program* (1944), 7, 45.

44   *NYWT,* October 28, 1944.

45   For the game, see *NYT,* October 29, 1944; *NYWT,* October 28, 1944; *NYHT,* October 29, 1944; *WP,* October 29, 1944.

46   Barney Poole interview (HMC).

47   Doug Kenna interview; *NYWT,* October 27, 1944; Clary, *Field of Honor,* 77.

48   Clary, *Field of Honor,* 77.

49   *NYWT,* October 30, 1944; Earl Blaik to Douglas MacArthur, January 1, 1945, Blaik Papers, USMA Archives.

50   Earl Blaik to Douglas MacArthur, January 1, 1945, Blaik Papers, USMA Archives.

51   *NYHT,* November 5, 1944; *NYWT,* November 4, 1944; *NYT,* November 5, 1944; *WP,* November 5, 1944.

10. Payback

1   *NYP,* November 4, 1944.

2   Lingeman, *Don't You Know There's a War On,* 253.

3   Rominger, diss.; *NYT,* October 27, 1944.

4   Murray Sperber, *Shake Down the Thunder: The Creation of Notre Dame Football* (1993), 219; Blaik, *You Have to Pay the Price,* 196–97.

5   *NYHT,* November 5, 1944; *NYT,* November 5, 1944.

6 Ernest J. King, *American Experience*, online; *NYP,* November 6, 1944.

7 *NYT,* November 5, 1944; *WP,* November 7, 1944.

8 *NYWT,* November 6, 1944.

9 Doug Kenna interview; Blaik, *You Have to Pay the Price,* 197; Earl Blaik to Douglas MacArthur, January 1, 1945, Blaik Papers, USMA Archives.

10 *NYHT,* November 10, 1944; *NYP,* November 9, 1944.

11 Thomas "Shorty" McWilliams interview (HMC); Doug Kenna interview; Goble Bryant interview (HMC).

12 Earl Blaik to Douglas MacArthur, January 1, 1945, Blaik Papers, USMA Archives.

13 *NYWT,* November 7, 1944.

14 *WP,* November, 1944; *NYWT,* November 7, 1944; ibid., November 9, 1944.

15 *NYWT,* November 9, 1944; *NYHT,* November 11, 1944.

16 Ibid., November 10, 1944; Hal Moore interview.

17 *NYHT,* November 10, 1944; *NYWT,* November 7, 1944.

18 Rominger, diss., 168.

19 *NYWT,* November 10, 1944; *NYT,* November 10, 1944.

20 Doug Kenna interview; Robert Richmond, Jr., interview (HMC); Robert Chabot interview (HMC).

21 *NYT,* November 10, 1944; *NYP,* October 18, 1944; *CT,* November 9, 1944.

22 *NYT,* November 12, 1944; ibid., March 1, 1998.

23 Ibid., November 12, 1944.

24 Glenn Davis interview (HMC).

25 For game details, see Blaik, *You Have to Pay the Price,* 198–99; *NYT,* November 12, 1944; *NYWT,* November 11, 1944; *NYHT,* November 12, 1944; *WP,* November 12, 1944; *CT,* November 12, 1944.

26 Doug Kenna interview.

27 Blaik, *You Have to Pay the Price,* 199; *The Pointer,* November 17, 1944.

28 *NYP,* November 13, 1944; *NYHT,* November 13, 1944; *NYWT,* November 14, 1944.

29 Ibid., November 13, 1944; ibid., November 14, 1944.

30 Goble Bryant interview (HMC).

31 *NYT,* November 16, 1944.

32 *NYP,* November 16, 1944.

33 Robert Woods interview.

34 Doug Kenna interview; Robert Woods interview.

35 "Notes from Tom Mesereau and Rodney Kerr," Tim Cohane Papers, USMA Archives; Blaik, *You Have to Pay the Price,* 199.

36 Doug Kenna interview; Robert Woods interview; Joe Steffy interview.

37 For game details, see *NYP,* November 19, 1944; *NYT,* November 19, 1944; *WP,* November 19, 1944; *NYWT,* November 18, 1944.

38 *NYT,* November 19, 1944.

11. Cause for Thanksgiving

1 *NYT,* November 22, 1944; ibid., November 23, 1944; ibid., November 24, 1944.

2 Ibid., November 20, 1944.

3   *NYWT,* September 2, 1944.

4   Rominger, diss., 261.

5   Ibid.

6   *NYT,* November 6, 1944; ibid., November 13, 1944.

7   Ibid., November 6, 1944.

8   For Roosevelt's health, see Doris Kearns Goodwin, *No Ordinary Time: Franklin and Eleanor Roosevelt: The Home Front in World War II* (1994), 491–93, 256–59; Kenneth R. Crispell and Carlos F. Gomez, *Hidden Illness in the White House* (1988), 75–78; and Robert H. Ferrell, *Ill-Advised: Presidential Health and the Public Trust* (1992), 28–32.

9   Samuel A. Weiss to Henry L. Stimson, August 19, 1944, RG 407, Army Adjutant General, National Archives, College Park, Md.; *NYT,* August 31, 1944.

10 See wires, Theodore R. McKeldin to Henry L. Stimson, November 15, 1944; Bernard Samuel to Stimson, November 13, 1944; Herbert O'Conor to Stimson, November 15, 1994, RG 407, Army Adjutant General, National Archives, College Park, Md.

11 *NYP,* November 14, 1944.

12 *NYWT,* November 13, 1944; ibid., November 14, 1944

13 Ibid., November 16, 1944.

14 *LAT,* November 16, 1944; *NYP,* November 19, 1944; ibid., November 17, 1944; *NYT,* November 14, 1944; ibid., November 16, 1944; *NYWT,* November 15, 1944; ibid., November 17, 1944

15 *NYP,* November 18, 1944; *NYT,* November 18, 1844.

16 Ibid., November 19, 1944; ibid., November 20, 1944; ibid., December 1, 1944.

17 *NYT,* November 21, 1944; ibid., November 22, 1944; *NYWT,* November 21, 1944; ibid., November 22, 1944.

18 Ibid., November 16, 1944.

19 *Army-Navy Program* (1944), 55.

20 Jones, *"Football! Navy! War!,"* 122.

21 *NYWT,* November 16, 1944.

22 Ibid., November 14, 1944.

23 Ibid., November 16, 1944.

24 *Army-Navy Program* (1944), 54.

25 *NYT,* November 30, 1944.

26 Robert Woods interview.

27 *NYWT,* November 28, 1944; ibid., November 20, 1944.

28 *NYT,* November 30, 1944; Blaik, *You Have to Pay the Price,* 202.

29 *NYT,* November 20, 1944; *NYWT,* November 28, 1944.

30 *NYP,* November 29, 1944; *NYT,* November 28, 1944; ibid., November 29, 1944; *NYWT,* November 30, 1944.

31 *The Pointer,* December 1, 1944.

32 *NYWT,* November 27, 1944.

33 *NYT,* November 30, 1944.

34 *NYWT,* November 28, 1944; *NYT,* November 28, 1944; *NYP,* November 28, 1944; *NYHT,* December 3, 1944.

35 *NYT,* November 30, 1944.

12. A Game for America

1   Robert Woods interview.

2   *NYP,* December 12, 1944; *NYWT,* December 1, 1944.

3   Ibid., December 1, 1944; ibid., December 2, 1944; *NYT,* December 1, 1944; Katherine Thomas interview.

4   *NYP,* November 2, 1944.

5   *CDN,* November 30, 1944; *NYT,* December 1, 1944.

6   Robert Woods interview.

7   Ibid.

8   *BS,* December 3, 1944.

9   Glenn Davis, "My Greatest Day in Football," in Schoor, Gene, ed., *The Army-Navy Game* (1967), 93.

10 *NYHT,* December 3, 1944.

11 *NYWT,* December 2, 1944.

12 *Army-Navy Program* (1944).

13 For the details of the game, see *NYWT,* December 2, 1944; ibid., December 3, 1944; *NYHT,* December 3, 1944; *NYT,* December 3, 1944; *NYP,* December 3, 1944; *WP,* December 3, 1944. I also relied heavily on two versions of the game film.

14 Earl Blaik to Douglas MacArthur, January 1, 1945, Blaik Papers, USMA Archives.

15 Eichelberger, *Our Jungle Road to Tokyo,* xxi.

16 Doug Kenna interview.

17 *NYHT,* December 3, 1944.

18 *BS,* December 3, 1944.

19 Ibid.; *WTH,* December 3, 1944.

20 Davis, "My Greatest Day in Football," 94.

21 Clary, *Field of Valor,* 56; Doug Kenna interview; Joe Steffy interview.

22 Earl Blaik to Douglas MacArthur, January 1, 1945, Blaik Papers, USMA Archives.

23 *NYHT,* December 3, 1944.

24 *NYT,* December 3, 1944.

25 Clary, *Field of Valor,* 79; Martin, "Portrait of a Fullback," 116.

26 Blaik, *You Have to Pay the Price,* 205.

27 Telegram from Douglas MacArthur to Earl Blaik, December 3, 1944, Blaik Papers, USMA Archives.

Epilogue

1   Blaik, *You Have to Pay the Price,* 200.

Index